I LIFT, THEREFORE I AM

How Philosophy in Fitness Can Transform Your Life

Manuel Gezalyan

Copyright © 2025 Manuel Gezalyan

All rights reserved. No part of this publication may be reproduced, distributed, or transmitted in any form or by any means, including photocopying, recording, or other electronic or mechanical methods, without the prior written permission of the publisher, except in the case of brief quotations embodied in critical reviews and certain other noncommercial uses permitted by copyright law. Any perceived slight against any individual is purely unintentional.

This book is provided for educational and informational purposes only and does not constitute providing medical advice or professional services. The information provided should not be used for diagnosing or treating a health problem or disease, and those seeking personal medical advice should consult with a licensed physician. Always seek the advice of your doctor or other qualified health provider regarding a medical condition.

For permission requests, write to the publisher at contact@identitypublications.com

Library of Congress Control Number: 2025901408

Orders by U.S. trade bookstores and wholesalers. Please contact Identity Publications:
Tel: (805) 259-3724 or visit www.IdentityPublications.com.

ISBN-13: 978-1-945884-96-2 (paperback)
ISBN-13: 978-1-945884-97-9 (hardcover)

First Edition, published in Buffalo, Wyoming, by Identity Publications. (www.IdentityPublications.com).

Contents

Acknowledgements — v
Preface — xi
Introduction — xvii

CHAPTER ONE
What Is Fitness and Why Does It Matter (Beyond the Obvious)? — 1

CHAPTER TWO
How to Think About Fitness — 19

CHAPTER THREE
How NOT to Think About Fitness — 39

CHAPTER FOUR
Cognitive Biases — 61

CHAPTER FIVE
Motivation and Optimization — 87

CHAPTER SIX
Your Inner Beast, Your Best Friend — 125

CHAPTER SEVEN
What You've Got & What You Want — 165

CHAPTER EIGHT
People, Please 183

CHAPTER NINE
Rest & Recovery 205

CHAPTER TEN
Starting Your Fitness Journey 233

CHAPTER ELEVEN
Tailoring Fitness 273

CHAPTER TWELVE
Ultimate Impact—The Ripple/Domino Effect 293

About The Author 305

Acknowledgements

- God

- Rubina, the love of my life and core source of power and motivation—thank you for your unwavering love and support ashxars. You've always been my muse. When I'm with you, everything just flows so smoothly and naturally. You kill my pain and give me clarity, allowing me to actually get things done. You are the greatest contributor to my deepest transformation yet. Imagining my future with you, being with you, serves as a perpetual engine—and though they say this concept is impossible due to the first law of thermodynamics, your love proves its reality.

- My parents and siblings: Mom, Dad, seeing the pain you've both endured raising the three of us while going through everything you did has given me an endless ocean of fuel. How I wish I can repay you in such a way that you forget what pain feels like, though I understand how impossible that is given that parents will always feel pain at the slightest hint of their child's discomfort. Mom, you're an incredible woman, and for you to achieve what you have through what you've endured laid the foundation of my understanding and development of resilience and familial love. You showed me what it means to truly care and to treat people how you want to be treated despite their lack of reciprocity. Dad, you were likewise an example of resilience, and you showed me what it feels like to keep pushing, to question myself and break past my own falsely perceived limitations, to look forward, and to do everything I can to be as good a man as possible. Thank you for buying me my first set of five-pound dumbbells from that garage sale, by the way—I bet you probably never imagined that would lead to this. Arpy, you were always a great example of excellence, responsibility, and accountability. Arax, you inspired me to let go of certain extremes and complemented my philosophical nature. I love you all so much, and if I were to fully express what you all mean to me, it would fill a book as thick as the Bible.

- Manvel Papi (My grandfather) and Armen Hopar (My uncle): Papi, thank you for my philosophical perspective, my love for reading and writing, and my ability to notice and appreciate both the small and the beautiful things in life. Hopar, thank you for taking me with you everywhere you went when I was a kid, answering all my "Why?" questions, and showing me how to prioritize the self so that we can better help those we love. For showing me what discipline is. For showing me how to build trust, and being patient with me despite all the frustration. For continuing to believe in and support me. Because of you both, I've had a more vivid and meaningful experience of life.

- My brother, Arthur, with whom I've spent a great deal of time philosophizing about most of these concepts. I love you, kiddo on a level you can't imagine. Though I lose my shit when I look around and see the garbage around us, you give me hope for the future by being a reminder that there are young men and women that have rich, brilliant minds that are capable of thinking deeply about things. You've challenged my thinking and taught me a lot—both directly and indirectly. Every time the thought of writing a book came up, you always responded with, "Bro, you should! I don't know why you're not!" Well, here it is. Thank you.

- My nephew, Leo, and Mets Papi (my great grandfather and author, Grigor "Geghuni" Gezalyan—may God rest his soul): They are the triggers for starting this book, and continue to be my sources of inspiration. Leo, when you're old enough to read and understand this, it was because of you, ultimately, that I started on this book. I wanted to do something that would make you proud to call me your uncle—and there's more I will do until you've reached that age, my boy. Seeing you the day you entered this world, holding you, filled me with more joy than I've ever felt before. And Mets Papi, I don't recall a single day where I didn't see you either writing, working on the garden, or both—that left a lasting impression. You gave me the nickname "Columbus," not so much because I was born on Columbus Day but because I was as curious and observant as I was. That curiosity only grew and led to my exploration and experimentation, though it's gotten me into more trouble than it's benefited me so far.

- Gregory Diehl—my dear friend, mentor, counselor in authorship, and source of inspiration. I read your books, reached out, we connected, and it's been great ever since. Thank you for challenging my thoughts and ideas in the constructive manner that you do. I appreciate all your support. Thank you.

- Ara Kirakosyan—my brother, supporter, and motivational source. Brother, thank you for forcing me to consider the harsh realities of life. For being a solid life mentor and confidante. Thank you for providing me with everything you could to support me, and for showing me what it means to do what a man's gotta do. Thank you for being an example of what it means to be a leader everyone loves. The lessons you've taught me are invaluable. And most of all, thank you for your love and patience.

- Dr. Jack Bayramyan and Armen Bayramyan—both authors and inspirations (and despite having the same last name, they are not related); Dr. Jack, I deeply appreciate the time you set aside to coach me despite your insanely busy schedule. You showed faith in me. The investment of your time in me left an everlasting impression and gave me a boost in my self-worth. Armen jan, though we too haven't spent much time together, every conversation we have had has been intellectually stimulating. Then when I found out you authored a book, I was even more inspired to do the same. Thank you.

- Samuel Cunado—my dear friend and inspiration. Sam jan, I looked up to you in high school, and I continue to do so. Even at such a young age, you taught me some very important, priceless life lessons that you learned along the rough road you'd traveled. What you've achieved after everything you've been through is miraculous and is a perfect example of someone who doesn't succumb to a victim mentality. Thank you for continuing to be such an inspiration for me and others, brother.

- Dr. Jordan B. Peterson: Your books and lectures saved my life and enriched my philosophy.

- And all my beta-readers who contributed to the improvement and refinement of my work. Thank you.

Preface

Why I Started Writing This Book

It all started when enough people asked me why I'm into fitness and why I put so much time, effort, and resources into it. At times, I'd catch myself diving into lectures and philosophical discussions, while most people would jump straight to more topical explanations like, "Oh, dude, the ladies love it" or "I just wanna get stronger." While these reasons are valid, they often miss the deeper, transformative aspects of fitness.

I want to reveal the depth within fitness, why it's worth exploring, and the significant impact this journey can have on you. **My aim for this book** is to leave you in a revelatory state, changing your perception of fitness from a surface-level activity to a deeper, more introspective, and profoundly effective practice. With that said, I want to be absolutely clear and state that **this book is NOT intended to convince you to get into fitness**. If this book inspires that action, wonderful. But even if it doesn't, simply understanding and appreciating the depth of fitness is a worthy goal.

My revelations about the depths of fitness didn't occur at the beginning of my journey. It was a combination of several years of experience in fitness, work, school, and life in general. For instance, I remember a particular moment in the gym when I was struggling to push past a plateau. A gentleman I was working out with at the time introduced me to the concept of the mind-muscle connection, explaining how focusing mentally on the muscle being worked could enhance physical performance. This simple yet profound insight not only improved my workouts but also made me realize the power of mental focus in achieving goals, both in fitness and other areas of life.

It didn't happen quickly, but I realized that if I had known some of these deeper, more philosophical insights earlier, I would have approached fitness differently—I would have approached *life* differently—accelerating my growth in the domains I strived to optimize most.

Why I connected physical fitness and personal growth. Don't other books cover this?

There are many fitness books out there, but for one reason or another, I have never been satisfied with the type of information or depth of perspective they offered. I feel there is so much more to fitness than tips on dieting, supplementation, lifting, and shallow motivational hoo-ha, as many people would imagine. Although you are likely familiar with many of these topics, this book attempts to provide a deeper look into them and aims to be more insightful than others generally have been.

Most other books regarding fitness focus on one of the following:

- **A single major aspect of fitness**, such as weight loss. Perhaps it may include techniques and lifestyle changes toward this goal—maybe even a bit on how to think about weight loss—but may fail to include some important and relevant variables and how to prepare for or handle them effectively.

- **Multiple aspects of fitness**, such as the various styles of training (strength, size, endurance, etc.), nutritional education or dietary tips, and the techniques and significance of recovery. This can all still be very helpful and insightful, but most of these books don't dive deep enough or encourage much introspection; they don't do a very good job at drilling into the thought processes, relationships, and reasons behind the topics they cover.

While I wouldn't say I've been *completely* let down by existing fitness books, they just haven't covered some of what I do in this book at the level that I do. Some authors might be aware of the more underlying layers of the core aspects but choose not to include them, perhaps thinking people wouldn't care or that it doesn't matter as much. But I believe it *does* matter, and it could make a significant difference for the right reader. There are people who have no idea that fitness can be approached from a deep philosophical perspective. If they only had an idea of what lies within the depths I'm referring to, fitness—and perhaps even life itself—might become more attractive and transformative for them. Many people can't imagine just how significant its impact can be across other domains of their life. They might think fitness is an inherently shallow pursuit, but there's so much more beneath the surface.

For some of us, the surface-level stuff is just not enough; we need a better, deeper, perhaps even more philosophical or psychological approach. But once we understand it at a deep enough level, we might become enthusiastic about it, and may even change fundamentally. Books such as *Mind Gym*, *The Mindful Athlete*, and *Sports Psychology for Dummies* come close to what I attempt to do with this book (with *Mind Gym* coming closest), but I still felt something is missing. Though they did touch some psychological concepts and draw connections, they were either more motivation-based or just not as thought-provoking as I'd like or expect. I'd like not only to explore further but to also draw even more connections to aspects of daily life while providing some personal examples.

The following are just a few examples of aspects in fitness and how they extend to other areas of life, and which will be discussed in further detail in their respective chapters:

- Tracking your progress may seem like a pretty straightforward activity—or so it's been presented that way. You just log your workouts to see if you're improving, right? However, it's not just about tracking for the sake of it. Keeping a journal of your workouts—recording sets, reps, weights, and volumes—or your diet significantly changes how you think about your fitness journey and other aspects of your life, outside of solely providing measurable data.

    Initially, tracking might seem redundant or pointless, but it soon becomes clear that it's the only way to know if you're getting closer to your goals. This process fosters a mind-muscle connection, similar to how handwriting notes might help you retain information better than typing. When you write things down, it creates a more intimate connection with your goals and results, which makes the whole process more impactful. When you see progress, even small improvements, it's rewarding and keeps you motivated. Without tracking, you might miss these small gains and give up before realizing your progress.

- Pushing past physical pain barriers in the gym can increase both physical and mental resilience, which can then translate into improved performance in other areas, such as work or relationships.

  For example, pushing a particular amount of weight and reps at the gym one week, overcoming the associated pain, and then noticing increased productivity at work the next day. This happened to me recently. I pushed through a perceived plateau at the gym, and the next day, I was hyper-productive at work. I completed tasks in hours that would usually take days. This kind of growth in the gym translated to my work life and even my relationships, allowing me to handle more and deal with challenges more effectively.

- Another important lesson from fitness is the willingness to ask for help. You may hesitate to ask for a spotter at the gym, as many do, fearing judgment or not wanting to burden others. However, you'd be surprised how many people are happy to assist—and this principle applies to other areas of life, too.

Becoming comfortable asking for help at the gym made it easier for me to seek assistance at work and in other domains. This not only improved my performance but also fostered a supportive environment. Recently, I finished my tasks ahead of schedule and offered to help my colleagues by taking some weight off their shoulders—pun intended. This willingness to take on additional tasks was appreciated and reinforced the idea that asking for and offering help benefits everyone. It's yet another lesson that applied to my life outside the gym.

By now, you may have already gotten the idea that the concepts in this book apply to *all* aspects of personal development in *any* area of life—such as how tracking your progress in the gym can teach you the value of measuring efforts in other pursuits, helping you avoid a willy-nilly approach and become more intentional about your actions.

I encourage you to apply these insights to achieve personal growth and understand the deeper significance behind everyday actions. This book is not for the faint of heart. By making you aware of these deeper connections, you can't help but take responsibility for your growth and transformation.

Introduction

Now, although you may already have a solid understanding of the book's purpose by now, as well as some idea of its contents up ahead, I will, in this section, give you a glimpse of the following:

- Who should read this book

- What to expect (and *not* expect) from this book

- How to get the most out of this book

- Who I am

- Introductions to this book's core concepts

Who Should Read This Book?

Although everyone can benefit from and enjoy this book, those who would do so the most include but aren't limited to those of you who:

- First and foremost, have (or have had) an interest in or curiosity toward fitness (or those involved in fitness who have ever wondered if there's more to it than meets the eye).

- Make an effort to continue and enjoy working on yourselves, expanding your perspectives, and growing as an individual.

- Strive toward and appreciate taking a deeper look into the impact of what you're doing or why you're doing it.

- Have already taken or continue to take steps toward self-actualization outside of fitness

- Enjoy philosophical or psychological approaches or styles of writing.

- Enjoy content that encourages introspection, self-reflection, and metacognition through both the content and its corresponding exercises.

- Find interest in the integration of topics that may, to some, seem unrelated—in this case, fitness and philosophy.

When the Right Kind of Person Reads It, How Should Their Paradigm and Their Life Be Different as a Result of Having Read It?

Even if you don't get into fitness after reading the book, I would at least hope that you would foster the perspective that the book introduces. Ideally, you will become more aware of not just how you do one thing and how it affects other things but also *why* you do it and *how* you do it. And finally, you will **start paying**

attention to more of the patterns in your life and **make a habit of looking deeper into things**. I'm not exactly suggesting that you look deep into every single thing in your life, but I also wouldn't discourage doing so if one felt so inclined—that's just a bit beyond what most people would want.

Sensing how much deeper you can actually dive into these concepts may act as a foot in the door, which may lead you to start looking deeper into almost everything else naturally if you develop enough of a habit of doing so. Especially if you have the kind of personality or mind for it, thinking deeply about things that most others normally wouldn't becomes quite a bit stimulating, or sometimes even therapeutic.

You may make significant discoveries through the in-depth exploration of some of these seemingly trivial matters—the depths of which may bring about certain ideas, through which you may form more connections, *deeper* connections, in your mind. This has its effect on creativity; the more you get used to thinking and thinking about thinking, the more it becomes kind of a blessing and a curse because sometimes looking *too* deeply into everything can be troublesome—one can go into dark places if they're not careful, though there's nothing really wrong with it if they can make it through.

After all, people *do* need to discover the dark corners of their minds, as it is their own internal world after all—and that's where just *some* of the "treasures" are hidden, as pointed out by Dr. Jordan B. Peterson, clinical psychologist, best-selling author, and easily the greatest influence on my life—but they *do* need to be ready for it. One must prepare oneself for some sort of out. They need to know how and be able to climb back out of that space if they need to "snap out of it," so to speak. Dwell too long in that space, and one may likely become a prisoner there.

What to Expect (and Not Expect) from This Book

This book will aim to give the reader a deeper understanding of the mentality, the philosophy, behind fitness, and how the understanding of which—as well as the application of the underlying, necessary introspective processes of that understanding—can significantly bolster the reader's efforts on their path to becoming the best version of themselves, which can then, ultimately, impact society as a whole. **The reader should gain a philosophical perspective on picking up patterns and using seemingly trivial instances in their life to create paradigm shifts in various domains of their life**.

The book will attempt to reach this goal by using a combination of the following:

- **Anecdotal and scientific evidence** for the concepts discussed, inferences drawn, and conclusions made

- **Personal examples** from both my own life and experiences, as well as from those with whom I've worked with and consulted

- **Introspective and self-reflective questions** which will be scattered throughout the book.

Unlike other fitness books, **this is not a technical guide** on achieving specific physical milestones, nor is it a simple motivational tool to start working out. It's also not *just* about the philosophy behind fitness, though that *is* a large part of it. Instead, **this book fills the gaps of what people commonly know about fitness**, introducing some uncommon insights and explaining why they matter on a deeper level. This depth of understanding is crucial because once you grasp it, you will likely experience a paradigm shift of sorts in a way that will only benefit you. You might even discover a newfound interest in fitness that you hadn't previously considered. At the very least, you will gain a new perspective on an important and commonly discussed topic among modern society.

If you embrace the concepts discussed in this book, you can expect significant personal changes, and with enough individuals experiencing this transformation, there could be a ripple effect with the power to influence society as a whole.

How to Get the Most Out of This Book

I wrote the book in such a way that it's both rich with material yet fairly easy to read for those of you who are either on the go, don't like overly complex text, or don't like going in order—so you can read it any which way you like. However, to maximize the benefits you gain from reading this book, consider the following suggestions:

- **Set aside time for introspection**: Dedicate quiet, uninterrupted time to read and reflect on the introspective and self-reflective questions presented. Use these moments to dive deep into your thoughts and emotions.

- **Keep a journal** (I'm working on a supplemental workbook which will be published after this one): Record your answers to the self-reflective questions, your thoughts on the examples provided, and your progress as you apply what you learn. This will help you track your growth and revisit your insights later.

- **Be open-minded**: Approach the book with an open mind, ready to challenge your existing beliefs about fitness and personal development. Be willing to explore new perspectives and ideas.

- **Apply the concepts practically**: Don't just read the examples—actively implement them in your daily life. Experiment with the techniques and strategies discussed to see what works best for you.

- **Engage actively**: Participate actively by answering the questions, reflecting on the anecdotes, and considering how the concepts apply to your life. Engage with the material as if you were having a conversation with the author.

- **Pace yourself**: Don't rush through the book. Take your time to fully understand and internalize each concept before moving on to the next. Allow the material to sink in and impact you.

- **Discuss with others**: Share your thoughts and insights with family and friends. Discussing the material with others can provide new perspectives and enhance your understanding.

- **Revisit key sections**: Revisit the sections that resonated with you most, as well as your journal entries, periodically. Reflect on how your understanding and application of the concepts have evolved over time.

- **Stay consistent**: Consistency is key to fitness and personal development. Make a commitment to regularly engage with the book's material and apply its principles to your life.

- **Seek further knowledge**: Use the book as a starting point for further exploration. Seek out additional resources and continue learning about the concepts and principles discussed in this book.

By following these suggestions, you can ensure that you not only absorb the knowledge presented in this book but also apply it effectively to achieve meaningful personal growth and transformation.

Who I Am

I am an unusual guy (in a good way), primarily kind of a nerd, who developed a passion for fitness, hyper-fixated on it, and eventually became someone from whom people would seek health and fitness counsel.

I used to be a small, timid kid—short, a bit chunky, and a bit awkward too—with low self-esteem. I'm still fairly short and can still be quite a bit awkward sometimes, so not *too* much has changed. I was teased and bullied often, and since I couldn't beat them, I decided to laugh at myself and play along. I developed a defense mechanism where I used self-deprecating humor, making jokes at my own expense so that it was *me* who took the first hit and not others—a "you can't hurt me 'cause I beat you to it" approach, so to speak. Over time, it took a toll… naturally. Thus, I developed a desire to be the kind of guy that can prevent others from going through what I did (or at least guide them through it), and to be as much like the heroes I looked up to as possible.

I've come a long way, and still have a ways to go, but I'm still an ordinary guy—just one who, after helping enough people, decided it would be great to write out and elaborate on everything I've discussed with those who I've trained and consulted. And because I know many of them have become much better versions of themselves, I believe I can expand my reach and help many more by writing this book.

The journey hasn't been easy, but through consistency and the implementation of other concepts covered in coming chapters, it has become less difficult over time. Just a few of the things that made my growth more challenging than it could have been include the following:

- **ADHD**: As a kid, for a while, I had more of the inattentive symptoms. As I hit adulthood, I took on more of the hyperactive symptoms. I learned of my condition through my own search for explanations regarding this feeling I had that something was "off" about me. I was different from other kids, and I was frustrated for making the same mistakes and being blamed for things that I felt were innate with me—things that I felt were helplessly out of my control. When I learned more about ADHD through my studies in psychology, it all made sense, and I started managing my own symptoms. Sometimes I feel like I may be on the spectrum, but I can't be sure.

- **Hypothyroidism**: Another condition I've had to live with since childhood. It consists of symptoms such as fatigue and lethargy, weight gain, muscle and joint aches, and depression, to name a few.

- **Poor sleep quality**: I normally don't get restful sleep, and it's primarily due to the fact that I've had (and continue to have) dark, convoluted dreams since I was a kid. Many of these dreams, which are often nightmares, wake me up at night—sometimes more than once. If I recorded these dreams, I would likely have enough content to write horror stories or screenplays. I'm not sure about the exact causes of these disturbing dreams, but I'm confident that fears, concerns, and insecurities (just to name a few) all play a part. Since I don't get good quality sleep, my muscles and nerves don't get the rest and recovery they need to perform optimally, thus slowing my progress.

- **The Armenian culture, cuisine, and hospitality I grew up in** (for which I consider myself blessed) was many times a hindrance to my nutritional regulation and frequency at the gym because of a few primary reasons:

    ☐ Armenian cuisine is actually quite healthy, but, in my household, my grandmother was the primary cook and loved using butter and oil a lot more than normal—"That's where the flavor is!" she'd exclaim.

    ☐ If you have watched *My Big Fat Greek Wedding*, Armenian hospitality is very similar to that presented by the Portokalos family in the movie. Saying "No, thanks" or "I'm not hungry" when being offered food is not well-received, and sometimes not even accepted—they'll slap something on that plate for you anyway, so you're either going to eat the food anyway or the guilt trip for not doing so.

    ☐ It is commonly perceived as nonsensical, weak, and sometimes insulting to whoever cooked, that someone, especially a male, would be selective or somewhat restrictive about what he eats.

    ☐ It is commonly perceived as nonsensical and impractical for someone to spend as much time, effort, and other resources on fitness as I was. "You want to work out? We have water jugs with handles. You can walk or exercise with them as you'd like in the backyard. Instead of focusing so much on building muscles, focus on building your brain," (which I actually did quite a bit of, but no one wanted to see that, or even could).

You will learn more about me throughout the book, as I have included my personal experience with the concept being discussed in each chapter. Much of the advice I've provided others has been based on my:

- Personal experiences

- Studies in fitness, the human body, and psychology

- Perspectives on life and self-development

Though most of whom I've advised—those who actually took the advice and stuck with it long enough to see results—have experienced positive outcomes, I will outright state that not everyone I've consulted did.

Those who have sought my advice did not do so expecting professional help, and I did not advertise myself or advise them as such. All of the consultation I've provided has been on a friend-to-friend basis, and the examples and evidence I've provided have been mostly anecdotal, stemming from my own personal experiences. People came to me for advice because they saw in me the results they wanted, and so trusted me, assuming that if I've reached such goals, I must know the steps it takes to get there—steps one can recreate in an attempt to reach the same goals.

Core Concepts

Self-Mastery Through Fitness

Fitness is a gateway to mastering the mind. The physical challenges we face in the gym are much like the psychological and emotional battles we face in life. By pushing through discomfort, we build resilience, discipline, and a greater sense of control over our thoughts and actions.

The Connection Between Physical and Mental Fitness

Physical exertion and mental clarity are inseparable. What you do in the gym—how you handle fatigue, pain, and failure—translates directly to how you handle stress, adversity, and setbacks in life. Building physical strength reinforces mental resilience, making you more capable in all areas of life.

The Importance of Recovery

Rest and recovery are not signs of weakness—they are integral to progress. The body, mind, and spirit require balance, and knowing when to step back is as crucial as knowing when to push forward. And to work optimally, it is crucial to acknowledge when rest is necessary because growth and sustainability depend on it.

Self-Love, Self-Care, and Self-Respect

Loving and respecting yourself involves making the tough decisions to prioritize your well-being. True self-respect comes from treating your mind and body with care, allowing recovery, and knowing when and how hard to push. Building a nurturing, trusting, and confident relationship with yourself is necessary for proper growth.

Discipline without self-care leads to burnout, and balancing the two allows for long-term growth and sustainability. Just as you would reward a hardworking employee with rest, you must apply the same principle to yourself. This concept is about having the discipline to know when to stop, recharge, and come back stronger.

As Above, So Below

How you do one thing is how you do everything. Small, seemingly insignificant habits and behaviors are reflections of larger patterns in life. If you introduce order, discipline, and care into even the smallest actions—like making your bed or completing daily tasks—you'll see that same order influence your greater pursuits, goals, and relationships.

Embracing Discomfort for Growth

Growth happens in discomfort. Embracing challenges, failures, and setbacks are key to evolving into a stronger, more capable version of yourself. This is often where the best lessons are found.

The Role of Motivation and Goals

Your goals determine the level of effort and resources you are willing to invest. And though motivation is important, it's the core drive, the discipline, and the habits that carry you through when motivation loses its strength. Understanding why you are doing something and aligning your actions with your goals allows you to maintain focus and dedication over time.

Transformation of the Individual

The journey of fitness is ultimately one of self-transformation—not just of your body but of your entire being. And the process of this transformation affects all areas of your life by aligning your external actions with your internal values.

The Ripple Effect of Self-Improvement on Society

Individual transformation has a ripple effect on society. As more individuals become disciplined, resilient, and capable, they influence those around them—creating a culture of strength, accountability, and collective progress. So it isn't just a personal journey; it's the power to shape families, communities, and societies as a whole.

CHAPTER 1

What Is Fitness and Why Does It Matter (Beyond the Obvious)?

What Is Meant by Fitness?

When you hear someone utter the word "fitness," what comes to mind? Probably a bunch of stereotypical images of gym bros, athletes, dumbbells, dieting—right? Well, those aren't *exactly* right, but they're not irrelevant, either. Fitness is broad, contextual, and can be both objective *and* subjective. Each of us has different ideas regarding what fitness means to us.

There's the **evolutionary meaning "survival of the fittest,"** which doesn't *necessarily* have to do with strength, speed, stamina, etc. (although those qualities *are* vital to survival, whether physical or mental). It has more to do with **adaptability**—how quickly, easily, etc., one can adapt or acclimate to their environment or to unexpected changes and unforeseen circumstances.

In this case, being fit enough to survive means that fitness must be context-dependent—*where* **are you trying to survive?** An intelligent computer programmer who works remotely and lives a predominantly stagnant life (given the nature of his work is sitting in front of a computer for the majority of his day) would quickly realize that the skills that contribute to his survival and domination in his work life (career fitness) would be useless if he spots a bear charging toward him during his camping trip (physical fitness).

He could train for such situations, but allocating resources—of which, and arguably for most people, time is most valuable—to be fit enough to outrun a wild predator in the woods may not be valuable enough for him to do so. Not to say that he can't or shouldn't spend some time improving his physical fitness, which may give him a slightly better shot at escaping such a morbid fate. But after weighing the chances or frequency of such occurrences, he may decide it's better risking getting mauled by a bear than being less than his best at doing whatever pays the bills and allows him his desired lifestyle. So, instead, and reasonably so, he may decide to **allocate most of his resources toward the optimization of what he most cares about**—in this case, his career.

In that context, survival of the fittest may likely mean, though isn't necessarily limited to, the following:

- Job safety during times of company layoffs, and even if the entire company shut down, the "fittest" would have little to no trouble finding another job.

- Much better chance at raises and promotions.

- Up to date with the latest updates and advancements in his domain, and thus adding significantly more value than his less-informed or outdated counterparts.

- Greater influence among team members, co-workers, and superiors.

The **objective** aspect of fitness comes in when, let's say, someone is applying for a job as a police officer, but they are so overweight, undertrained, and mentally unprepared that, if put in a situation where they have to chase a suspect on foot or witness a gruesome crime scene, they can be at high risk of heart failure or mental collapse. They would, therefore, be objectively unfit for the job.

Objective fitness is **measurable** with data and is **directly connected to your anatomical and physiological capacity**. Take two healthy gentlemen, call them Cane and Abel, and say they are the same in age, weight, and height. They are performing the same exercise, side by side. If Abel is able to lift the same weight for more repetitions before hitting failure than Cane, or if Abel is able to lift *heavier* weight for the same amount of repetitions than Cane can with *less* weight, Able is objectively more fit than Cane—and that can be due to differences in their physical fitness, mental fitness, or both.

The **subjective** aspect, on the other hand, comes in when someone decides for themselves or others how fit they are relative to what they consider being fit enough is physically, aesthetically, mentally, etc. A basic example I've witnessed many times: A group of women are hanging around together at a pool party, and they spot a gentleman coming out of the pool after a nice, cool dip. One by one, they take turns assessing this man and sharing their opinions on his level of attractiveness, which usually begins by his physique, followed by his behavior. This man doesn't have perfectly carved abs but has a flat tummy. His chest doesn't look like it lactates but isn't saggy and has decent shape. His arms are not like those of Superman, but they appear full and tight. Now, one of the ladies may say that for her to consider him fit, he would need to have washboard abs and nice, tight, prominent, and perky pecs. Her friend, on the other hand, argues that what she expects is perfection, even unhealthy to a degree, and that this gentleman really is fit.

To be clear, perfection is not, by any means, the same as optimization. <u>Perfection</u> **is the unattainable ideal that in the process of striving toward, brings you closer to becoming your best self.** So although no one can really reach perfection in fitness, they can and should continue to strive toward optimal fitness in the domain they've chosen. In the context of this book, <u>Fitness</u> **is the optimization of the body, mind, and soul toward the thing you care most about.** So then this raises the question, **"What do you want to optimize?"** which may raise even more questions, such as:

- How do I choose what to optimize?

- Can I choose to optimize more than one thing?

- Can I optimize one thing that has an overlapping effect on more than one domain? Does that count as optimizing for more than one thing? Would it be efficient?

In later chapters, I'll go into more detail with optimization and how to approach these questions, but there are a few things to keep in mind until then. First, you have a finite amount of resources to allocate. Second, even though you can choose more than one thing to optimize, **the less things you choose to optimize, the more optimal the chosen ones will become because you'll have more resources for which to allocate.** Lastly, even if you choose to optimize just two things, one of those is going to be favored and optimized more than the other—albeit not significantly, but it will be nonetheless, whether you like it or not. This isn't to say that there's anything wrong with being a Jack of all trades, just as long as the individual understands they'll be a master of none—in other words, well-rounded but not optimized in any domain.

The process of choosing what to optimize and how to do so is yet another example of both the subjective and evolutionary nature of fitness. It is just one of the many processes involved in forming a strong foundation toward the development and adoption of the fitness mentality. The fitness mentality, as I refer to it in this book, is a mindset that values growth, improvement, resilience, fortitude, extreme ownership, integrity, and honesty—just to name a few, and it is the mark of an individual who wishes to be on, and maintain the path of, strong character development— one who, with the application of the principles discussed, has the potential to become a beacon for those who surround him/her.

For example, encountering a problem in a relationship you haven't faced before might motivate you to work on your communication skills and empathy. Just like in the gym, you face certain challenges and, in the process of trying to overcome challenges or find solutions to new problems, grow stronger from them in every sense: physically, mentally, *and* spiritually. The growth comes primarily from two sources: pain and newly acquired knowledge, which will be covered in more detail later on.

This mindset begins with a seed that makes its way into your mind. The seed can be considered the first sign of a new Will to change something about you or your circumstances. Some may even think of it as a little squirming bug in your head or gut that makes you feel like 'somethin just ain't right,' and urges you to do something about it. The seed may come from a feeling or realization, perhaps a moment of self-reflection or introspection, or even simply a particular challenge that motivates you to develop yourself. It can even come from a single thought or idea that was inspired by some external factor. The seed is not exactly enough, of course, but ***it's what is necessary to give birth to the chance at the potential fruit upon the successful execution of the will***—the most vital piece of the puzzle that makes up the fitness mindset.

The Will to change is not just a momentary thought; it's a powerful force that **originates deep within the soul**. This force is often born from a sense of dissatisfaction or an awareness that something is out of alignment in our lives—an internal signal that our current state no longer serves us or that we are capable of something greater. It's the soul's way of communicating its desires for growth, pushing us to break free from the chains of stagnation and urging the mind to explore new perspectives and possibilities.

Communication from the soul is not always loud or clear. It can reveal itself as a subtle, almost imperceptible yearning or a **persistent discomfort that we can't quite put our finger on**. This is where the psychological aspect comes into play—the mind, driven by this inner voice, starts to rationalize the need for change and goes on to imagine its approach. It starts to ask questions, to seek answers, and to challenge the existing state. The mind becomes a battlefield where old habits and beliefs clash with the emerging Will to evolve. This internal conflict is not just a mental struggle but a philosophical one as well, involving themes of identity, purpose, and the nature of self-improvement itself.

When the Will aligns with the soul's deeper values and intentions, it creates a harmony that resonates throughout the entire being. The once scattered and doubtful mind begins to focus its energy on strategic thinking—planning, analyzing, and setting goals that align with the soul's desires. This alignment is critical because it ensures that the changes we seek are not temporary or superficial but are rooted in our core values and are, therefore, sustainable.

The body, in turn, responds to the orders of the mind. It **becomes the vehicle through which the Will is enacted, translating thoughts and plans into physical action**. This is where the connection between mind and body is most apparent. The discipline required to push the body to endure discomfort and pain clearly demonstrates the strength of the will. Every rep in the gym, every mile run, every disciplined meal is a physical manifestation of the Will's determination to reshape not just the body but the entire self.

Philosophically, this interconnectedness between will, soul, mind, and body makes apparent the comprehensive nature of true transformation. It challenges the common idea that fitness is merely about physical appearance or athletic ability. Instead, it presents fitness as a process that involves the whole being—where physical exertion is as much about building character and mental resilience as it is about sculpting the body. In this context, fitness as an integrative process means developing a stronger, more integrated self, where each aspect—body, mind, and soul—supports and enhances the others.

Psychologically, this process also touches on the concept of self-actualization—the realization of one's full potential. The Will to change, then, can be considered a **drive toward self-actualization**, which would mean we are **acknowledging that we are not yet fully who we are meant to be**, and that the journey toward that ideal self requires us to engage every part of our being in the process of growth. This deeper understanding of fitness, then, is not just about how we look or how much we can lift but about how we live, think, and, ultimately, grow into the people we are destined to become.

To really understand the full spectrum of fitness, however, it's important to acknowledge how our **internal transformation manifests externally** as well. As the will, soul, mind, and body get stronger and align, their inner workings will often result in noticeable changes on the outside. Such changes may manifest in the following manner:

- **The Will**: It becomes easier to do things you know you should do that you don't feel like doing, such as canceling that one subscription you were forced into that makes it incredibly annoying to cancel—ahem, like SiriusXM.

- **The Soul**: Leads to internal peace, which leads to clarity on your values and makes it easier to cope with stress. For example, you may have felt guilt towards a certain family member, and so you may have avoided going to certain family functions where that person would be present. Since you value family, you felt even more conflicted for not going, or the guilt was enough to cloud your value. With more internal peace, you may have the clarity to remember you value family and will be more inclined to confront that feeling of guilt, make peace with yourself, and—combined with a stronger Will—have that much-needed conversation with that member because you've also become more empathetic.

- **The Mind**: You will notice that you learn faster, retain more, and recall more easily. You will become more inclined to understand yourself and others. You will also be better able to protect yourself from ideological parasites (Hat tip to Dr. Gad Saad, and his work *The Parasitic Mind*). Say, for instance, you are presented with a valid argument—one that flows logically—but the conclusion of which is false, even if the argument *seems* sound. With a clear mind and a better understanding of yourself, you will be better able to see through beautifully crafted and otherwise persuasive arguments, catching their falsities. You will be more intellectually aware, less susceptible to bullshit, and better able to think for yourself without being unnecessarily stubborn.

- **The Body**: If nothing else, you will experience increases in pain tolerance, immunity, recovery, and vitality. You will also appear healthier and more attractive. Anyone I know, including myself, who works out consistently and has a decent diet rarely gets sick—and when they do, they are less affected by the symptoms and recover much faster than others. These individuals also tend to be happier and, at least upon first impression, receive better treatment from others.

In the next section, we'll explore how these external manifestations of fitness, especially aesthetics and confidence, play a significant role in not just how we see ourselves but also how the world perceives and interacts with us.

Aesthetics, Confidence, & Fitness

Though having an aesthetic physique may occur naturally as a byproduct of other fitness goals, physical fitness encompasses multiple aspects, such as strength, endurance, cardiovascular health, immunity, and flexibility. And **just because someone looks beautiful on the outside doesn't necessarily mean they're healthy**. They might appear fit but could have underlying health issues, possibly due to extreme diets or drugs they've used to achieve a particular look. For all we know, their sleep, diet, and hormone levels could all be terrible. I've known people with great physiques who passed away due to conditions no one would have imagined they had. This serves as a reminder not to judge a book by its cover but also doesn't mean you should assume anything else either. If you're curious about someone's health, simply ask, but it's just better to focus on your own journey.

Not judging a book by its cover applies not only to health but also to how we perceive fitness and beauty more broadly. Fitness is subjective, and what one person finds attractive or ideal might be very different from another's perspective. There's plenty of evidence backing the idea that being overweight isn't healthy, but does that mean there's something wrong with having a preference for curvy men or women? No, of course not. If that's what you're attracted to, then so be it. It's like looking at an unconventional piece of art and saying, "That's my favorite painting. I love it. It's beautiful to me." However, though some people may prefer plus-sized bodies, a significant majority of people would choose body types closer to cultural ideals of attractiveness (Swami & Tovée, 2012).

When it comes to art and beauty, most may assume it's an *entirely* subjective matter, but—surprise, surprise—I'm here to tell you there's an objective aspect to all this as well. You see, if standards exist, and the majority share the opinion that such a painting grossly misses those standards, then questioning the judgment of someone who loves it wouldn't be totally uncalled for.

It's a bit absurd to say *everyone* or *everything* is attractive. If that were the case, there would be no such thing as masterpieces of art. So, yes, **there are objective qualities to aesthetics**—like symmetry, for example—but it's still largely subjective. Good news is, whatever you look like, it's likely that someone somewhere out there will find you attractive.

Societal norms and subjective preferences naturally extend to how physical fitness impacts not just appearance but the way you feel about yourself as well—your confidence, ultimately. The connection between physical fitness and confidence should not be underestimated. **The way you carry yourself—your posture, your presence, your demeanor—is *heavily* influenced by your physical fitness**. For example, when my girl and I are out walking somewhere, and I catch other men glancing over (she is a beauty; it's inevitable), I glance back at them, and most of them quickly turn their eyes away. I wouldn't have had that level of confidence if I wasn't aware of what I'm capable of. This confidence isn't about intimidation but about a sense of security and a strong presence. It's like having a weapon sheathed, drawn only when necessary, and always there in case I ever need to use it. Being physically intimidating can be helpful, but I don't *want* to be an intimidating guy—that's *not* the goal. It's just something I know I can use if I have to.

Physical fitness doesn't just change how you perceive yourself; it alters how others perceive you as well. There have been men who, to my surprise, expressed that I had an intimidating presence until they got to know me. That's the kind of unspoken power that comes with physical fitness. If you're a mugger, and you see two men walk by—one slanky and unconfident, the other muscular and confident—who are you going to target, all other things being equal? Posture gives off *huge* signals, and physical fitness will help correct it. First, because well-developed muscles will pull the ligaments and skeletal system in an upright, healthy form, and second, because the confidence you'll have will naturally lead to you standing up straight with your shoulders back. As a result, your body will physically appear tighter and stronger.

But it's not just about the look. Even when a man looks at another confident man, there's a psychological effect that takes place. I call it the "Holy shit, now *that's* a man!" effect. It's that moment of recognition where you can't help but acknowledge the intense presence and power of someone who exudes immense strength and confidence. And thank God he's a nice guy, right? Because if he were an asshole, you wouldn't want to be around him, so thank God he's on our side. And just to be clear, the confidence I'm referring to is the authentic type—not the compensatory.

This reaction is part of what I call the **Superman archetype— the world's strongest and nicest man simultaneously**. It's an ideal that many strive for in fitness, not just to look good but to embody strength, confidence, and kindness in equal measure. But remember, this isn't just about *physical* fitness. The mind and soul are deeply interconnected with the body, and true confidence comes from the harmony of all three. The journey to fitness, therefore, is not just about building muscle or losing fat but is more about developing a strong, resilient, and capable sense of self, both inside and out.

What is Meant by Personal Development?

When I think about personal development, I think about it in as many ways as you can develop yourself: your skills, relationships, career, and any other domain of your life, which leads you to become a better citizen among society. A citizen who has honed a particular set of skills can offer something valuable to society. A citizen who has the ability to form and maintain good, strong relationships has the power to influence and unite others, especially due to the self-reflection, empathy, openness, and humility required from them to do so. This enables them to consider a wider range of perspectives beyond their own, and so forth. Through their process of self-development and optimization, the individual learns how to think and reflect more deeply on their own thoughts and actions, and how those may affect the people around him. By doing so, he becomes more conscientious, mindful, and intentional. And since individuals influence everyone they interact with to some degree, those who interact with the kind of individual I'm describing will be left with a slightly better version of themselves after being influenced. We tend to want to be more like those we like and respect.

But what is meant by personal development? You can start by asking yourself what it means to be better in a given role or domain. Once you explore that, you can begin to explore your strengths and weaknesses, as well as other elements within that domain that have a significant impact on your growth—resources, blockers, etc.

You can then start paying attention to see if you notice any patterns in your behavior in various domains and contexts of your life. When you're ready, consider the following questions:

- Are these patterns apparent in a single domain, or do they show up in other domains as well?

- What are some of the common mistakes I've made or continue to make? Why do I keep making these mistakes?

- Has anyone in my family, including the last three generations, had similar patterns or made similar mistakes? Who may have endured hardship or trauma that may potentially be connected to *my* patterns or mistakes?

- How can I prevent those mistakes going forward?

- How can I use the strengths I already have to do so?

- Is there a way I can make up for my weaknesses that may be contributing to my patterns/mistakes?

- Who can I work with whose strengths can make up for my weaknesses?

- Who's feedback matters to me? Would this person's feedback make sense, and can I actually apply it? Is this feedback coming from a good place?

These are just *some* things to consider when thinking about personal development, but there is so much more. I'll go into more detail in later chapters, but, in a nutshell, **I define personal development as increasing your fitness in the various domains of your life that matter most to you—ultimately becoming a better human being and having as positive an impact on the world around you as possible.**

The Broader Impact of Fitness

Fitness creates a ripple effect. When you see someone who is fit—mentally, physically, or spiritually—it inspires you, and you naturally become more inclined to be as much like those you're inspired by as possible. And keep in mind, too, that the promotion and normalization of being fit would benefit society because then anything outside of that would be abnormal. I say this because I often witness someone spotting a very fit person and looking at them in awe. Being very fit is not the norm—it's not so common, which is why it's also admired the way it is by many. This is also why people feel comfortable not striving toward becoming fit: As of now, it's normal not to be.

In fact, quite the opposite—being unfit and obese—is being normalized in the West by those who sympathize with people who struggle with body image issues and don't want to make them feel marginalized. However, I—among many others—find it wrong on a deep level because it's a gateway to the normalization of other counterproductive lifestyles, which can easily lead to the degradation of society. It's already apparent that good values—such as family values—are becoming less common.

Now imagine if the norm becomes fitness of not just the body but also the mind and soul. It may finally cause the necessary discomfort for people to start taking action toward becoming the best version of themselves—but since the majority still won't reach their best, considering how much effort and resilience it takes (that's why the top 1% of any group of people is the top 1%), they will still be much better versions of themselves than if they didn't feel the need to start that process to begin with. This will contribute to a society of individuals who value development and strive for constant improvement, and because they understand what it takes, such individuals are more likely to respect and support the development of others, creating a sense of community. This willingness to help others becomes contagious and inspires further growth and improvement in society.

CHAPTER 2

How to Think About Fitness

As Above, So Below

How you do one thing is how you do everything. **The smallest weak decision made where it seemingly matters least will inevitably bleed into an area that actually matters most**—like micro-macro systems, where small, seemingly insignificant actions (micro) influence larger, overarching outcomes (macro). As above, so below.

I lead the section with this point because fitness in one domain of life, likewise, becomes fitness in others. This does not mean that someone successful in physical fitness is also necessarily successful in, say, business and vice-versa. It *does* mean, however, that if the successful businessman were to get into fitness, he would go about it the same way he does in business, and he would likely hit his goals once he gets a grasp on what his body, schedule, and diet allow. And, for the same reasons, he who is successful in physical fitness would likewise have a higher chance of succeeding in his career.

Just one of many examples is my friend and coworker John.

John

When I first met him, John wasn't into fitness. But while working with him, I noticed he had a strong work ethic, a deeply passionate drive for what he cared about, laser focus, and lots of fuel he channeled through productivity. One day, he expressed his interest in getting into fitness to flatten his belly and put on some muscle. I reinforced the idea but didn't push. I invited him to join me at the gym whenever he'd feel up for it.

The day came when he finally joined me. He said he'd had enough and that he wanted to hit his goal. He asked me to give him a breakdown of exactly what he needed to do. This is when I knew he was serious about it because these are precisely the steps he took that led to his success at work. He would set his target, figure out exactly what needed to be done, and then he'd hunt it down like a predator after its prey—only time was the matter before he hit his goal.

John experienced the most pain and discomfort in the first two weeks as his body adjusted to new movements and resistance, but he did not give up. I pushed him enough for him to realize the potential strength, endurance, pain tolerance, and overall resilience—both in mind and body—that he had within.

Just a few weeks after that, he expressed how much better he felt mentally and physically because of the routine. I even noticed that he was more resilient at work—the things that would easily trigger his irritability now seemed to have significantly less impact. He had been going every single day for just over a month and already began presenting noticeable results:

- Significant strength and endurance gains
- More defined chest and arms
- Slimmer waist overall
- Increased impulse control
- Better overall mood

John is just one of many people with whom I've had the pleasure of witnessing this development—and the impact of which on other domains of his life—first-hand.

The Mind-Body Connection & the Pain Barrier

How does repeatedly pushing your body to its limits transform your mind? This question is relevant whether you're a weightlifter or an Olympic sprinter, but **regardless what sport you choose, the confrontation with pain will always be there**. This isn't to say that the sport doesn't matter at all; each activity challenges the human body in its unique way, but, at the core, they all test our limits. **It's conquering the pain and obstacles that come with pushing those boundaries that leads to transformation.** In the documentary *Pumping Iron*, Arnold Schwarzenegger talked about crossing the "pain barrier," which is what he believes **separates the champions from the rest** (Gaines & Butler, 1977).[1] Crossing the pain barrier is a concept I strongly believe in, not because Arnold said it—though, coming from such a man, it definitely carries weight (pun intended)—but because I've personally experienced tremendous growth as a result of its application. It's not about suffering through pain until you're incapacitated but rather overcoming a level of discomfort that promotes growth and builds resilience. Each time you feel pain you're not used to, endure it a little more than you normally would've each time. **Your mind and body are much more resilient than you might think.**

For the sake of an example from my own experience, I'm going to toot my own horn a little. If you know how rare an achievement it is, you'll understand why I must use it as an example. At the time of writing this, I am able to bench 325 lbs while weighing just 165 lbs, all without boosters, steroids, or other performance-enhancing drugs—just good old-fashioned macro- and micronutrients. I lost count on how many people have asked if I "juice" (a slang term that refers to the use of steroids)—some of whom still don't believe me when I say I never have. Quite honestly, it's a hell of a compliment. Those who *do* believe me have asked how I'm able to lift as much as I do. I will tell you what I've told them.

When I lift, I become hyper-focused on the movement and the muscle being worked. I blur everything else out and do my best to form a connection between my nerves, my thoughts, my blood pump, my breaths, my movement, and the muscle itself—everything involved in producing the optimal rep and result. To catch a boost, I just look at my fiancé. Some folks may catch a boost when there are attractive members of the opposite sex within their vicinity—and that's healthy and natural, as long as they're not being creepy. I just hope their clothes don't show prints of that which is utilized for the primary purpose of our existence as human beings.

As I go through the motions, I imagine the oxygen and blood flowing through my arteries to my muscles, as well as the nerve signals traveling to and from my mind and muscles—often with my eyes closed. Eventually, I get to a pain barrier. This isn't when it starts to hurt; it's where it burns and sucks so much that it feels like I can't lift even one more. This is the point where my facial expression mirrors one of paying the price for having Taco Bell. However, this does not mean pushing yourself to injury; it means there is a level of pain you can handle that you're just not used to. I push to the point of what I call **the "Bee Sting"** (because it really does sting, and it rhymes with beasting) for all sets except the first, which is a warmup and not meant to tax my macro stores. If I can push about 12 reps—the last few being bee stings—I know I can attempt a heavier lift, and **I anchor my mind** to push the new weight for at least six or seven reps. Even if I'm only able to hit four reps, my mind and muscles won't stop trying because the goal was higher.

To push the same pain barrier every time I attempt a higher amount of weight, I need **to access the next level of that mind-body connection**, which actually involves **speaking to each part involved** in this movement—especially the mind and the muscle. I begin to personify the contractile units of my muscle (known as sarcomeres), and I literally engage in an internal dialog with them while also imagining how they look, how they work, and how they'd be responding to my communication. What do I tell them? I actually start to empathize with them, I motivate them, and I remind them why we need to do this together—and then I tell them of the coming reward. **This builds a strong relationship and level of awareness between you and your parts**, and it significantly increases your ability to push past seemingly unbreakable barriers.

So why focus on the pain that comes with fitness, especially the grueling task of lifting weights over and over again? Because this relentless, intense pain is a stark contrast to the more unpredictable and emotional pains of life—like surviving a war, losing someone you love, or enduring a catastrophe. And though each type of hardship requires its own unique resilience, the toughness you build from repeatedly lifting heavy weights is special. It trains your mind to go beyond what you think you can handle and to keep growing but does so **in a safe and controlled environment**.

Discussing pain in fitness introduces a comparison between specific resilience (like what you build in the gym) and the general resilience needed for life's unexpected challenges (like finding out your mother-in-law needs to move in with you). Inside the gym, you're provided a controlled setting where you can plan your battles with pain and face it head-on, increasing your endurance step by step and systematically working to increase your tolerance. Outside the gym, you have to adapt to whatever comes your way and still find the strength to push through—but **the increased pain tolerance developed *in* the gym will surely transfer to your resilience toward challenges you face *outside* the gym**.

Although pushing the pain barrier and understanding the mind-body connection is crucial to growth, it doesn't come without risks. Consider the story of athletes like bodybuilding legend Ronnie Coleman, among many others, who, despite medical advice, pushed beyond safe limits, and injured themselves. This is not by any means a knock on Mr. Coleman or any of the other legends; they've achieved great feats and inspired many. I'm just saying that we should use their experience to warn us of the risks of pushing too hard and remind us that ambition needs to be balanced with wise judgment.

By now, you might be asking, "Well, how do I know how much pain to endure? How do I know at which point I will or will not injure myself?" And you'd be asking rightfully because it's a fine line and it's not hard to get lost in the moment of the pump—in a moment where you're so motivated that you want to prove to yourself more than you should—and injure yourself.

I will now guide you through how you can start using and understanding your mind-body connection, and how to cross your pain barrier in a manner I've personally found both safe and effective.

Using the Connection

To effectively use the mind-body connection, you must first become aware of it. This isn't something that happens overnight, but with consistent practice, you'll start to notice the signals your body sends during your workouts. The trick is to not just go through the motions but to actively engage with each movement, each rep, and each breath.

Start by honing your focus. When you lift, don't just lift. **Lift with intention**. Feel the weight in your hands, the tension in your muscles, and the rhythm of your breath. Picture the muscle fibers contracting and expanding with each movement. Imagine the blood flow, rich with oxygen, fueling your strength. Engage your mind in the process—this is where the real connection happens.

Physical effort and literal muscle building aside, learning to channel your mental energy into the task at hand drastically enhances the effectiveness of the workout—or whatever it is you're doing. **The mind should be as involved as the body**, in such a way that it is directing and refining each action. This focus turns a regular workout into a deeper, almost meditative one, where you're sharpening your mind, training it to be more disciplined and resilient.

As you practice mindful lifting, you'll notice that you've become more in tune with your body in everyday life. You will be more aware of how your posture affects your mood, or how stress affects your breathing. This awareness is foundational to mastering not just your physical form but your mental state as well.

Breaking the Barrier

Breaking the pain barrier involves pushing through both physical discomfort and the mental limits you've unconsciously set for yourself. Many of these barriers are psychological, even if they feel physical. Your body can usually go further than your mind tells you it can—it's capable of much more than you might imagine. **The key is learning to recognize when your mind is giving up before your body actually needs to**.

When you get to the point where the discomfort becomes intense—when your muscles are screaming and your mind is begging you to stop—that's when the real growth begins. This is where you start to **negotiate with your own limits**. It's much like having a conversation with yourself: "Can I do one more rep? Can I hold out for just a few more seconds?" Often, the answer is yes, even when your mind initially says no.

But this is also where you need to be careful. **It's crucial to differentiate between the pain that leads to growth and the pain that leads to injury**. Pain that is sharp, sudden, or feels like something is tearing is your body's way of telling you to stop immediately. However, the dull, burning pain that comes from lactic acid buildup or the deep muscle fatigue after a long set is where I've felt I can safely push a little further. The goal is to **break the barrier without breaking yourself**. It's a fine line, but one that becomes clearer with experience. By continuously pushing slightly beyond your comfort zone, you condition both your body and your mind to handle more stress, more discomfort, and more challenges.

How Physical Fitness Can Affect Aspects of Personal Development

It works on both a physiological and anatomical level as well as a figurative and metaphorical level.

When you exercise, various physiological functions take place—one of the primary ones being an increased flow of blood and oxygen. With this increased flow, blood transfers nutrients much more effectively and efficiently, and your brain gets more blood and oxygen flow than normal, which contributes to its optimal performance.

Consider what happens when you hold your breath. You kill brain cells. If you hold your breath long enough, if you deprive it of enough blood or oxygen, you'll die. And if you don't die, you'll definitely give yourself brain damage. On the other hand, and as with the appropriate supplementation for anything else, if you supplement with blood and oxygen, the brain and body are going to work even better than at their regular state (ScienceDaily, 2019; Hyder et al., 2013)[2].

Physical resilience is yet another outcome on the physiological level. You're essentially getting your bones, muscles, and other tissues used to a *controlled degree of stress*, through the recovery from which they become stronger and more resilient. Some might ask, "What's the point? Why would I need increased physical resilience?" Maybe you'll perform better at work. You'll definitely do better in your sex life because your endurance, blood flow, and vitality are up—among other things... At the very least, I imagine you'll live longer.

Consider the following scenario. Maybe your wife complains that you don't mow the yard. Maybe you don't mow the yard because you don't want to admit that you can't—maybe because you run out of breath every time you push the fucking mower just part of the way through the yard. But if you get fit, you could potentially complete that task without huffing and puffing, and then you'll have made your wife happier. And if your wife is happier, perhaps that may make your day a little less painful and a little more enjoyable. And that's just *one* example of a potentially practical outcome of fitness.

Metaphorically speaking, the routine of driving to the gym, working out after a long day, and gradually seeing results reflects the virtues of sacrifice, discipline, and delayed gratification. You might not notice changes immediately, but persistent effort over time deeply reinforces these principles. Setting a goal, like a hundred pushups a day or a week, and sticking to it regardless of immediate outcomes, teaches you a powerful lesson in perseverance. You don't always need a strict deadline either because even just committing to consistent, incremental effort is enough to catalyze change.

Such a disciplined approach has a ripple effect that extends beyond the gym. In the workplace, for instance, mundane tasks often pile up—tasks that anyone could do, but that no one steps up to handle. Using the same discipline that you do in fitness, you could take the initiative to clear a large pile of mail or paperwork that makes people nauseous every time they lay eyes on it. Maybe you could pick up that responsibility and think, "Okay, if I just clear like five envelopes a day, that stack will no longer be such a big stack. It'll be a smaller pile. Or, hey, the pile might even go away," and it'll be better for everyone because you've gotten rid of an eyesore. And then people will commend you for it because it was something that perhaps nobody else felt like doing. But, you did it, despite it not being a part of your job, and it benefited everyone. And maybe the boss will see that, and he'll notice you. Sure, it's also possible he won't notice or even give a shit, but *not* doing it gives you ZERO chance at making ANY impact at all. As Wayne Gretzky said, "You miss 100% of the shots you don't take." In the end, you'd not only be clearing the clutter but also demonstrating your capacity to manage and lead—qualities that are sure to be noticed.

Throughout your fitness journey, you learn to break down larger challenges into more manageable actions. Just as you might see muscle growth after two months of consistent workouts, you might also see that a once-overwhelming pile of work has been handled over two weeks of consistent work. This kind of progress feels amazing, and reinforces the value of long-term, incremental efforts

You can use the same approach when trying to commit to going to the gym—you may begin to face a series of internal battles. Initially, it's uncomfortable and challenging, but as you persist, the process becomes more natural. You may find yourself thinking, "I'd rather do other things at that time" or "I don't feel like it. I'm too tired after work"—and that's perfectly natural, guys. It *does* suck to get started, and it *also* sucks to keep it going sometimes. There are *many* days, even after you've developed a routine when you're really not going to feel like going. Although it's not an unforgivable crime to skip a day here and there, it's easy to fall into that habit and get back into a slump— fight through it! And some people may have the confident thought process that, "Well, I know how to fight the pain and get into it, so even if I stop for some time, I can get right back into it." That's not *complete* bullshit, but I've known avid gym-goers, including myself, who after being out for just a couple months, still found it difficult to get back in. Sure, it won't be *as* hard as it would for anyone getting in for the first or second time, but it's still pretty fuckin' challenging to get out of comfort and back into the grind zone.

The following thought process was one I've personally had—perhaps you've had a similar one:

"Fuck, I'm too damn tired man… But if I don't do it, I'm just gonna feel worse… and then this is just gonna constantly haunt me. Is there anything more valuable that I can do if I don't go to the gym that will give me the same satisfaction or outweigh my not going to prevent feeling shitty about it later? No? Fuck… Okay, well, it's looking like the better idea is to get my ass over there."

And so you begin. It's annoying, it's hard, it's uncomfortable. But, **the first benefit is you're not beating yourself up for not doing what you know you should be doing**. And then the physical aspect of it kicks in and you feel better for actually going because your body feels more alive, more alert, a little bit more focused. Endorphins are rushing, there are dopamine hits, and you feel good. And you're like, "Okay, this isn't so bad."

The next day, it's kind of the same battle—and it's going to continue until you eventually get used to it. If you can build enough resilience and get used to facing that internal battle, I promise it becomes easier to face more challenging things over time. Then, when you do it for long enough and see the results, it's so rewarding that it leaves a lasting impression and conditions you—and then your mind automatically starts looking at everything else that way. This process also leads to the development of self-trust. Every time I've won that battle, I've built more trust in myself, which led to having more confidence in myself. I became more resilient to the weaker, tempting thoughts that tried to keep me at the teat of comfort. This resilience transforms into a habit, making it easier to tackle increasingly difficult challenges.

The satisfaction that comes from seeing the results of this discipline is unlike any other. It not only boosts your self-esteem but also changes the way you approach most problems, if not all—encouraging a systematic, persistent method to tackle various other issues in life. In essence, the principles of physical fitness are directly transferable to personal development. Whether it's handling responsibilities at work or managing personal challenges, the discipline, resilience, and ability to see through long-term goals developed through fitness can significantly enhance your effectiveness and satisfaction across other domains.

The Mental Prison: What It Is and How Fitness Can Be a Way Out

When speaking of the mental prison, I'm referring to **the feeling of being shackled by your thoughts and emotions**. It often feels as if the various internal voices of your different selves have control over you, acting as the wardens of your psyche, so to speak. And to be clear, these internal voices are *not* the same as the symptomatic, imagined voices apparent in Schizophrenia. They are *your* voices—your hypercritical self, empathetic self, anxious self, existentialist self, *collectively*—all having their say, sometimes all at the same time.

This mental state can manifest anywhere, and, for many of us, it's often our default state. You could be at a party, a supermarket, at work, or in class, but you're absorbed in your own thoughts. You're not present, not fully aware of your surroundings, and are thus usually slow to react. And this is often externally visible. Someone deeply entrenched in their mental prison might appear withdrawn, aloof, or constantly looking around nervously. These characteristics are more common in, though not limited to, those who are heavily self-critical—who have an *unhealthy* degree of self-awareness.

To get a better understanding of this mental prison, or even to gauge the degree to which you've attempted to understand, consider the following questions:

- When did you get there?

- Have you been there so long you've forgotten? If so, has it always been the same, or have you adapted to or understood it to some degree? How would you describe the difference between how it felt when you first got there versus now? Has it helped you or hindered you more? In what way(s)?

- How did you get there in the first place?

  - Was it due to a traumatic event?

  - Was it due to trouble understanding people's reactions toward you, or particular outcomes or consequences?

  - Do you have any family members who are also stuck in their head, so to speak?

  - Are you just naturally a deeply introspective person?

    Note: In case you confuse introspective with introverted, while they are both *similar* personality traits, they are *not* the same thing. *Introspective* folks have a tendency to spend lots of time in their head—thinking, reflecting, conversing with themselves, etc.—while the *introverted* have a tendency toward being more reserved, quiet, limited in social interactions, and focused more on inner experiences as opposed to outer ones. Introverted people *can* be introspective (and have a higher tendency to be so, compared to their extroverted counterparts) and vice versa, but introspection is not limited to the introverted types.

- How much have you explored? What's it like?

- Are there parts you're afraid of exploring?

That last question is especially important. If there are parts of you that you're afraid of exploring, or parts of you that you know for a fact will scare you, perhaps that's *exactly* where you need to look and what you need to face. **Perhaps that's where the key to freedom lies**. But also, maybe not. It's possible that after facing trouble, there is no key to be found after all, but now at least you know you looked and know for sure it's not *there*, and that you must look elsewhere. It feels like wasted effort, but it's not—think about it like the process of elimination. You may run into this problem several times before you find the key, but by knowing which places you've already searched and which problems you've already faced, you get closer to the place or problem that contains what you're looking for. And even if the other searches don't provide what you're looking for, they *do* provide other valuable lessons and intangible resources—such as a better understanding of yourself, at the least—that you inevitably pick up along that mysterious, unpredictable, and often troublesome road.

However, is intense introspection necessarily a prison? Or is finding joy in being in your head and thinking a lot necessarily a bad thing? No, not necessarily. *The **critical factor** is whether you control your thoughts or they control you.* **Being in control** *means having the ability to delve into deep thought* *and surface at will, without being overwhelmed by those thoughts*—and if you can't, you are the prisoner of your own mind. It's not the deep thinking itself that's problematic—it's being so consumed by these thoughts that you can't **stay present** in the moment.

For many, the mental prison is a dark, unnavigable space—especially daunting for those who don't know how to face it. It's like groping in the dark for a flashlight, which, once found, illuminates your surroundings and helps identify paths forward. This exploration involves pinpointing the specific characteristics of your personal prison—understanding its appearance, its terrain, the feelings it evokes, and how you found yourself there.

What you find might be terrifying, which is often why some of those memories or aspects of yourself that contribute to this mental confinement become repressed. **Are you ready for that?** If not, how can you become ready? So you start facing things that are not *as* terrifying but are still challenging enough that you could recover from without much injury. If directly confronting these issues seems too overwhelming, start with smaller, less intimidating challenges to gradually build the fortitude necessary.

Now, while understanding your mental prison is essential, it's the steps you take toward breaking free that will ultimately free you. **You need to act; understanding alone is not enough**. Whether it's confronting social anxieties, applying for challenging job positions, or embracing new experiences, these actions are critical. Think of them as workouts for your mental strength. For example, if social interactions intimidate you, ask about the cashier's day at a store you don't frequent until you're prepared to converse with the cashier at the one you do. After every small interaction, take a moment to reflect on what happened—did you die? No. It may have been awkward, but who cares? You don't have to see them again. And if it wasn't awkward, if it went better than you had imagined, even better! You might even look forward to the next experience. Actions like these are the practical exercises that help you break free.

To sum it all up, escaping your mental prison requires a blend of deep self-understanding and proactive behavioral changes. By combining introspection with practical action, you can pave your way to freedom and come out the other side completely transformed. As you go through some of the later chapters, you will come across tools and techniques that can seriously help you navigate your prison.

Endnotes

1. Gaines, C., & Butler, G. (Directors). (1977). Pumping Iron [Film]. White Mountain Films.

2. ScienceDaily. (2019, December 4). Respiration key to increase oxygen in the brain. Retrieved from https://www.sciencedaily.com/releases/2019/12/191204090817.htm

    Hyder, F., Rothman, D. L., & Shulman, R. G. (2013). Total neuroenergetics support localized brain activity: Implications for the interpretation of fMRI. Proceedings of the National Academy of Sciences, 110(9), 3549-3554. https://doi.org/10.1073/pnas.1222165110

CHAPTER 3

How NOT to Think About Fitness

Many of us have had, or at least are aware of, one or more stereotypes, fears, or negative associations of sorts surrounding fitness and gym culture—and this may have played some role in one or more of the following:

- Your attitude toward or perspective on fitness

- Your decisions (or lack thereof) toward fitness

- Your opinion and experience of others already in fitness

If you have negative associations, fears, or misconceptions toward fitness, you're gonna have to burn those down before you can move forward. And I will help you with that by picking apart the common ones many of us might have toward fitness—where they come from and how they planted themselves in our minds. I will then reintroduce how to look at fitness through a cleaner lens.

All Brawn/Beauty and No Brains

There are many people who think that those who work out a lot and have nicely built physiques necessarily have little to no intelligence—as if the physique is some kind of trade-off or compensation for the falsely perceived lack of brains. This is just the same kind of misconception people have about models. Even if there may be a trend, it isn't true for all. Many of those who have made these generalizations, I've noticed, had neither the intelligence *nor* the body. So, shitting on those who have at least one major thing they *wish* they had makes them feel better.

If there was a free magic pill that, POOF, gave them a God-Bod sculpted by Michaelangelo himself, don't you think they'd take it? I can bet the majority would. The problem is they'd lose it within just a month or two because **they don't realize the effort, skill, and discipline necessary to keep it up**. This may remind you of lottery winners, particularly those who frown at the rich, who go broke soon after because they don't have the financial literacy or know-how to manage that money wisely. Those who seek quick and easy solutions are the reason there exists a multi-billion-dollar industry to serve them.

The ones that do realize it, however, might naturally and reasonably think, "Well, instead of investing that much in my physique, I'd rather spend it doing something else, something more worthy, more intelligent, more valuable." Aha! That's the word. Valuable. People have different *values* and different *goals*. These are what determine what you spend your resources on, and it doesn't make someone more or less stupid or intelligent for having different goals and values than yours—so long as they are diligently realizing and standing for those values. There is respect in acting in accordance with your values, being aligned with them, protecting them, and maintaining your integrity. The right people notice that.

I've been subject to this misconception before. It used to hurt. But there were reasons why it didn't stop me:

1. Even if at the time I thought it might be true, I started to think, "Fine, even if I *am* retarded, should I not *at least* have the brawn?"

2. Through different skills and experiences, I started seeing evidence that I wasn't as dull as people might have thought, so that motivated me further. Then I began to think, "God, I can't wait 'til these turd nuggets see me when I get there (there, meaning the peak of my success) and think, 'How is this possible? He's got a nice body, *and* he's intelligent??' or even 'Shit, he made it.'"

3. I wanted to have a nice body very badly. I wanted to at least *look* like one of the heroes I admired, and I knew that that would boost my confidence.

4. That was the only guarantee I had. I knew that if I just continued to lift weights and follow the known steps and science of bodybuilding, I would surely achieve notable results in just a matter of time. Saying "Just follow the recipe" makes it sound easy, and in some way, it is (the steps are laid out, and you know what you have to do),

but the difficulty comes with the inevitable pain and the necessary discipline.

5. I started noticing that those who judged me that way were either a) very ignorant of what it takes to build such a physique, b) jealous/insecure, or c) upset that their woman would keep glancing at my thick, veiny muscles. Therefore, the opinion no longer affected me unless I allowed it, and the only way I'd allow it is if I actually still felt slow or incapable to some degree.

I'm sure there are still people who see me and think I'm all brawn and no brain, and I don't care because **their opinions carry no weight**—pun very much intended... Yep, I think I'm gonna keep that one going.

I'm sure you've heard people scoffing at nerds and academics as well, saying things like, "All you do is read books. What's that give you? Do something useful, stupid. Bet you can't use a hammer to hit a nail." Or hell, even the typical, "Can you even lift, bro?" Who the fuck cares? These comparisons are not in the same domain and are, therefore, incomparable and nonsensical. What one *can* or *does* do that the other *cannot* or *does not* do doesn't make either person good or bad, smart or stupid. Just because someone *can't* or *doesn't* do what *you* deem more practical or valuable does not make the other person a dimwit. How about finding a way to work with that person, befriend them? Perhaps you'll fill in each other's gaps and teach each other a thing or two. Perhaps you'll both become better human beings.

So that's one of them. People don't want to be falsely perceived as being potentially stupid just because they're going to the gym or working toward a nice physique. There's no shortage of dumb jocks, but there *are* people who are very fit, who frequent the gym, who are also academics, designers, engineers, programmers, accountants, etc.

So, stop giving a fuck about the opinions of those that busy themselves judging others in such a shallow manner. They don't matter. They don't carry any weight.

It Becomes an "Us vs. Them" Thing / I'll Become Categorized

This misconception revolves around how others perceive you and with which group you identify. People often fear being associated with or placed into stereotypes, such as being seen as part of the "bro" community. This group is often caricatured for its intense focus on physique and body-building, complete with its own slang (known as "bro-talk") and anecdotal fitness advice known as "bro science." While their vernacular or mannerisms might be annoying to some, it's worth noting that many individuals within this community are genuinely supportive and well-intentioned. That's been my experience anyway, though that's not to say there aren't bad seeds—every bunch has them.

Beyond just the "bros," the fitness world is diverse. It includes communities like CrossFit enthusiasts, powerlifters, and more, each with its distinct culture. However, embracing fitness doesn't necessarily mean you have to take on a singular identity. You can be a multifaceted individual—a professional in any field, an artist, or someone with several hobbies—who also cares about fitness. Approaching fitness with this perspective will make it easier for you to see past the stereotype that fitness enthusiasts belong to a particularly generalized group.

The diversity in fitness is very similar to specializations found in professional environments where each department has its strengths and weaknesses that ideally complement each other—like an ecosystem, so to speak. However, people are often attracted to those similar to themselves, which can limit the benefits of interacting with diverse groups who have differing skills and perspectives. This is much like an engineer saying, "We don't talk to the design team," and vice versa, yet each has valuable contributions that complete the other's work.

For example, some may compare themselves or feel similarly to figures like Arnold Schwarzenegger or Isaac Asimov, who excelled in seemingly opposite fields—bodybuilding and science fiction, respectively—but whose ardent approach was the same. Schwarzenegger's dedication to body sculpting and Asimov's prolific writing demonstrate that excellence can manifest in different forms, regardless of the domain.

To address these stereotypes, we need to realize that everyone has unique strengths and can contribute in unique ways in multiple areas. Understanding that labels such as "nerds" or "jocks" are simplistic can lead to viewing individuals' capabilities and interests with a more nuanced perspective. The more we engage with diverse groups, the richer our personal experiences become and the broader our perspective.

The fear of being categorized should not slow you down or stop you from integrating fitness into your life. Whether you balance a medical career with artistic hobbies or explore fitness for the first time, you don't need to conform to a stereotype. Fitness is a personal journey that can complement various aspects of your life and enhance both physical and mental well-being.

Through this discussion, I want to encourage readers to see fitness as an inclusive, adaptable, and enriching activity that can be suitable for everyone, regardless of their background, goals, or interests. If we could just embrace the intricacies of our identities and the many different motivations behind physical activity, we can change what it means to be part of any fitness community and eliminate the "us vs. them" mentality that usually holds people back.

Fitness Requires Too Much Time & Ideal Conditions

Incorporating regular physical activity into our daily lives often involves getting around personal and environmental challenges. Of course, everyone's circumstances are different and are influenced by a number of things—living conditions, job demands, and personal preferences—but there are adaptable strategies to help overcome these barriers. You can begin by considering the following questions:

- Are there things you spend time on that are less valuable than this goal? These may include doom-scrolling on your phone

- Can you cut any of those things, at least temporarily? If not, can you cut at least *some* of the time you spend on them? And if not, still, can you find a way to incorporate some form or amount of exercise into those things you can't or are not willing to cut?

- Can you think of valuable things you spend time on, but that which you can modify in a way that allows you to incorporate exercise?

For example, let's consider the routine of someone who spends considerable time in front of a computer for leisure activities such as video games or watching movies. One might think this time is lost, but it presents an opportunity for integration. You could reduce your leisure time slightly, say by 15 to 30 minutes, and allocate that to a workout. Alternatively, during the inactive moments like loading screens or commercial breaks, you could perform exercises like dumbbell curls or squats. With this approach, you can continue to enjoy your leisure activities while incorporating fitness—effectively hitting two birds with one stone.

The concept extends to family environments, especially for those of you who have children at home. Whereas you might typically engage in passive activities like watching TV, this time can be transformed into active play with your little ones, which not only serves as quality family time but as an effective workout that can significantly increase your physical activity levels as well. Besides, that **time you spend with your kids is especially important in their formative years**, and which will contribute to some of the best memories they will have with you. Using this approach, you may think, "What's the point? Like that's gonna do anything... I doubt I'll see results at that rate." And understandably so. However, though it may seem insignificant, and though you may not be spending as much time as you need toward your fitness goal, ***it is a step forward nonetheless***, which can be increased over time.

If finding time for exercise seems nearly impossible due to family or work commitments—fair enough—***leveraging the support of those around you can be instrumental***. If you're in an intimate relationship, I highly recommend talking to your significant other about the need to share responsibilities, such as childcare or household chores, to free up some time for you to get into a more structured exercise routine. If they are aware and supportive of you and your goals, they will work with you to look for ways to give you that time.

And there are a number of other benefits that come from this mutual support. It can help you overcome barriers, develop supportive environments, and contribute to improved levels—and the very crucial habit of—communication in your relationship. Before you can even discuss these challenges with your loved ones, you should first understand how you perceive your daily schedules and priorities. Incorporating a workout routine isn't just a fun thing to do—it's a very important element of our overall well-being.

For those facing significant barriers, the most practical approach—as I mention frequently throughout the book because of how incredibly effective it is—is to break down these challenges into smaller, more manageable parts. Assess which obstacles are the easiest to tackle first, and then set realistic, incremental goals for overcoming each one.

I also always encourage people to adopt a mindset that sees physical activity as a *necessary* part of life rather than an optional add-on. You can find less demanding tasks that can still encourage movement and activity, such as standing while reading or taking short walks during breaks, which can cumulatively contribute to your fitness goals.

Now, if you're finding yourself trying to think of every possible objection instead of spending that effort on finding—or at least considering the idea of—potential solutions, that's fair, but if that's the case, then perhaps you should reevaluate your goals. This is a sign that either you don't value your physical fitness enough, or even if you do, you may also be too deeply embedded in your comfort zone—in which case you'll have to choose a less intimidating challenge to slowly get yourself used to discomfort. Or, you can take my favorite approach—the don't-think-just-do cold plunge approach—which REALLY sucks the first several times but feels amazing after and straightens you out faster than all other approaches. If you're like me and you're willing to pay the price for speed and efficiency, then this may also become your preferred approach.

Finding more time is crucial, but it's more important to creatively modify existing routines that will seamlessly integrate into your daily life and create a supportive environment that prioritizes physical health. This approach makes it a lot more possible to maintain an active lifestyle and move closer to your goals amidst your busy and obstacle-filled lives.

Cultural Judgment and Societal Expectations

The influence of cultural and societal expectations can significantly deter individuals from pursuing physical fitness beyond activities considered to offer more practical benefits. It often doesn't make sense to people why someone would choose to spend a significant amount of time and resources on activities like weightlifting purely for aesthetic reasons. For such folks, choosing to become a boxer or professional swimmer might seem more understandable because they perceive those as having clear, practical value. However, the idea of repetitively lifting weights just to have a nice body puzzles many. I've often heard criticisms myself, suggesting that instead of spending all that time building muscles, I ought to engage in martial arts, play soccer, take up dance, or devote more time to academic pursuits.

On the contrary, however, there exists a whole 'nother culture that pressures those who *aren't* into fitness to *get* into fitness. For example, I live in Los Angeles County near Hollywood, CA, where fitness for the sake of vanity is popular—so both cultures exist. And to be clear, I am NOT part of this culture. As I have mentioned earlier, this book is NOT intended to get you into fitness but is instead meant to broaden your perspective on it instead.

This mindset **stems from a societal valuation of activities deemed more practical**, while being completely ignorant to the practicality of weightlifting and other activities that don't fit that criteria—and this can *significantly* influence individual choices. There's an Armenian term I've heard used many times, "parap,"[1] which loosely translates to pointlessness or without reason and is often used as an adjective to describe someone who is idle and has nothing better to do—and that's how many perceive those who lift. So allow me to present you some of the practical benefits I experienced, among many others, from lifting weights, even if (or even especially if) it's just to build an aesthetic physique:

- **Strength gains**: this allowed me to perform better in certain jobs, such as construction and massage therapy; and, at the very least, I can carry more bags at once from the trunk of mom's car to the kitchen.

- **Favorable responses from others**: having a more aesthetic appearance has significantly changed the way people respond to me. People are nicer, they trust me more easily, they're more inclined to help, and it's easier to negotiate—and there are studies to support my experience.

    Research[2] indicates that physically attractive individuals are often judged more favorably compared to their less attractive counterparts. For instance, one study found that attractiveness can influence perceptions of trustworthiness and likability, which may lead to leniency in various social and legal contexts (Beaver et al., 2021). Similarly, another study highlights the multimodal nature of attractiveness, noting that visual, auditory, and olfactory cues collectively influence perceptions, thereby affecting attitudes and decisions toward individuals (Groyecka et al., 2017).[3]

- **Significantly slows aging**: I've met several gentlemen, both at work and the gym, who I could have sworn were 20 years younger than their actual age (which I found out later in conversation). I myself have been told by many that I look about 5-7 years younger than my actual age. Here is some research to help you understand:

  Research has demonstrated that regular resistance training or weightlifting has significant anti-aging benefits. A meta-analysis by Liu, Lu, and Yang (2020) concluded that such training can substantially decrease the likelihood of premature mortality, specifically noting that even 30 to 60 minutes a week could lower the risk of dying from all causes, including cancer and heart disease, by 10% to 20% during the study period. Additionally, resistance training has been shown to improve physical performance and muscle strength in older adults, particularly those diagnosed with sarcopenia, suggesting its potential to combat age-related decline in muscle mass and strength.[4]

- **Better sex**: Yes. I've personally noticed that my sex drive went up—among other things—due to increased blood flow, increased testosterone, increased endurance, and more. And it's not just better sex for men but for women as well. The experience I've had with women who would frequent the gym was significantly better than with those who did not, but I can't be sure if that was due to their active stimulation-seeking personality, from their overall health and body, or both.

Research supports that regular resistance training can indeed enhance sexual function in men. Specifically, a systematic review found that resistance training, among other forms of physical activity, can significantly improve erectile function in men. This is attributed to resistance training's capacity to improve vascular health and overall physical strength, which are important factors in sexual health (Gerber et al., 2020)[5].

Studies have also found that regular resistance training can improve sexual health, especially for women. For example, a study on obese middle-aged women showed that those who engaged in resistance training reported improvements in their sexual function (Bortz et al., 1990)[6].

Now, unfortunately, many people aren't aware of these benefits, and remain fixated on the idea that working out is a parap activity for parap people. This perception can deter someone worried about how they're perceived by their friends and family—it can make individuals feel like they must choose between their health goals and social acceptance. The fear of being mocked or seen as boring for choosing to have salad over steak or water over wine at a party is real. For instance, in cultures where social gatherings often heavily revolve around food and drink (Armenian, Italian, Greek, and Hispanic, among many others), maintaining a fitness regimen *can* be challenging. In such cultures, declining food or drink can lead to tensions and make one feel like an outcast at gatherings where what most would consider indulgence is actually the norm—I say this not just from my own experience but from witnessing many others go through the same experiences. These cultural barriers are significant, yet they often go unaddressed in discussions about health and fitness.

It's also important to understand the different therapeutic benefits and personal development opportunities that various physical activities offer because it's essential to consider what will genuinely work for you. For example, someone such as myself who finds meditation torturous might benefit more from high-intensity martial arts because the stimulation from which—for some of us—can provide a more calming effect. You need to find what activity aligns with your personality, what's true to your nature, and what helps you unwind—whether that's a quiet hike, a competitive game of hide and seek, or a challenging yoga session.

Fitness isn't a one-size-fits-all kind of deal, and neither is the way we integrate it into our lives. It's vital to tailor your approach to your personal needs, goals, and specific challenges that you face within your cultural context. Consider my own experience as an example: despite the apparent contradiction, I smoke cigarettes, yet I usually maintain a rigorous fitness regimen not so much for health but for vanity. It's a balance—my vices and disciplines counter each other, which allows me to enjoy my lifestyle without compromising my appearance, health, or pleasure. This surprises many, given the rigid stereotypes associated with fitness enthusiasts. However, I view it as embracing a balanced lifestyle that accommodates both discipline and indulgence and challenging the common idea that fitness requires absolute purity.

An entirely personalized strategy can help overcome the barriers put forth by societal norms and lead to more sustainable and fulfilling experiences with fitness.

Fitness Is All-or-Nothing

Many people adopt certain goals because they merely *think* they should, not because it's inherent to what they value—like the short-lasting New Year's resolution of going to the gym that everyone makes. A lot of people do it because it's kind of the thing to do, the thing that people *expect* them to do, or because it's some kind of trend. Some others just like the idea of a new beginning and don't care what society thinks, but because they haven't built up the right habits or the right lifestyle to sustain it, they quit soon after starting. What many people make the mistake of doing is going all in, all at once, and then crashing because they feel there is no point in doing it otherwise. That's likely because they know if they give themselves even a *little* room, they might slack off and not take it seriously—but **taking it seriously doesn't necessarily mean going all in, all at once**.

After the initial excitement dwindles down, many of these folks find themselves questioning the point of their efforts; they begin to recognize a pattern of starting and stopping that they almost knew would happen. It's right around this time that thoughts such as, "Of course... What was I thinking?" usually begin to present themselves. So instead of diving headfirst into intense routines, it's much more effective and definitely more sustainable to develop incremental habits that prime the mind and body for upcoming changes. While some of you, like me, are more effective with the tear-off-the-band-aid approach and embracing the suck, this approach isn't suitable for everyone. Most require a gradual build-up, a warm-up phase, before fully committing to a new routine—and there is absolutely no shame or weakness in that. We are all built differently, each of us with our own unique set of abilities.

Besides the tear-off-the-band-aid approach, for a while, I combined it with an all-or-nothing approach—as if the former wasn't extreme enough—because I thought that's the only way anyone should approach anything they do. It works if you have the personality for it and want that to be the sole focus of your life—and there was a point where it *was* my sole focus—but when I started prioritizing other things, it didn't take long for me to learn that it was not a sustainable approach.

A large number of people are so afraid that if they don't take the all-in approach, they won't see results. Perhaps it doesn't occur to them that even painfully slow growth is better than no growth at all—and so they continue to think, "If I can't have it now, I don't want it at all..." Well, whaddaya want? Didya think it was a cakewalk? Many of those who quit early or don't even start are just not *patient* enough to gradually build the necessary skills and habits to sustain their new lifestyle. These habits take lots of time and effort to build, and though you are the captain of your ship, the people closest to you have a major influence on your time and effort. For someone who's naturally agreeable, the casual invitation to skip the gym for a movie night or a drink can be tough to resist, especially when it comes from someone close, like a best friend or family member. Imagine mentally preparing yourself at work, getting yourself pumped, and coming home ready for the gym, only to find your brother inviting you to relax and watch a movie instead, drink already poured. You may start to remind yourself that you've indeed had a hard day at work and may find it easier to convince yourself that you deserve a break and ought to join your brother—especially since it's not every day you spend time together.

This situation presents a nudge of temptation, like an ice cream sundae on a hot summer day, with guilt being the cherry on top, forming the perfect recipe for a seemingly reasonable excuse. I say seemingly because it depends how much you value that goal; if it's a high enough priority, that's not enough reason to be excused. Of course, this isn't to say you should be very rigid and not take time for leisure, but the pressure to conform and the guilt of turning down a loved one can still be overwhelming, which usually throws off even the most committed intentions. It's in these moments that the support—or lack thereof—can make or break you.

Let's say you find yourself relenting and skipping the gym—or whatever fitness activity you've chosen to engage in. The next day, the regret compounds, which can either make you want to go even more, or it can further demoralize you and destroy the trust you have within yourself. This is when open communication with your closest peeps becomes essential. Discussing your goals with your loved ones, like explaining the importance of your gym time, scheduling movie nights on non-gym days, or even inviting them to join you at the gym, can strengthen your relationship with them and make them more likely to support you.

Here's an example of how I've communicated with my father—a man I love dearly, who I hate saying "no" to but who's had a hard time wrapping his head around my approach to fitness:

Me: "Dad, yesterday I wanted to go to the gym, and you knew I wanted to go, but then you offered to watch a movie together. I enjoy watching movies with you, and it's very difficult for me to turn you down because I love spending time with you. If you could let me know ahead of time, I'll be able to plan my routine accordingly. That way, I can go without the pain of turning you down, and I can enjoy my time with you without the pain of skipping my workout."

Dad: "I don't see why it's a big deal—the gym is not going to go away if you don't go one day. But if you don't want to watch, that's okay tghas (Armenian for "my boy"), I'm not saying anything. I just don't understand why you spend so much time on that. What's the point? What does it give you? Same thing you can do at home, and instead of wasting so much time on that, work on your brain. I'm not saying *don't* do it, but I think it's just *too* much. I don't know, whatever I say, anyway, you will do what you want."

Me: "Pap (Armenian for "Dad"), I know you don't see the point of me doing what I'm doing in the way that I am, but that gives me what I need for me to function optimally. And when I feel my best, I can be my best for everyone around me. You always say you want the best for me, and I know that which is why I'm trying to explain why this is so important for me and how this leads to me being my best. This makes me feel better mentally and physically, it builds trust and confidence in me, and when I have that, I can think clearly—and as a result, I can retain more from what I learn and I become more creative."

Dad: "Okay, I guess you know better—I hope so."

Me: "You'll see. Trust me."

And he did see. It's even come to a point where if he notices I haven't been going, he shows concern because he sees that I'm an overall better person—mood, behavior, productivity, etc.—when I train regularly.

However, if your attempts at compromise and communication are ridiculed or discouraged—say your brother dismisses your efforts and predicts your failure—it's a clear sign that stronger boundaries are necessary. In such cases, prioritizing your goals over appeasing others becomes not only a matter of attaining the desired outcome of that goal but of asserting your autonomy, making a point, and even filtering what doesn't serve you out of your life—all of which are essential to personal growth. ***If your dedication makes someone uncomfortable, it often reflects their insecurities, not your inadequacies***. Having these discussions and negotiating time for fitness amidst social obligations requires ***clarity about what's truly important to you and the resilience to uphold these priorities***, even in the face of heavy opposition. More on social support and resistance in chapter eight.

These misconceptions are still surface-level biases. There are deeper cognitive biases at play here, which will be discussed in the following chapter. It's important for me to bring awareness to these biases before you can effectively begin understanding the concepts in the book, as well as how they're all integrated so that you can finally be ready to navigate parts of your mind that may normally trap you.

Endnotes

1   The "p" in "parap" is pronounced the same way that the "pp" is pronounced when saying "Hopped"—it's a quick, tight p.

2   Beaver, K. M., Schwartz, J. A., & Nedelec, J. L. (2021). Beauty is only skin deep: An examination of physical attractiveness and criminal justice outcomes. PLOS ONE. https://doi.org/10.1371/journal.pone.0259135

3   Beaver, K. M., Schwartz, J. A., & Nedelec, J. L. (2021). Beauty is only skin deep: An examination of physical attractiveness and criminal justice outcomes. PLOS ONE. https://doi.org/10.1371/journal.pone.0259135

       Groyecka, A., Pisanski, K., Sorokowska, A., Havlíček, J., Karwowski, M., Puts, D., ... Sorokowski, P. (2017). Attractiveness is multimodal: Beauty is also in the nose and ear of the beholder. Frontiers in Psychology, 8, 778. https://doi.org/10.3389/fpsyg.2017.00778

4   Liu, C., Lu, Y., & Yang, Y. (2020). Resistance Training and Mortality Risk: A Systematic Review and Meta-Analysis. American Journal of Preventive Medicine, 59(6), 792-799. https://doi.org/10.1016/j.amepre.2020.05.012

5   Gerber, M., Brand, S., Lindwall, M., Elliot, C., Kalak, N., Herrmann, C., Pühse, U., & Jonsdottir, I. H. (2020). Concerning a pandemic: Physical activity and mental health in the Swiss population before, during, and after the first COVID-19 lockdown. Frontiers in Psychology, 11, 2943. https://doi.org/10.3389/fpsyg.2020.589543

6   Bortz, W. M., Angwin, P., Mefford, I. N., Boarder, M. R., Noyce, N., & Barchas, J. D. (1990). Exercise-induced changes in plasma catecholamines and sexual function in women. Journal of Sex Research, 27(3), 409-417. https://doi.org/10.1080/00224499009551557

CHAPTER 4

Cognitive Biases

Understanding Cognitive Biases

Our brains process an incomprehensible amount of information every second. To manage this massive task efficiently, the brain relies on shortcuts—like templates or mental rules of thumb—that help it make quick decisions. These shortcuts are formally known as heuristics. They can be incredibly useful, but their major downside is that they can lead to errors in thinking—and we refer to those errors as cognitive biases.

A cognitive bias is like a trick that our minds play on us, which leads to deviations from logical or rational decision-making. Instead of analyzing every piece of information carefully, our brains take shortcuts—since humans, like other animals, are programmed to conserve energy—which can result in poor or inaccurate judgments or twisted interpretations of reality. Also, these biases are not random; they are consistent, somewhat predictable, and affect us all to some degree.

Cognitive biases influence our everyday decisions, from the trivial to the life-changing, affecting how we perceive the world, interact with others, and make choices. They must, therefore, be well understood, and by recognizing these biases, we can make more rational and effective decisions.

Sapir-Whorf & Cognitive Consonance

I'm a big believer in "You are what you think," primarily due to two major concepts: the Sapir-Whorf hypothesis and cognitive consonance. I will explain them briefly before discussing exactly why I believe one becomes what one thinks, as well as how it happens. Let's begin with Sapir-Whorf.

The **Sapir-Whorf hypothesis** presents the idea that the language we use can influence—consciously or subconsciously—the way we think and perceive. Upon learning this, I thought, "Of course! Each language has its own unique words and phrases for things or ideas that other languages don't, that can't be translated to any other language." I'm sure you can think of some words or phrases that are unique to *your* language. This idea doesn't stop at general languages either; it includes the various jargonic, cultural, and dialectical differences that exist within the larger bodies of language.

One clear example is the stark difference between street talk and academic speech or even the difference in the words chosen by lazy folks versus those chosen by their productive counterparts. I encourage you to make a habit of paying attention to the words you're choosing to think with—even go so far as to pay attention to others' chosen words.

Also consider the fact that, of all the words we know and of all the data we're exposed to, we choose very specifically what to pay attention to and what to use. Once we've sifted through all the data and have chosen what to use—a process that takes more effort than you might think—our mind does what it can to retain and stay consistent with what we've invested in, which leads us to the concept of cognitive consonance.

Cognitive consonance basically states that the alignment of your thoughts, actions, and beliefs leads to a sense of mental peace and harmony. The **opposite of this** is called **cognitive dissonance**, in which case your thoughts, actions, and beliefs are *not* consistent with one another. So, your mind—of which one of the primary purposes is to protect you—does everything it can to make sure those three are aligned.

Finally, the combination of these two concepts brings us to their impact on our intention and perception, collectively. If the words we choose to use influence our thoughts and perceptions, and—at the same time—our thoughts and perceptions influence our actions and beliefs, all while the mind does its best to keep them aligned, then the goals we think of and how or whether we decide to act on them are significantly influenced by what we tell ourselves right from the start. In a nutshell, **you harvest the fruits of the seeds you choose to plant**—where your thoughts are the seeds, and the outcomes you achieve are the fruits. If you plant seeds of doubt and negativity, you'll likely harvest disappointment and failure. But if, for example, you plant seeds of determination, optimism, and self-belief, the fruits you reap will likely be success, growth, and fulfillment.

So, to hit a goal we ***thought*** of, we can only do so through the ***act*** of aiming (Peterson, 2024)[1]. I like to think of aiming using the acronym **AIM: Align, Investigate, Mobilize**—a concept I'll explore further[2] in a later chapter. What you choose to think about is essentially what you choose to aim at, and that aim directly influences your subsequent thoughts, decisions, and actions. Then it follows that **your thoughts are not just passive reflections of your inner world but are rather *active forces* that shape your reality and direct the trajectory of your life**.

I'll aim to portray the significance of these concepts as they relate to fitness and how they do so in the following example, drawn from my own experience:

My fitness journey **began with the idea** of looking like one of the heroes I admired. I **thought**, "To be anything remotely close to them, *I can* at least **begin** to **be as fit as them**." And because I admired their resilience, discipline, and intelligence, I not only began working on my physical fitness, but I put a great deal of time and effort into my mental fitness as well. ***I aimed*** toward the ideal of what I valued, and my subsequent thoughts, actions, and decisions followed suit. Obviously, I could never be as strong as Superman but having him or others as my north star guided me toward the results I wanted.

I thought "***I can***," and my mind did its best to align the rest of my thoughts, actions, and decisions to keep them consistent with my belief. So, be very careful with what you think because if you **think** you **can't**, well, the **mind is going to try and stay consistent with that**. And if you're having a hard time thinking thoughts—or planting seeds—that would serve you, then it's well worth dedicating some time to figure out where your current thoughts, actions, and beliefs came from. Get as close to the roots of the existing tree as possible to understand why it's been producing undesirable fruit—or no fruit at all.

The most effective way to do this yourself is to be in a place where you can write your thoughts down on paper as they come to you. This makes it easier for you to keep track of your thoughts. And there is something about physically writing out your thoughts—as opposed to typing or talking it out—that makes it as effective as it is. I found this to be true mostly from my own experience, as well as from other anecdotal evidence. My curiosity about this grew, and so I needed to see whether there was any science to back this or if it's just limited to the experience of a select group of people. During my research, I came upon an article by Mueller and Oppenheimer (2014)[3], which explained the effectiveness of this technique based on the connection between the mind and muscles used to write. Their research indicates that handwriting enhances learning and retention because it involves deeper cognitive processing of the material, a concept known as "desirable difficulty."

But don't think too much about the writing process. Don't worry about grammar, structure, spelling—none of that. Just dump your mind onto paper and pay attention to common, recurring themes. Frequently ask yourself, "Where did this thought come from? Why did I feel this way?" Think back on memories. Are there any memories that you still hold onto because of feelings of guilt, trauma, or other negative emotions that you've had a hard time letting go of? This introspective practice isn't just about emotional or psychological well-being—it's crucial for fitness too. **Our relationship with fitness—or anything else, really—is often a reflection of deeper thought processes and beliefs we've internalized over time.**

For example, if you've always struggled with body image issues or have been criticized for your appearance, those negative experiences can shape how you approach—or avoid—fitness. Maybe you see working out as punishment or a way to "fix" yourself, whereas for others, it may be an empowering activity that makes them feel grateful for what their body is capable of. Or perhaps you avoid the gym because it makes you feel like you're lacking in some way, maybe due to past failures or comparisons with others. These thought patterns can be traced back to earlier experiences that were burned into the core of your mind and, since then, have been dictating how you should feel about yourself and your capabilities. So what can you do?

Try visiting childhood. There might be some dark, repressed memories that you don't want to face. It's possible there may be significant experiences that your mind has chosen to repress in order to prevent you from re-experiencing the pain, fear, or confusion caused by those events—and perhaps these are what's giving rise to your current system of beliefs. Maybe it wasn't traumatic; maybe it was just so repetitive that it became part of you. It could have been a seemingly trivial experience in childhood, maybe a normal thing that you and your family did, that—though it didn't seem like a big deal per occurrence—with **enough occurrences, can add up to have a significant impact** the same way enough droplets make up a pool of water that can damage the floor you stand on.

By peeling back the layers and understanding these underlying thoughts, you'll be much better equipped to reframe your mindset, which in turn can transform your approach to fitness, making it more true to you and your long-term goals. For instance, if you learn that your avoidance of fitness stems from a fear of failure based on your past, you can start to consciously shift that mindset. Instead of seeing fitness as another intimidating challenge you'll probably fail, you might see it as an opportunity for growth and accept every small step forward as a win. This shift can make the process of getting fit feel less like a chore and more like a rewarding climb to self-discovery and -actualization. Outside of the naturally resulting mental clarity, **the effort you put into understanding and reshaping your thoughts sets the stage for a more successful, fulfilling journey** in any domain of your life.

So how long do you keep writing? Well, there is no exact amount. I can't tell you that if you write an hour a day for a week that you'll come to some golden key that unlocks everything you need to know about yourself. Only *you* would know if you're truly being honest with yourself when you've reached a deep enough understanding of the sources of your thoughts and actions.

Writing down your thoughts isn't necessarily the only way, nor is it the most effective for some. You may discover more by talking to the right person, but the right person is hard to find. Besides that, most people don't have the skill of being able to truly listen and ask the right questions without trying to relate or throw out some sort of unsolicited advice. Another downside about talking it all out is that it's easy to lose track of your thoughts, whereas when you're writing, it's all in front of you. If you must talk to someone, maybe **find a good psychologist; they listen for a living, and the questions they ask will be far more effective than anyone else's—they're not just there for treatment or diagnoses.**

Exploring & Reprogramming Your Thoughts Through Writing

Before diving into the process of self-discovery and reprogramming your thoughts, you need to be ready to get to the core of some of these things. The core of certain thoughts might be dark and could bring up heavy emotions. So, you have to ask yourself: "Am I ready to face this? Am I ready to confront something that might scare me or evoke intense feelings?" Until you're ready to do that, you can't truly be free. To do anything meaningful with your thoughts, you first have to understand where they come from and why they exist. Once you've identified the source, you can decide, "Okay, this makes sense, but it hasn't served me. Now that I know this, what can I do about it?"

My preferred method for doing this is writing it down because I can see what thought led to the next, and that makes it easier to follow the progression of my thinking.

But what if you're much more into fitness and not so much into writing? Writing isn't the only option. You can also talk to someone about it, but that person needs to be someone you trust—someone who has your best interests in mind, not just someone you're cool with. Even then, talking can be tricky because the person might unintentionally guide you in a direction that strays from your true path, making it too easy to get distracted. There are very few people who can sit there, shut up, and listen without trying to steer you somewhere. Some people just need an ear, someone physically present to listen without saying much back, maybe the occasional, "And then what happened?" or "Go on." But since not everyone has that person, it basically leaves you with writing or typing.

I've personally found writing to be the most effective way for reprogramming *my* thoughts because there's an actual connection between my mind and muscles when I physically write out my thoughts—it keeps me more focused than anything else. You could sit on the couch in the dark and think about these things, but if you're scatterbrained like me, it's too easy to digress, go off on tangents, or decide, "Maybe I'll just watch a movie."

It takes a considerable amount of effort to think about your thinking—try it if you haven't, and you'll see what I'm talking about. **That's why most people don't do it**. And when you see that your thinking is wrong, you might freak out, think it's bullshit, and stop. When someone else tells you your thinking is wrong, it's easy to deny it. But when *you're* thinking about your thinking, you might realize, "Oh, shit, something's not making sense here." That's a very unsettling feeling. It's not comfortable. That's when you have to endure and **push past your own pride** because **catching yourself in your own bullshit is not an easy thing to do**.

There's an internal battle that happens. Which thought is going to win—the wrong one or the right one? The easier path is usually to go with the wrong one, but it will then be simmering in the back of your mind, bothering you because you've already realized it's wrong. **It's very much like creating your own hell—each poor choice fueling the tortuous scorching of the soul**. The easy thing to do is to justify it, gloss it over, and move forward. The most constructive thing to do, however, is to really ask yourself, "Okay, where did this wrong thought come from? How did I come to realize it was wrong? And now that I know, how can I think differently about that experience that caused this wrong thought process?" This is how you shift your thinking, own your thoughts, burn the old ones, and create new ones. Our minds are full of shit—much of it coming from our past experiences—and they need a good tidying up.

Each person looks at the world through a unique set of lenses that have been specially shaped by their individual experiences, personalities, and temperaments. This is why even siblings who grow up in the same household often see and interpret things differently. These differing viewpoints are incredibly important to understand because they tie back to the thoughts we carry—especially toward understanding others and their intentions. And if we don't actively monitor and challenge these thoughts, they can easily lead us astray.

However, our thoughts aren't formed alone by themselves, and it's not just about the words *we* choose to think or speak but also those of the people around us. The social environment we surround ourselves with plays a significant role in whether we continue to pursue our goals or give up on them. The language, attitudes, and behaviors of others can deeply impact our mindset and actions. Therefore, it's important to pay attention to:

- The people you spend most of your time with
- The words people around you use

- The words you choose to accept

- The way you interpret them

- The words you use to think about what they said

- The words you choose to respond with

Just as the words of others can shape your thoughts, the way you think about yourself and your level of self-trust are equally crucial. If you catch yourself thinking, "I don't trust myself," challenge that thought. Ask, "How can I start trusting myself?" instead of passively accepting the doubt. A thought like "I don't trust myself" is particularly dangerous because it can quickly spiral into self-doubt, inaction, and eventually dissolve the trust others have in you.

The point here is that your thoughts will affect your habits, your social life, your perceptions of fitness and diet, and how people respond to your lifestyle changes, which will in turn affect your success. Take my friend Sam, for example. He was homeless *multiple* times but managed to turn his life around because of his thought processes. His faith-based mindset allowed him to get back up *every* time and push forward to where he is now—a successful fitness coach who is a good husband, a good father, lives in a beautiful home, and drives his dream car. His faith saved him, both literally and figuratively.

Faith, in this context, has almost nothing to do with religious doctrine or ritual. I'm referring more to a deep and genuine trust in a power both within and beyond yourself—perhaps a belief in an ideal or a force that aligns with your deepest values. Whether you call this force God, the universe, or simply your highest self, faith is trusting that this power is real and is within you. You can feel this power from time to time. It may feel like a tickle across your body when you do something much better than you thought you could. Consider faith as the anchor that keeps you from deviating from the right path. When you pray, it's not just wasted effort and recited words; you're planting the seeds of your intentions and nurturing them with the conviction that they will grow if tended with love, trust, and consistency. Where and when you pray or find this connection doesn't matter; it's the faith itself that matters—the belief that the force you're speaking to knows what's in your heart and mind—and that's what guides you toward your goals.

If your thoughts consistently focus on gratitude and asking for strength and wisdom, that language manifests itself in reality. Your mind then becomes more focused on finding the strength, wisdom, patience, or whatever else you need because it is powerful enough to pick up on what you're asking for and thinking about. That's how thoughts manifest into reality.

Selective Attention

Selective attention is a cognitive bias where we focus on certain aspects of a situation while ignoring others. You will *only* see what you *want* to see. This bias can significantly influence the way we perceive ourselves and the world around us, particularly when it comes to fitness. This brings us to a form of selective attention called **confirmation bias**, where your mind, without realizing, begins to notice *only* the instances that *confirm* a particular belief or reality, whether real or imagined. If, for instance, you think, "If I get into fitness, *this* is how I'll be perceived," (whatever "this" is), you will find or twist evidence to confirm that belief.

Even if you're not worried about stereotypes or what people think about you, selective attention still has an influence. It often presents itself in the form of self-doubt, with thoughts like, "I'll probably just give up before I even start... What's the point?" This mindset is dangerous because it creates a negative feedback loop. The more you focus on the possibility of failure, the more likely you are to notice signs that confirm this fear, which can paralyze you into inaction, inevitably leading to failure and advancing your descent into the maelstrom of poo.

Selective attention is also one of the major reasons why people quit soon after their New Year's resolution. They start with enthusiasm—buying gym memberships, new supplements, and workout gear—but they haven't addressed the underlying thought patterns that have held them back in the past. They're still surrounded by the same environment, with the same circle of people who might be weighing them down instead of supporting their goals. Such an environment makes it much easier to focus their attention on discomforts and obstacles, while ignoring the progress they *have* made or even the potential benefits they *could* gain.

For instance, imagine you've committed to a new fitness routine, but your friends or family start questioning your choices: "Why are you wasting your time with that?" or "What's the point?" If your mind is already predisposed to doubt, or if, deep inside, you're looking for the perfect way to rationalize your way out, these comments can easily reinforce your fears and lead to your quitting. You might start to think, "Yeah, maybe Jim's right. Life's too short and I already work enough at my job... Plus, if I go now, my muscles will be sore and I'll be tired at work like last time. On top of that, I want to spend more time with my girl." At the same time, however, you chose to ignore the compliment your girl gave you the other day about having a tighter chest, a nicer back, or hell, maybe even better performance in bed. Perhaps you chose to ignore the fact that you've gotten a bit stronger, maybe a bit leaner too.

To combat this, it's crucial to catch yourself by paying attention to what you pay attention to and then immediately shift your focus when you notice that what you're thinking about is not serving your goal. I'm not saying that there is absolutely no reason for stopping—life happens, and priorities shift—but you need to be as real as possible with yourself. When you catch yourself, do your best to consciously redirect your attention to your achievements, no matter how small. Remind yourself of the benefits you're already experiencing, as well as why you started the journey in the first place. By doing so, you will be able to reprogram your thought patterns and, with enough time, significantly decrease the influence of this cognitive bias, and thus, you will ensure that your focus remains on the positive aspects of your journey rather than its potential pitfalls.

Sunk Cost & Stockholm Syndrome

Stockholm syndrome is a psychological phenomenon where hostages develop a bond with their captors, often to the point of defending or even loving them. In the context of fitness and personal growth, it is surprisingly common for people to develop a form of Stockholm syndrome with their own self-imposed limitations. How could you tell if you were one of them? Imagine the following.

You've imprisoned yourself in a comfortable little cage, a routine or mindset that feels safe because it's all you know or have ever known. It doesn't let you explore, but at least everything's predictable. Over time, you've become attached to this prison despite knowing deep down that it's not good for you. The thought of straying away from it—stepping out of your box—makes you feel uneasy, alienated, and even a little afraid of the unknown.

But who is the captor in this scenario? Is it society? Your environment? Ultimately, it's you. You are the captor who keeps yourself from growing. Yes, your environment plays a role, but you've chosen to create and remain in that environment. You've selected the people you surround yourself with, and while it may seem like you're stuck with certain negative influences, like harmful family members, there is always a way out, even if it's difficult—just depends on the price you're willing to pay.

This attachment to your captor-self, the version of you that holds you back, is deeply ingrained. There's sentimental value attached to it because it's been with you for so long. It's filled with memories and experiences, making it hard to let go. This is similar to how some prisoners, after serving long sentences, become institutionalized—they grow so accustomed to their environment that they struggle to adapt to life outside of it.

In fitness, this can manifest as clinging on to old habits or routines that are no longer effective but feel comfortable. For example, someone might stick to a workout routine that produced results for some time but eventually plateaued. The familiarity of the routine makes it hard to let go, even though trying something new could potentially lead to better results. Besides that, attempting a more challenging regimen or even an entirely different approach can feel like abandoning the safety of the known for the uncertainty of the unknown can be horrifying. This self-imposed limitation prevents progress, keeping you locked in a cycle of mediocrity rather than allowing you to reach your full potential. To truly break free, you must recognize this attachment for what it is: a barrier to your growth. It's not easy to let go, but acknowledging it is the first step toward escaping the prison you've created for yourself.

The **sunk cost fallacy** occurs when someone continues to invest resources—whether time, money, or energy—into something with the hope of achieving a particular outcome, even when that outcome doesn't materialize, thinking that just a little more effort or time will produce the desired results. This behavior is especially common in business, where failing ventures are desperately kept up by additional resources in the hope of eventual success. The same pattern is often seen in gamblers who keep betting, convinced the next win is just around the corner.

But what I'm addressing here is slightly different. It's about how people spend so much time living life a certain way, becoming accustomed to that state of being, and developing a comfort zone they are reluctant to leave. This comfort zone becomes their norm—a state they've invested heavily in, even if it no longer serves them.

For example, someone might continue following a fad diet like keto despite not seeing the desired outcomes, thinking, "I've already put in this much effort. If I just stick with it a little longer, it'll eventually work." This mindset can be detrimental because it prevents you from making necessary changes that could lead to better results. Instead of acknowledging that the approach isn't working and adjusting course, you might double down on the same ineffective methods, ultimately hindering or halting your progress and potentially leading to burnout or giving up altogether.

In fitness, the sunk cost fallacy might look like sticking to an unsustainable diet and a suboptimal workout routine, despite investing months without seeing results. This is especially true when they've enthusiastically told people about their routine—making them more inclined to want to stay consistent with what they've advertised. Thus, when someone suggests a different approach, they resist and cling to the belief that more time will yield success, despite evidence to the contrary.

This is a dangerous mindset because it can lead to giving up entirely and coming up with seemingly rational reasons to justify doing so. When their flawed approach doesn't work, they may conclude that fitness itself is the problem, not the method they chose. It's like someone who fails in business and decides that business itself is not worth pursuing, rather than acknowledging that their specific approach was flawed.

Now, in the following example, I will try to show you what the combination of Stockholm and sunk cost might look like since I believe they are cousins who hang together more often than you might think. Consider the example of prisoners who've spent years behind bars. For them, prison life becomes all they know. It becomes familiar, even comforting, despite its harsh realities. When released, the unpredictability of the outside world often drives them back to the only environment they truly understand. Similarly, people can become so entrenched in their comfort zones that the thought of stepping into the unknown feels overwhelming.

This leads to a form of sunk cost. In this case, it's not about expecting a specific outcome from staying in the comfort zone but rather a fear of leaving it because of the time and energy already spent there. People think, "I've already invested so much into this life; changing now seems too risky." It's not insanity—characterized by repeating the same actions expecting different results; it's the unwillingness to abandon what's familiar, even if it's no longer fulfilling or effective.

Imagine living in a shitty apartment most (if not all) of your life. It's not in a good neighborhood, and maybe the neighbors are annoying. However, because you've been there so long, you've somehow grown sentimentally attached to it, and though you want a new place—and there is a good chance you'd move if you could afford to—it presents some challenges:

- You'll be abandoning the sentiment associated with the current space.

- You'll have to allocate more of your finances to the new place, which means you'll have less to spend on things you normally would otherwise.

- To avoid the reallocation of those resources, you'll have to make more money, which means you'll have to allocate more time to work, leaving you less time to spend on things you normally would have otherwise.

- The new place might come with neighbors you're not used to or even HOA that may have rules and expectations you're not used to or willing to abide by.

- A bigger space means more to clean.

And these potential challenges are more than enough to deter someone from making that move, even if the price of staying may be greater than that of moving.

I've observed that people often reach a crucial decision point when they're on the brink of a breakthrough. It's in these moments of fear and uncertainty that many go back to their old ways, defending the very prison cell they were once so eager to escape. This behavior reminds me of wisdom attributed to Buddha: when confusion, chaos, or fear strikes, you instinctively go back to the beginning. For many, that beginning is their comfort zone—the familiar place they know best, even if it's holding them back.

I've noticed this pattern in myself as well. Whenever I feel uncertain or off-track, I find myself slipping back into the same uncomfortable situations that initially motivated me to change. For example, financial difficulties often push me into a spiral of stress and anxiety, yet they also reignite my drive to take action. It's as if I'm trying to regain control by revisiting old pains, even though they are the very things I sought to overcome.

To get around this, I've learned to implement controlled moments of regression—short visits to the old self or the old state—so that I don't feel completely alienated from the person I once was. **This *conscious indulgence* in old habits serves as a safety valve that prevents unconscious breakdowns and allows for a more gradual change instead of a jarring one**.

But what does this have to do with the sunk cost fallacy or Stockholm syndrome? The connection lies in the fear of change and the comfort in familiarity. Stockholm comes in when people spend years in a particular state, becoming attached to it, even if it's no longer beneficial. The thought of abandoning it, of risking the unknown for something better, feels too uncomfortable. And then the sunk cost fallacy follows when the investment in the old way of life makes it hard to justify the leap into something new.

It is crucial to recognize when we're holding on to something simply because we've invested so much in it or become attached, rather than because it's the right thing to do or the right way to go.

The Boiling Frog

Following the discussion on the sunk cost fallacy and Stockholm syndrome, another cognitive bias that can subtly undermine your fitness journey is the "boiling frog" phenomenon. This concept, although simple, has deep, long-term effects when it comes to understanding how we slowly get used to our comfort zones, often without realizing the potential danger until it's too late.

The boiling frog metaphor suggests that if you place a frog in a pot of water and gradually increase the temperature, the frog doesn't notice the change until the water is boiling and it's too late to escape. In contrast, if you throw the frog into already boiling water, it will immediately jump out to save itself. The lesson here is that when changes happen slowly, we may not perceive the threat or discomfort until we're seriously affected by it.

This concept applies to fitness and personal growth in the following manner. Many people, myself included, start strong and enthusiastic—whether it's a new workout regimen, a diet plan, or a lifestyle change. We see results quickly and feel the initial high of accomplishment. But then, over time, that enthusiasm subsides. We start skipping workouts, making excuses, indulging in old habits, and before we know it, we're back in our comfort zone. The change is so gradual that we hardly notice it until we've lost all the progress we made. You can also look at it the other way around, which is to gradually get used to aspects of the fitness regime rather than the comfort zone—slowly get into the habits that serve your fitness goals, and, before you know it, you're fully immersed.

In my own experience, I've always been an all-or-nothing person. I'd dive headfirst into something and then burn out soon after—whether I saw results or not—retreating to the comfort zone I thought I had left behind. This cycle repeated itself until I recognized the pattern and made a conscious decision to implement controlled breaks or "comfort days." But even these breaks needed to be managed carefully. I'm still the type to dive right in—that hasn't changed, and some of you may be like me—but many of you would benefit from starting slow and building up to a point where you're fully engaged in your routine without feeling the sudden and painful heat.

When it comes to fitness, these controlled breaks might mean not skipping the gym entirely but allowing yourself a lighter workout or a rest day. Maybe even indulge in a treat, but don't overdo it—the key is moderation. This is where the concept of the shadow comes in, representing the parts of ourselves that, if ignored, can seriously disrupt our efforts. By acknowledging and feeding this shadow in a controlled manner, we can prevent it from overpowering us.

This actually ties into the concepts of sunk cost and Stockholm syndrome. Just as we can become attached to how much we've invested, or the comfort of familiar surroundings, we can also slowly acclimate to behaviors that lead us away from our goals. Not recognizing this slow descent until it's too late, just like the frog in the pot, is what makes it so dangerous.

As we move forward, it's important to recognize these subtle shifts in behavior and patterns of thought. The challenge is to stay vigilant and self-aware, ensuring that we don't slowly boil ourselves in our own comfort zones—and it really is a challenge to do that when we're often so hyper-focused on the moment.

In the next section, we'll explore another common pitfall—waiting for the "right time" to start. This elusive "perfect moment" often never comes, leading to endless procrastination. Understanding how to overcome this bias is crucial in taking action and sustaining the momentum needed to achieve your fitness goals.

Procrastination: Waiting For "The Right Time"

I've spent a lot of time wrestling with this thought process, not really knowing what to call it or how to explain it. But when someone finally pointed it out, it clicked. This is procrastination, plain and simple, dressed up as "waiting for the right time." And to some degree, it ties into the sunk cost fallacy.

Think about it. You've spent all these years in this comfy little lifestyle, and now you're about to throw it all away. Maybe you've just spent a bunch of money refilling your pantry with all the goodies you love indulging in. You might tell yourself, "I can't start my new diet and lifestyle just yet—I've got all this stuff to munch on, and I don't want it to go to waste." How convenient... So you delay the change, lying to yourself, thinking you'll start after you've emptied the pantry. But then, when it's empty, the motivation to change has waned, and you're back to restocking and repeating the cycle.

The "right time" does not exist. It's just a convenient excuse that keeps you in your comfort zone. For many folks, waiting for perfect conditions is often a way of avoiding the discomfort of change. If you really wanted to change, you'd find a way to make it happen, regardless of the circumstances. This mentality isn't limited to fitness either. It's the same in other areas of life, like travel. I've heard too many people say, "I'm going to start traveling next summer when I have a break from work," or "I'll travel after I finish college." But then something else comes up—a new job, a new project, whatever it is—and suddenly, travel is postponed again. The reality is, if you wanted to travel badly enough, you'd find a way to make it happen, just as you would with fitness.

In fitness though, this tendency to delay can be especially damaging; you don't have to build muscle, necessarily, but if you're not at least maintaining your fitness, you're letting it decline—it's just that you don't feel the consequences just yet, like the boiling frog. Waiting for the right time often means never starting at all, and that's a hell of a trap. And even if you start, stopping for a while and trying to start again can be detrimental to long-term progress because there's a very high chance you'll fall right back into the same "right time" trap.

Don't wait for the perfect moment. The right time is now, and the only way to make progress is to start, even if the conditions aren't perfect. After all, the most successful people in fitness—and in life—aren't the ones who *waited* for the right time; they're the ones who started and adapted along the way. *They created the right time.*

Endnotes

1   Peterson, J. B. (2024). How To Set Goals. YouTube. Retrieved from https://www.youtube.com/watch?v=R3SgWagstL4

2   Chapter Section: Defining Failure, Success, Good Enough, Ideals, & Where You Stand (A & B)

3   Mueller, P. A., & Oppenheimer, D. M. (2014). The pen is mightier than the keyboard: Advantages of longhand over laptop note taking. Psychological Science, 25(6), 1159-1168. https://doi.org/10.1177/0956797614524581

CHAPTER 5

Motivation and Optimization

Motivation

The Will lies at the core of every one of our actions—it is the most vital element in the motivation to act. The Will is the inner force that pushes us to move, to strive, to reach for something beyond our current grasp. It's **the spark that ignites the fire of determination**, setting us on a path toward growth and transformation. Without the Will, even the most rigorous training or the best-laid plans are meaningless. As Liam Neeson's character Ra's al Ghul says in *Batman Begins*, **"The training is nothing. Will is everything."** This quote does an amazing job at exemplifying the Will as being responsible for transforming potential into reality—the thing that turns mere intention into action.

But where does this Will come from? It originates deep within the soul, that intuitive gut feeling, the wellspring of our emotional health. The soul, in many ways, really is like a deep well from which the Will draws its strength. When the soul is aligned with our values and desires, it fuels the Will to act, to aim higher, and to achieve more. This alignment is critical because the Will is directed by our deeper intentions and beliefs. This is where the concept of **AIM** comes into play: **Align, Investigate, Mobilize**. First, we **align** our Will with our deeper values and intentions to make sure our goals resonate with our true selves. Next, we **investigate** the paths available to us, evaluating the challenges and opportunities that lie ahead. Finally, we **mobilize**, putting our Will into action and turning our plans into reality.

Through proper aim and alignment, The Will becomes an unstoppable force, driving us to overcome obstacles we may have thought too large, push through pain we never believed we'd endure, and ultimately achieve goals we thought impossible. It's the bridge between thought and action, as well as between desire and achievement.

The Will to improve is an incredibly important aspect of fitness—so much so it can't be emphasized enough. Something makes you think, "Ya know, I feel like I want/need to do better." This could stem from simple curiosity about your own potential, or it may be conceived through self-reflection, introspection, or some particular challenge that presents itself in your life, and you may feel like you're not ready to face such a challenge—thus motivating you to reflect further. Perhaps you don't want to take on this challenge but you have to because too much depends on its outcome, and you don't want to simply just give up, in which case you may finally be motivated to take your first action toward improvement.

Consider the example of growing through a particular problem in a relationship that you haven't encountered before. Although you've had many relationships and many different problems, you haven't faced this particular kind of problem. Maybe you don't want to lose that relationship, so you start reflecting again, and maybe you start working on your communication skills. Maybe you have to learn how to be more compassionate and empathetic, whereas before you were a little *less* empathetic. Maybe you start thinking things like, "You know what, is it possible I'm being selfish? Why would a reasonable person think, act, or speak this way? Where are these thoughts and emotions coming from? What purpose are they serving?" etc.

This internal dialog is a form of introspection, and improving your level of fitness in any domain involves *a lot* of introspection—a lot of willingness to work on particular areas that you may otherwise haven't had to before. So now I'd like you to imagine these domains as being parts of your body and life as being one big gym. You must lift certain burdens and face certain pains to grow, to develop particular skills, and to develop that mental or emotional strength, flexibility, stability, etc.

This introspective process doesn't just help you understand what you need to improve but also uncovers the deeper motivations that really make you want to change. The Will to improve is often stimulated by a realization or challenge that forces you to confront areas of your life that need growth. But **why do we choose to act on certain challenges and not others?** The reasons behind our actions are complex and varied, but they all start with one core motivation.

We may decide to start a business because we want to be our own boss. "Can't someone decide to do so simply because they want to make money?" Yes, but to make money, they could have just gotten a job or set up a garage sale. Very few decide, all willy nilly, to start their own business just to make some money—there are deeper motivations, other reasons they would be willing to take on such responsibilities that come with the territory. And we'd typically see this behavior in the entrepreneurial types. As Lori Greiner from *Shark Tank* so accurately stated, "Entrepreneurs are the only people willing to work 80 hours a week to avoid working 40 hours a week."

Now, likewise, the same logic applies to why people decide to enter the world of fitness. We may decide to follow Arnold's blueprint because we want a massive yet extremely sculpted body. "Can't someone decide to do so simply because they want a nicer body?" Yes, but to have a nicer body, they could have just gotten a little leaner and put on some more muscle. Very few decide to endure such intense training just to feel good topless. Behind such a decision likely lies a much deeper reason.

The person motivated simply by the desire to have a nicer body would not be motivated enough to take on an extreme training routine; it would be more work than he wants out of it. But what gave rise to this motivation? Perhaps he wants to feel more confident or attractive. Why? Maybe to give himself a better shot at asking his coworker out. On the other hand, the person motivated by the desire to look like Arnold would be much more motivated to take on a far more intense training routine. Why? Perhaps he wants confidence too. So both of these guys are doing it for confidence? How does this make sense? Why does one decide he needs a Schwarz-bod to feel it, while the other feels just enough is enough? The underlying motivations depend on their values, their self-worth, their environment, their upbringing, and many other variables. I've seen very attractive people who have little to no confidence—some of whom are aware of their aesthetic and can care less, while others, even when people tell them how attractive they are, don't believe they are.

So we see that even motivations have motivations. And as much as I'd love to dive deeper into the thought processes behind these motivations and the behaviors they incite, I will have to do so in another book.

There are, essentially, **three primary motivations for getting into fitness—general health, physical capacity** (strength, size, endurance, etc.), **and vanity**. So why these three? How do they interact with each other? Do you optimize for one at the expense of the others? Do you have to choose *one*?

I'll tell you why I chose those three and how they interact with one another, but the latter two questions will be answered in the section about optimization. But before I answer those questions, I will provide some brief examples for each of the primary motivations.

General Health

- "I need to lower my BMI to qualify for life insurance."

- "My doctor made me."

- "Sex breaks my heart. Literally."

Physical Capacity

- "I need to be able to carry heavy loads at work." (Strength)

- "I'm a twig." (Size)

- "Sex takes my breath away. All of it." (Endurance)

Vanity

- "I want to be more attractive."

- "I need to qualify for an acting role."

- "I want her turned on with the lights on."

Whether your motives are one of these three or something completely different, you don't *need* to choose one over the other, but optimizing for one *does* affect the others. We'll discuss optimization more in-depth later on, but for now, let's stick to motivation.

Like many others, my primary motivation was to become more attractive, to feel more confident. And, really, the motivation of achieving a nice body is a very primal one. Not many people work hard at getting abs and defined muscles strictly for health purposes. They want to look more attractive to the opposite sex. They want to increase their chances of propagation. This is especially important for women because men don't care as much about their status. Women, on the other hand, may select a slightly less attractive man, but normally *only* if he's of higher status than she is and if she feels safe and secure with him. But even though women care more about the man's status, even then, a man's physical attractiveness is still the first impression. She looks at us first and then decides, "Yeah, I would" or "Nope, not in a million years"—and you can often tell how they feel toward you based on the way they look at you. "The eyes, Chico, they never lie," as Tony Montana declares in *Scarface*[1].

Now, I'll answer the first two questions regarding the three primary motivations mentioned above:

1. Why these three?

There's not much complexity behind this finding, and if you pay attention to people's reasons, you may also find it to be true. The majority of reasons I've heard from people I've interacted with (probably thousands, if not more) who want (or wanted) to *get* into, *were* into, or *are* into fitness, drilled down to these three core reasons.

It's much less common for someone to get into fitness for a bet or some other cause. Yes, there are company competitions, but even that's not as common—and most of those who participate either give up mid-way or stop when the competition ends. Also, you won't really hear someone saying, "If I get into shape, Santa will get me the glow-in-the-dark Fleshlight I wanted." More common would be, "If I get into shape, my wife would get better sleep and will thus be nicer to me."

2. How do they interact with each other?

For anyone going into fitness for the first time, training for any one of the three will—at least in the beginning, for some time—have a positive impact on all three. You'll see improvements in general health, physical capacity, and vanity.

Training for general health somewhat warms you up for the other two paths. It focuses on achieving overall well-being through regular exercise, balanced nutrition, and activities that support cardiovascular health, flexibility, and mental well-being. This approach naturally enhances both physical capacity and vanity.

For physical capacity, general health training lays a solid foundation. By improving basic strength, endurance, and mobility through light resistance work and aerobic exercises, your body becomes better prepared for more intense physical challenges and primes your body to perform well in any physical task.

When it comes to vanity, training for general health subtly but effectively improves your appearance. Regular exercise and a balanced diet do lead to noticeable changes in body composition, such as reduced body fat and improved muscle tone. While the focus isn't on achieving a specific look, you'll usually at least develop a more vibrant and balanced physique that aligns with many aesthetic goals. However, these aesthetic improvements are fairly minimal when compared to those achieved through a vanity-focused regimen. Still, the changes from general health training are more sustainable and contribute to a healthier, more resilient body overall.

Training for physical capacity involves focusing on strength, endurance, agility, and overall performance. When you prioritize physical capacity, you're pushing your body to handle more weight, run faster, or last longer in any physical activity. This approach naturally affects the other two areas—general health and vanity.

For example, as you train to lift heavier weights or run longer distances, your cardiovascular health, muscle mass, and overall energy levels improve, which ties back to general health. A stronger, more capable body is normally a healthier body, since increased physical capacity usually means better heart health, improved metabolism, and greater resistance to injuries.

At the same time, training for physical capacity can enhance your appearance, even if that's not your primary goal. As you build muscle and reduce body fat, your physique becomes more defined, which can improve how you look and feel about your body. Even with an enhanced appearance however, this approach doesn't always align with the typical standards of vanity-focused fitness. For instance, someone training for powerlifting might prioritize strength over aesthetic symmetry, resulting in a body that's incredibly strong but not necessarily meeting conventional beauty standards.

Training for vanity focuses primarily on appearance—sculpting the body to achieve a certain look. This could mean working toward overall muscle definition, reducing body fat to reveal abs, or shaping specific areas of the body like arms, legs, or glutes. While this path is often seen as superficial, it still interacts significantly with both general health and physical capacity.

When you train for vanity, you're likely to engage in activities that also improve your general health. For example, reducing body fat through a combination of diet and exercise lowers your risk of chronic diseases like diabetes and heart disease. Additionally, building muscle mass can boost your metabolism and increase your overall energy levels, contributing to better health.

However, the interaction between vanity and physical capacity can be a double-edged sword. While training for aesthetics often requires lifting weights and performing resistance exercises that build strength, the focus on appearance can sometimes lead to imbalances. For instance, someone might overtrain certain muscles to achieve a specific look, neglecting other areas that contribute to functional strength and overall capacity. This can lead to a body that looks good but doesn't perform as well in physical tasks or could be prone to injury due to muscle imbalances.

As we go through the different motivations driving us toward fitness, it's clear that these reasons—whether they stem from a desire for better health, increased physical capacity, or enhanced appearance—are not always straightforward or purely positive. Sometimes, beneath the surface of these motivations, there lie deeper, darker emotions that fuel our drive. These can be powerful forces, often born out of pain, frustration, or unresolved issues from our past. Understanding and harnessing these darker motivations can be just as crucial to our fitness journey, as they can push us beyond our limits in ways we might not have anticipated.

Exploring Dark Motivations

Motivation isn't always positive. Negatively charged motivations exist, and they're usually far more powerful than their positive counterparts. When exploring these darker motivations, you might find yourself diving into deep, shadowy places within your psyche—places associated with your childhood events, traumas, or the roots of your reactive nature. Getting to the core of such things, exploring such places, can be a heavy journey that may or may not yield a desirable outcome. But of all the mediums you can use to travel these roads on your own, fitness has been the most promising because it's by far the only one that's helped me and others I know climb back out of our darkest places. On the physiological level, fitness releases endorphins, neurotransmitters, and hormones responsible for stress relief and mood regulation, which offers a natural boost that can help pull you out. It's not a cure-all, but it's a powerful tool in your arsenal.

But what happens when you sit with these dark thoughts? If you're not accustomed to fitness or any other physical outlet, trying to find your way around these mental landscapes can seem heavier than they really are. Sitting alone in your room, replaying dark or debilitating thoughts over and over, can make you feel like a ten-ton cloud is looming over you, making it extremely difficult to escape from. Fitness, however, offers a way to channel those emotions in a way that transforms that darkness into strength—you lift that cloud at the same time you lift the literal weight.

Okay, so you have this dark motivation you want to use, and you have this weight you want to lift, but you need aim, and you need to know what makes up the weight on your shoulders. Some folks, whether in fitness or some other domain, feel the power of these motivations, and they do channel it into something—feeling the urge to keep pushing hard—but without real purpose. I've found myself asking, "Why do I feel the need to push myself so hard? What am I trying to prove to who?" And the process through which I thought about those questions revealed a lot about my deeper motivations.

What would you reveal about yourself if you asked yourself the same questions? Perhaps you're trying to validate yourself because you've never felt validated by someone important in your life. Maybe you're trying to prove that you're not the failure some people once made you out to be. These were some of the themes that presented themselves during that process, and these thoughts can be unsettling—at times, even terrifying—but acknowledging them is the first step toward transforming them. But how does *trauma* show up in the pursuit of fitness? I can't say for sure how large a part trauma plays in the gym community, but I imagine many people who frequent the gym have experienced some form of trauma.

Trauma is a part of life, after all, and people deal with it in different ways. Some might engage in fitness as a way to compensate for trauma, while others might find that their trauma is exacerbated by the pressure they put on themselves in the pursuit of their fitness goals. For some others, the gym becomes a sanctuary—at least one place where they can control details or aspects of their lives, even if just for an hour a day. But for others, it can turn into a battleground where they're constantly wrestling ghosts from their past and trying to exorcize demons through sheer physical exertion. And once in a while, a few of them might even wonder, **"Am I really doing this to get stronger, or am I just masking one form of my pain with another—one I know the cause of and recover from more clearly?"**

Think of it like how some people use sex as a coping mechanism, sometimes in unhealthy ways that might even worsen their trauma. Fitness can have similar effects. Some might hit the gym with a chip on their shoulder, feeling the need to prove something to the world because they've never felt validated or capable enough. They push themselves to extreme lengths, sometimes even to the point of injury, in a desperate attempt to lift that metaphorical chip off their shoulder. **That's when the pursuit becomes unhealthy**—when you ignore your body's natural limits, you negatively impact your life (or even that of others) just to prove a point. In those moments, you might catch yourself thinking, "If I just lift a little more, run a little farther, push a little harder, then *maybe* I'll *finally* feel like I'm enough." But that's a dangerous game because **there's no finish line when you're running from yourself**. Injuring yourself in the process can throw you into an even darker place, especially if fitness was your primary outlet for coping with your trauma. Then you're left wondering, "Now that I can't train, what the hell do I do with all this pain?" And it's not like you can really spend that downtime reflecting because the injury will likely produce a physical pain that will distract you from doing so.

On the other hand, there's a healthy way to channel those negative emotions through fitness. Instead of letting trauma control you, you can choose to push through it in a constructive way. Maybe you decide, "I'm not going to lie down and let this beat me. I'm going to see what I'm capable of, but I'm going to do it with discipline and self-awareness." You can set realistic goals, reach physical and mental milestones, and feel the fulfillment that comes from that without the risk of falling into a hole you dug for yourself. The rush you get from endorphin and dopamine releases, the balanced hormones, and the overall vitality that comes with a healthy fitness routine can seriously help you heal the wounds you're trying to patch up. You'll know when you're on the right path when you begin to think along the lines of, "I don't need to prove anything to anyone. I'm just trying to become the best version of myself. I can give a shit about someone else's expectations." And that's a powerful realization, one that can turn fitness from a mere coping mechanism into a vehicle that will drive you towards genuine self-improvement.

I'm not saying fitness is a magic pill that makes all your problems disappear—I wish. We're human, which means we'll continue to face struggles and frustrations. Fitness is a supplement to your overall well-being, but too much of any supplement can be harmful, in much the same way you can get vitamin poisoning. Approach it with balance, use it as a tool for growth, and make sure it complements rather than controls your life.

However, just as fitness can be a surprisingly useful tool for processing trauma and navigating our minds, it can also become a form of compensation—a way to fill perceived gaps in our self-worth or to mask deep-rooted insecurities. When we look beneath the surface, it's normal to find that the drive to push ourselves to our limits is fueled by a desire to compensate for something we feel is missing or lacking in ourselves. This brings us to the next layer of motivation in fitness: the complex and sometimes hidden urge to compensate.

Compensation as a Motive

It's fairly common for people to see someone who's incredibly fit and maybe assume they've got it all figured out. But for people to compensate for perceived shortcomings in their lives by overachieving in other areas is more common than you might imagine. Take, for example, my friend's narcissistic boss who defines his value by the size of his bank account and strokes himself every time he checks it. Whenever he feels threatened, he quickly resorts to statements like, "I could buy and sell that guy without breaking a sweat." His wealth becomes a way to assert his superiority and mask his deep-seated insecurities. In much the same way, there are those at the gym who might be doing the same thing—just that they use the numbers on the barbell instead of their bank account. The weight they lift, the muscles they build, all become ways of compensating their perceived lack of self-esteem in other areas of their lives.

This compensatory behavior is more common than you might think. It's where the stereotype of "brawn versus brain" comes from—the idea that people who spend all their time lifting weights must be doing so because they have nothing else to offer. But this stereotype is far too simplistic; although these kinds of folks exist, it is important that we **do not generalize** and assume that every muscular or hyper-fit individual must be compensating. The reality is that many of these individuals might be incredibly intelligent or have some other incredible skills. Some may either fail to realize that, or may still be compensating for something else entirely. For some others, building a strong, intimidating physique becomes a way to protect themselves from a world that feels threatening. It's like a sexy suit of armor that they think hides the vulnerabilities underneath. I say "think" because fake confidence reeks—if not at first glance, then definitely during enough observation or interaction. Aside from the compensation, however, many of these so-called "gym rats" might *seem* intimidating on the outside, but once you get to know them, you may actually find them to be some of the most agreeable and kind-hearted people you'll ever meet. They may have just built up the tough exterior not because they're inherently aggressive or unapproachable but because they've learned to mask or counterbalance their softer sides with muscle and grit.

Speaking of aggression, when you're at the gym, it's easy to mistake focus and determination for anger or intimidation. When you see someone lifting heavy weights with a serious expression, it might look as though they're pissed off at the world, but really, they're just deeply concentrated. This is sometimes referred to as the "resting bitch face" of the gym—or RBF for short. Outside the gym, this same person might walk around with a similar demeanor, not because they're trying to be intimidating, but because it's simply an involuntary external expression of their internal focus.

But let's get back to compensation. What causes it? Are *you* compensating for anything? If so, why? It often stems from feeling inferior in an area that you value highly enough and where you might feel the need to prove something—either to yourself or others. It's not the feeling of inferiority in just *any* area, though, because many folks are lacking in many areas. It's the real or perceived deficiency in an area you'd feel embarrassed for people to know about and that you feel the change for which is out of your control. And the areas to which you assign that importance, as well as how you feel about your deficiencies in them, depends on your immediate surroundings, both now and in the past—who you grew up around, who you looked up to (or look up to now), who influenced you and how, and what you felt was important to them. Maybe you were never respected, acknowledged, or validated by someone important in your life, no matter what you did—or because what you did just wasn't good enough and you knew it. Or hell, maybe you've *always* felt inadequate in some way. Whatever the reason, you've channeled that insecurity into some form of production, say fitness, and you're pushing yourself to extreme lengths to build a physique—or some other outcome—that compensates for what you feel is lacking.

However, there are two sides to this. On the one hand, pushing yourself to extreme levels in the gym—or anywhere really—especially when driven by a need to compensate for something else, can lead to unhealthy behavior. Ignoring your body's signals, overtraining, or neglecting other important aspects of your life in pursuit of an outcome you feel will make up for your deficiency can all result in serious consequences. Physical injuries, burnout, and even mental health issues can arise when fitness, at your core, becomes more about proving something than about what you're telling others you're doing it for—say, strength or general health.

On the other hand, compensation in and of itself doesn't have to be a negative thing. After all, the body, like most things in nature, has its own balancing system known as homeostasis (Cannon, 1932). Whoever is familiar with that system might only think of it in the physical sense—meaning, only relating to the body—but there exists a homeostatic process that occurs at the psychological level as well (Kohut, 1977; McEwen, 2006)[2]. This refers to the mind's ability to balance itself out after facing some kind of stress. And compensatory behavior is a prime example of just one form of psychological homeostasis, as it is the mind's attempt to manage some cognitive or emotional distress or imbalance (Baumeister et al., 2003; Kohut, 1977)—in this case, the stress of feeling deficient in some way. When our body feels deficient in some nutrient, we may suddenly have the urge to eat the thing that will satisfy that need. Similarly, when our mind feels deficient in some area, it should not come as a surprise if it nudges us to make up for it. But, just because it is a completely natural process, it does not mean it's okay to go about it thoughtlessly. By becoming aware of this process, we can catch ourselves in whatever compensatory behavior we've adopted, and ask ourselves:

- What is the behavior I use to compensate?

- What am I compensating for?

- Why am I compensating for that?

- Am I doing that for me, for someone else, or for others?

- What is it about what I'm compensating for that's so important?

- If I'm choosing to continue compensating for it, does the compensatory behavior I've chosen most optimally serve my higher goals and values?

- Has my life been better, stayed the same, or gotten worse since I started compensating?

- Would my life be better, stay the same, or be worse if I stopped compensating?

I strongly suggest you take the time to think about those questions, as they will help you dive deeper into understanding your own behavior—and only good can come of that, especially when the behavior is part of an incredibly vital survival mechanism.

Compensatory behavior in fitness is a reflection of our broader human tendencies, and we all have areas in our lives where we fall short—for me, quite literally, as I stand only five feet, six inches. For many, fitness becomes a tangible, measurable way to feel some control over these shortcomings, to build a more complete, more powerful version of ourselves. But the major danger that comes with compensation is that you can fall into an endless cycle of never feeling good enough in its pursuit. Your numbers, your size, and your workout intensity can become obsessions. Eventually, you may even find yourself chasing an ideal that's always just out of reach, which inevitably leads to a constant state of dissatisfaction, which may spark another behavior to deal with that dissatisfaction—one that is commonly self-destructive.

It's crucial, then, to recognize when you're pushing yourself beyond healthy limits. If your self-worth is tied too closely to your physical achievements, you might be compensating for something without even realizing—in which case, you would do well to step back and reassess.

My Motivation

The Punisher was the first person I ever wanted to emulate, and then it was some of the other heroes, like Thor or Wolverine, who had amazing physiques—physiques I personally thought were beautiful—like a work of art. It wasn't even like, "Oh, it's because I know girls like it." That was just something that I wanted, that I would have loved to look like someday, so I started working toward it. Even outside of physique though, I have an affinity toward aesthetics in the world around me. I guess I can say it's just a natural personality trait I've had since childhood, which also showed up when I took the Big Five Personality Test—a psychological assessment that measures five major dimensions of personality: openness, conscientiousness, extraversion, agreeableness, and neuroticism.

As a kid, I wasn't exactly fat, but I *was* kinda chunky. I was meek and timid, and I was bullied for some period of time and teased around a lot—and that was also due to my very naive nature. So it wasn't just the aesthetic I loved and wanted. Being fueled by these negative experiences, I also wanted to develop the confidence I never had before, which I felt upon achieving a particular level of physique.

After experiencing the rewards from some degree of development—such as admiration from others—my motivation to continue on my path to optimal fitness grew. As I continued to develop physically, I noticed a growth in my desire to develop as a person overall. And because of my increased tolerance to pain, I was able to push myself through the pain of overcoming challenges I otherwise wouldn't have. Once I noticed this change in me, I began to seriously consider all the areas in which I want to improve. However, I also knew that attempting to improve all those areas simultaneously would spread me too thin, and my progress toward each would be very slow and ineffective. So, I decided I needed to choose just one, maybe two, to focus on because that would be the only way to effectively optimize the areas I cared most about.

Optimization

Optimization is the most effective use of your resources on what truly matters. But deciding what's worth optimizing isn't as simple as picking one area and going all out. It's important to understand the interplay between different aspects of your life and be intentional when deciding where to direct your focus.

Balancing this process is critical, but the more balance you want across the board, the less optimal everything will be. However, focusing too heavily on one area—like physical fitness—can lead to unintended consequences in others, such as your relationships or career. Keep in mind that every action has an equal and opposite reaction, so when you dive into one aspect, be mindful of what you might be neglecting.

God being the exception, no other Earthly being can realistically be optimized in all areas. Even the most iconic figures of strength and success are often idealized beyond what's realistically achievable. Take Batman, for example. He's portrayed as the epitome of human optimization, impossibly excelling in damn near every physical capacity. He's depicted as the world's greatest detective, an unmatched martial artist, a world-class gymnast, and a hyper-intelligent, incredibly busy billionaire. But there's a contradiction here: You can't hold the world deadlifting record and also be the most flexible gymnast while maintaining peak mental acuity and running a billion-dollar empire. You could be *one* of those things and be the best in the world—two if you're a freak of nature—but you couldn't be *all* of them.

Similarly, think about Arnold Schwarzenegger. He built a body that became a global symbol of physical excellence, but that doesn't mean he'd be suitable for military combat, where endurance, agility, and other factors play a crucial role. It's essential to acknowledge this when setting your own goals and choosing where to focus your efforts.

How to Choose What to Optimize

It's essential to acknowledge that the resources we have are limited—whether those are time, energy, or finances. We can't excel in every area simultaneously, and sometimes, we have to make tough choices about where to direct our focus—especially for those of us who want to do it all. Personally, I chose to optimize toward an aesthetic physique. I'm not at my peak, but I'm content, and that's because it's not my number one priority right now. To reach my peak, I'd have to make it my top priority and dedicate a significant amount of time and resources to that goal. But I can't afford to do that—at least not now—because I've got bills to pay, and bodybuilding isn't my career.

When we talk about optimizing our goals, the first step is figuring out what we want to achieve and what's standing in our way. For most people, fitness immediately conjures up images of physical improvement—getting stronger, bigger, leaner, or increasing stamina and endurance—but they shouldn't ignore the mental and spiritual aspects of fitness. They're interconnected, and they influence one another more than most people realize.

Survival of the fittest doesn't necessarily mean just physical fitness; it's referring to the most optimized version of yourself in the context that matters most to you. Think about this for a moment. If you live in a jungle, survival of the fittest could mean how fast you can run from a tiger. But in the corporate jungle of New York, it's more about intelligence and strategy—survival often comes down to who's more clever, tactical, or even willing to bend the rules. Thus, fitness and optimization depend on your environment and what's required to thrive there. It is the *context* that defines what "fitness" means.

So, how do you choose what to optimize for? It starts with asking yourself, "What area of my life do I want to improve the most right now? What's the most valuable domain for me to focus on?" This question is crucial because that determines how you allocate your finite resources. For instance, if you work in construction, physical strength might be more practical than just having an aesthetic physique. But in business, having a well-toned body can actually give you an edge, as people tend to trust and respect attractive individuals more easily. I call it pretty privilege, and based on my experience, it's a real thing.

Indeed, attractive people often experience more opportunities and better treatment simply because of how they look. It may be a harsh reality for many, but it's something that can be leveraged. People are more likely to do business with someone who presents themselves well. The world's perception of you, by and upon which you are judged, might seem solely based on vanity, and it may not seem fair, but **you can use that perception to your advantage**. Besides the benefits that come from aesthetics though, improving your physical appearance can boost your confidence, which might, in turn, help you in your career. But since you can't optimize everything at once, the challenge becomes deciding which goal to prioritize. It helps to first figure out and distinguish what you want and what you need.

When it comes to the practical side of optimization, there's plenty of information out there about different workouts and diets tailored to specific goals. But I do things a bit differently. For example, I don't follow a traditional workout split like chest day, leg day, or push-pull day. I focus on what I feel my body needs. Some days, I might target one muscle group from each section of the body—chest from the upper body, lower back from the midsection, and hamstrings from the lower body. Other days, I might mix it up just to keep things interesting. I might even throw in a few extra sets for other areas, depending on how I feel.

Now, I've found that this approach works for me, but it might not work for everyone. Everybody is different, quite literally, and what works for one person might not work for another. However, the basics do apply to everyone—if you want to *gain* weight, you need a calorie surplus; if you want to *lose* weight, you need a deficit. For example, if you're regularly eating 3,000 calories a day but burning only 2,300, you're at a 700-calorie surplus, meaning you'll gain weight over time. On the other hand, if you want to lose weight, you need to increase your caloric expenditure while reducing your intake. Cutting down on calorie-dense foods, like switching from milk to water in your protein shakes or reducing the amount of creamer in your coffee, can make a big difference. I use nonfat milk for my shakes which contain 90 calories per 8oz I use for my shakes, and I have up to three a day. That's 270 calories I can cut from substituting milk with water—tastes fantastic, just not as thick and creamy. My favorite creamer cups are at 30 calories each, and I normally use between four to six a day. If I switch to black coffee, which I still love, I'm cutting roughly another 150 calories a day. It's these small, consistent changes that add up over time and help you reach your goals faster. To figure out which of the small things you can cut out, get a little bit introspective and think about what small but regular things you consume that you can and can't live without.

Weighing the pros and cons is just one part of the optimization process, but you should think deeper about the underlying motivations driving your decisions throughout it. For example, you might want to build an impressive physique because you can imagine the confidence and admiration that could come with it. But then you might ask, **"Am I seeking this for genuine self-improvement, or am I trying to fill a deeper void?"** Or take your career, for instance. You might be at a point where you're comfortable, but what does "comfortable" really mean? Does it mean you're satisfied, or **have you simply settled because you're afraid of failure?** You might ask yourself, **"Am I avoiding the next level in my career because it's not truly what I want or because I'm scared of the challenges that follow?"** Maybe your comfort in your career is actually a mask for complacency, and what you really need to do is breakthrough.

Similarly, when it comes to relationships, you might feel like you're being pulled between the desire to grow physically and the need to maintain strong personal connections. Here, introspection could lead you to ask yourself, **"Am I neglecting my relationships because I'm genuinely focused on my fitness goals, or am I using fitness as an escape from unresolved emotional issues?"** Are you pushing yourself in the gym to avoid dealing with a failing relationship, maybe even trying to convince yourself that the gains from the former will somehow make up for losses in the latter?

The real challenge, though, is having the willpower to start and sustain the effort required to make it through those deeper thought processes. I recommend constantly evaluating and re-evaluating your priorities, your progress, and your motivations. It's also good to keep asking yourself these questions:

- Why am I doing this?

- Is this the best use of my time and energy?

- What am I really trying to achieve here?

These questions help you stay aligned with your goals and ensure that your efforts are actually leading you toward the life you want to live. Now, as promised, I will return to the latter two questions mentioned in the section about motivation above.

1. Do people optimize for one at the expense of the others?

Yes, in most cases, they do. It's almost inevitable that when you focus on optimizing one area, others may take a backseat, at least temporarily. For example, if you're solely focused on building physical strength, you might find yourself spending less time on cardiovascular health or flexibility. Similarly, if vanity is your primary motivation, you might prioritize aesthetics over practical physical capacity or overall health. The diet, workout routine, and overall approach varies for each domain, which is why the optimization toward one is inevitable. The key is to recognize these trade-offs and decide whether they're worth it for you in the context of your goals. It's important to understand that every decision comes with a cost—so choose wisely.

2. Do I have to choose one?

Not necessarily. You can strive for a balance, attempting to work on multiple areas simultaneously. However, the more areas you try to optimize, the thinner your resources will be spread. You can do it, but it requires careful planning, more discipline, and an honest assessment of what you can realistically manage. Sometimes, it's better to focus on one area for a while and then shift your focus to another.

When considering what to optimize, you need to be brutally honest with yourself. Self-deception is a common trap that can lead to misguided, even wasted efforts. You might say to yourself, "Well, I'm enough"—and perhaps you are—but I encourage you to take a moment to carefully consider the following questions:

- Are you really content?

- Can you not be *more* fit?

- Can you not optimize your most valued domains even more?

- What makes you think you're already fit in a given domain?

- **How real are you being with yourself?**

Answering these questions requires a truthful, accurate evaluation to cancel out the possibility of self-deception. It's easy to convince yourself that you're doing fine, but the real challenge is to look deeper and ask, "Am I really as fit as I could be? Or am I just comfortable?"

Tuning the Optimal Amount

After you've identified what you want to optimize and how much time and energy you're willing to devote to it, the next step is tuning the optimization process to the point between effective effort and overexertion. Optimally, you should weigh your goals and your capacity to make sure that your pursuit of improvement doesn't come at an expense you can't afford. This comparison requires just as much attention and introspection as the initial decision to optimize.

In my own fitness journey, I've realized that my balance involves pushing myself to peak performance but not beyond the point of burnout—something many have actually considered extreme but are unaware of why or how I approach it the way I do. It took a long time for me to tune my approach. In that time, I did experience burnouts and breakdowns, and I was learning what to pay attention to and how to tune my routine for **maximum impact and minimal damage**. The lessons learned and skills acquired gave me the freedom to adapt to any changes life would throw at me—a freedom that came with a hefty but worthy cost, which will be discussed further in the next chapter. It's an approach that involves negotiating with myself. It's up to you to tune your approach to *your* sweet spot—the amount of effort that provides the biggest bang for the buck.

Now, just as many folks wouldn't spend 16 hours a day writing, no matter how passionate they are, they also likely wouldn't (and shouldn't) put that much time or effort in the gym every single day; that would be overkill. Even with something like amazing sex, you wouldn't want to have it all day, every day, as good as that may sound—trust me, you will come to a point where it starts to hurt. Still, there are many who end up pushing far past their healthy limits.

Keep in mind, too, that balance cannot apply the same way to everyone; what's balanced for me might be extreme for someone else. Finding your personal sweet spot requires going through the introspective and physically demanding processes, carefully testing your limits, and seeing how your mind and body respond. If you find yourself dreading your workouts or feeling burnt out, then perhaps it's time to negotiate with yourself. But let's be clear. This isn't about justifying laziness—not at all. Especially if you're new to fitness, you're not going to feel like going to the gym every day. That's not burnout, just the growing pains of starting out. However, if you've been consistent for a while and start to feel exhausted or mentally drained, that's when you need to reassess and get back to tuning.

Also, **you don't need to hit peak performance all the time**. It really depends on your goals. If your goal is to achieve a specific body fat percentage or reach a certain weight, you need to consider your schedule and responsibilities. If you've only got two or three hours a week to dedicate to fitness, trying to hit an ambitious goal in a short time frame is unrealistic and potentially dangerous. You might get overwhelmed and discouraged, either before you even start or after realizing it's not feasible. That's why I emphasize the importance of understanding your priorities. For me, fitness has been a high priority, and I've been willing to dedicate up to 20 hours a week to my routine. It's practically a part-time job, but not everyone can or should do that. Take my friend Shaun, for example. He's been working out consistently, following a strict diet, yet he's frustrated because he's not seeing the idealistic results he wants. He compares himself to others who might be on supplements, steroids, or who have different genetics and entirely different routines—and it's having a significantly negative impact on him. The lesson here is that pushing too hard without considering your unique set of abilities and circumstances can lead to burnout or injury. Don't blow your motor, folks.

So, how do you know where your limits are? It comes down to asking yourself the right questions, not just when you're tired or struggling but also when you're at your best:

- Why do I feel the way I do?

- What's keeping me at that level?

- What did I do to get there?

- How can I adjust or maintain it?

Understanding these factors can help you recognize when you're approaching your limits. And when you're feeling tired or off, it's worth considering the following—some of which may sometimes seem insignificant, or may simply not occur to us.

- Did you eat anything before your workout? If so, what and how much?

- Did you sleep well? If there were bad dreams, what could they be trying to tell you?

- Is there something on your mind that's draining your energy?

- Could it be that maybe, just maybe, the goal you're pursuing isn't as important to you as you thought?

- When's the last time you had a blood test to check your hormone and micronutrient levels?

Answering these questions can help you adjust your routine, as well as how much leeway to give yourself.

For those just starting out, it's much better to start by making small adjustments, like cutting back from three sodas a day to two. Making drastic changes overnight is, in many cases, nonsensical and unsustainable. It's better, therefore, to *gradually* find what works for you. As you get used to small sacrifices, you can challenge yourself more, maybe even cutting out soda entirely for a week. Or maybe you don't cut out soda completely but reduce it to a level that feels manageable. Do your best to consider an approach where you can be genuinely productive without being overly restrictive. The goal here is to progress steadily without the crash.

Potential Risks or Drawbacks of Over-Emphasizing Physical Fitness at the Expense of Other Aspects of Personal Development

The more you prioritize physical fitness—especially if you're aiming for rapid results—the more you'll need to sacrifice in other areas of your life. The more time you spend in the gym, the less time you spend with loved ones, advancing in your career, or engaging in hobbies that stimulate or relax your mind. Overemphasizing physical fitness can lead to neglecting mental and spiritual development, both of which are vital aspects of holistic health. **Every choice has a cost**, and the more you push toward one goal, the more other aspects of your life may suffer.

If you're not careful, you may start to resent your fitness goals if they begin to take away from things that still hold significant value in your life. This resentment can gradually build and lead to frustration as you feel torn between competing priorities. Left unchecked, this frustration can snowball into exhaustion. You might find yourself dreading the workouts you once loved or feeling exhausted by the heavy demands you've placed on yourself. The exhaustion will likely lead to feeling like no matter how hard you push, you're not getting anywhere—or worse, feeling a loss in areas that once brought you joy and fulfillment. This can lead to a deeper emotional exhaustion, where you begin to question whether all the sacrifices were worth it to begin with.

The tunnel vision that drove you can leave you feeling isolated, as if the rest of your life has slipped away while you were hyper-focused on one aspect.

Newton's Third Law: Every Action Has an Equal and Opposite Reaction

Newton's Third Law—every action has an equal and opposite reaction—applies to fitness and personal development, not just in terms of optimization but also in how we understand and harness motivation.

In fitness, **every effort you make to optimize your body triggers a reaction that is equal in power to the invested effort**, whether it's muscle growth, fatigue, or injury. The harder you push, the more pushback you're going to get, both physically and mentally. This is where your deepest, strongest motivations come into play. Yet, no matter how crucial this drive to push through pain and fatigue is, we must also recognize that this same drive can lead to an equally hot crash if not balanced with the same degree of recovery—an aspect of fitness so important it deserved its own chapter. Likewise, in the context of personal development, Newton's law suggests that every step toward self-improvement has its counterforce. **The force with which you decide to approach your task, challenge, or goal determines the level of counterforce you should expect and prepare to handle.** This is why it is imperative to consider the deeper motivations behind your actions, which you can do so by considering the following questions:

- What is the true motivation behind the force with which you decide to act?

- Are you pursuing a goal that truly aligns with who you are, or are you distracting yourself from confronting something darker within?

- When you push yourself to the limit, is it really about self-improvement, or are you punishing yourself for past failures or insecurities you refuse to acknowledge?

- What part of you craves this challenge?

- Is it the side that believes in your potential, or is it the side that seeks to suppress the fear that if you stop, even for a moment, you'll be consumed by doubt, regret, or a sense of inferiority?

- When you push through pain, is it because you want to grow, or because you're afraid of what might come up if you allow yourself to rest?

- Are you truly pushing toward a better version of yourself, or are you driven by a subconscious desire to escape a part of yourself you can't face?

The answers to these questions determine the intensity of your efforts and whether the resistance you encounter is truly worth the resources required to overcome it. What happens when you realize the goal you're pursuing might not be what you truly want but rather what you think you need to feel whole? As we move forward, this understanding of Newton's Law primes us for the next exploration—The Beast within. This inner shadow represents the darker side of our motivations and reactions. It is the part of us that can either be a powerful ally or a destructive force. Understanding this is key to mastering both our motivation behind and our effort toward optimization.

Endnotes

1   De Palma, B. (Director). (1983). Scarface [Film]. Universal Pictures.

2   Cannon, W. B. (1932). The Wisdom of the Body. Norton & Company.

Kohut, H. (1977). The Restoration of the Self. International Universities Press.

McEwen, B. S. (2006). Protective and damaging effects of stress mediators. The New England Journal of Medicine, 338(3), 171-179. https://doi.org/10.1056/NEJM199801153380307

Baumeister, R. F., Heatherton, T. F., & Tice, D. M. (2003). Losing control: How and why people fail at self-regulation. Academic Press.

CHAPTER 6

Your Inner Beast, Your Best Friend

Bee Sting to Beasting

Growing up, it was too easy for others to pick on me. Some of those who did didn't realize how much it bothered me because I wouldn't show it, and that was either because:

- I was afraid of conflict and consequence.

- I thought I was in the wrong or that maybe I was taking it the wrong way.

- I sometimes thought I deserved it.

- I thought since some of the things they'd say about me were true, no matter how it made me feel, that I couldn't say anything back.

- I wanted attention and interaction, and if that was the only way, I guess beggars can't be choosers. Even if it hurts, perhaps feeling pain is better than feeling nothing at all.

- I feared damaging or losing the relationship.

- I thought I was wrong for being hurt.

Looking back, each of these instances felt similar to bee stings—sharp, burning pains that drained me as I endured them. I was small, slow (because I was in my head all the time), highly distractible, and quite naive, which gave these people plenty to feed on. Ultimately though, it was my agreeable nature that made me an easy target; they knew I wouldn't retaliate—it was all fun and no consequence. This is a typical pattern. Bullies often target those who don't fight back, and they continue until the person either snaps or finds another way to cope. Unfortunately, I didn't snap.

In my case, I developed a defense mechanism where I would start laughing along and even making jokes at my own expense before anyone else had the chance. Eventually, I became the joke, and that did not fare well for my self-worth. At the time, I didn't know how to fight back, and deep self-doubt made it easy for others to manipulate my perception of the interactions. The fear of potential consequences if I dared to retaliate was paralyzing, and it's a fear that has clung to me over the years. I still feel a profound sense of shame for not being able to stand up for myself or others at the time, constantly questioning whether my actions or lack thereof were ever justified.

Perhaps this shame is a natural part of growth and maybe even serves as a reminder of where we've been. As I drew closer to adulthood, not much had changed except that I had started showing some teeth. Even then, people were able to tell that

I was unsure of myself—too scared to take definitive action. This uncertainty stemmed from a deep-seated fear of the consequences, especially when I depended, to a degree, on the person I might confront. Doubts lingered, like a nagging voice asking, "What if I'm wrong? What will happen if I respond aggressively? What would the consequences be? Would I be able to handle them?" These questions may seem trivial, but to me, they've been crucial in assessing the worthiness of a potential confrontation.

Yet, over time, something in me shifted. I started to realize that each of these bee stings, these small moments of embarrassment and self-doubt, could either slow me down or be channeled as fuel. That's when the idea of "beasting" occurred to me. The sting of a bee burns just the same as the burn you feel during an intense workout. Whether you're hit with an unexpected problem or a harsh truth in life, the sting will cause an inflammatory reaction—in some cases, even a dangerous, allergic one.

However, what if I told you there is a way to become more resilient to these stings, to where you can significantly reduce the adverse reaction? Well, there is. I've learned that **you can desensitize yourself to the effects of the sting through consistent micro-exposures over time** (immunotherapy is a form of this and is used to desensitize people to literal bee stings). I've personally noticed that repeated exposure to and endurance through stings of varying degrees has desensitized me to their effects—especially true for the more common stings. So then I decided to use the pain of the sting as fuel to push through even more pain, and found that I emerged stronger on the other side—a process I consider part of what I like to call "Beasting." The sting is inevitable, but how you respond is largely in your control. Fitness taught me to take control of that choice through repeated and constant stinging in a controlled and predictable environment. In essence, a large part of "Beasting" is transforming pain into power. I like to think of this as beasting through bee sting.

Currently, however, especially in situations where the stakes are clear and high—such as when someone threatens to harm someone I love—I find clarity and resolve. In these moments, it's either me or them, and I choose me without hesitation. Yet, I still believe many conflicts can be resolved through understanding rather than aggression. Some might disagree or say I'm looking for excuses, but this cautious approach has kept me alive and out of unnecessary trouble.

Now, if faced with a direct insult, my first reaction is to question whether I've provoked such a response. If the answer is no, I consider that the other person might be struggling with their own issues. Recognizing that a healthy person wouldn't intentionally hurt others without reason allows me to control how I react. If I know the accusations aren't true, I can easily let them go, acknowledging that the person is perhaps dealing with unresolved personal conflicts and might either be displacing or projecting. Or if I dislike a joke or comment, particularly from someone I don't share a close relationship with, I might confront them to understand the intent behind their remark or simply cut ties if necessary. This often catches them off-guard, leading them to reconsider their approach with me in the future. However, there are some things for which I have absolutely zero tolerance, regardless of an individual's state of mind, health, history, motives, etc.—I will deliver a consequence I see fit for that offense. Besides edge cases though, my overall understanding has transformed how I handle potential conflicts.

Through these experiences, I've learned the importance of tailoring my own communication to the dynamics of each relationship. What is acceptable banter with a close friend or sibling might not be appropriate with someone else who might interpret it differently. Recognizing and respecting these boundaries has become crucial in maintaining my dignity while dealing with difficult interactions.

Consider the following:

- What are some "bee stings" that have shaped your sense of who you are? How have these experiences influenced your choices and behaviors?

- Have you ever wanted to give up, but pushed through the discomfort to achieve your goal anyway? If not, why not? Think deeper than, "I didn't feel like it." Well, why didn't you? If so, what worked? How did that experience shape your mindset and resilience?

- When deciding whether to face conflict or if already faced with one, what factors influence your decision? What do you typically think and feel in those moments, and why?

The Beast Within

Dark motivations often arise from the depths of our most primal instincts—those raw, unfiltered impulses that lurk beneath the surface of our consciousness. When we dig deep into our motivations, we might discover desires embedded in fear, pain, or a thirst for power. These are the whispers of The Beast within us, the shadow force that drives both our most heroic and most destructive actions. For most of us, these dark impulses are something to be feared, controlled, or even suppressed. But what if, instead of fearing The Beast, we learned to understand and harness it? What if we recognize this dark force as not just a source of danger but also one of strength and resilience?

I've always wanted to see peace and harmony, and so I've also never liked conflict. I understand the necessary and usually, in many cases, constructive nature of conflict, but if I can handle something without it—or if I can avoid it entirely—I usually do. This is mostly due to my generally agreeable, enthusiastic, and open personality (though my agreeableness has dropped significantly over the years due to experiences wherein, which conflict was the only way through which resolution could be reached).

Even from a young age, we can identify certain core values and patterns that our lives are likely to follow. So if you could see why you found a certain character or a real person you knew, really inspiring, really profound, and impactful, **it's revealing something about you**—something you either possess or deeply want.

Many people with my personality traits may naturally avoid or have trouble making friends with guys who can be described as being highly resilient, principled, and disagreeable in nature; industrious, orderly, and gritty; powerful and highly skilled. However, because of my deep self-awareness and acknowledgment of my strengths and weaknesses, I knew it would do me well to befriend such characters. I was inspired by them and wanted those traits myself. And that's why I was so inspired by the Punisher because you have to have those traits to be able to do the things the Punisher does. But I was wrong in that. Instead of trying to partner up with someone with those traits and *appreciate* the strengths of my own, I wanted to completely *swap* my traits for those because I was *ashamed* of my own.

It was initially because of this that I decided to join the military in my early 20s—there was nothing more motivating for me—and not just any part of the military. Specifically, I wanted to be in a special unit. I started with the goal of getting into the Air Force, but they told me I didn't qualify due to a couple speeding tickets (but they can fly at Mach speeds... go figure). Next in line was the Navy. I trained and qualified for the SEAL training, and I scored high on the ASVAB, meaning I could take any job I wanted. However, I eventually received word that I couldn't get in because of certain health records. I could have gone to another branch, but at that point, I didn't want to anymore. I was too torn, and then it just felt like fate was stepping in.

Later, I kept asking myself, "Why was I so motivated to join the military to become a seal? What was I really after?" And it was because I wanted to become the kind of man that I admired—a good man, intelligent, kind-hearted, but very dangerous. I wanted to be loved and respected, to be someone capable of protecting and standing up for others when most others can't or won't, someone with credibility and influence, and someone people would be lucky to know.

Well, I did become *some* of those things, and I'm now definitely capable of protecting my loved ones, but I wouldn't call myself a "badass." I am a respectable man with a good heart and mind, and my ability to write and influence people makes me potentially dangerous. I can't think of much that's more dangerous than the ability to influence thoughts and actions—that is, without having anyone at gunpoint. And as it is in the same case with any kind of power, I use my knowledge and pen... or keyboard... constructively rather than destructively while keeping my Beast under control (though I'm well aware of the danger he's capable of if he ever needs to be let loose).

What Is "The Beast," Exactly?

Most of you have heard of the shadow—the dark side—that lives within us. I believe the concept of the shadow was first introduced by psychologist Carl Jung, notably in his work *Psychology and Alchemy* (Jung, 1944). I don't just consider it the shadow, however—instead, I like to think of it as The Beast. Some of you may naturally form a negative feeling or association, or even a sense of denial, upon the thought or imagination of The Beast as a part of your being, but I assure you—when understood, tamed, and befriended—The Beast can be an incredibly powerful ally.

The presence of The Beast becomes apparent when you think of or experience the following—though the list is not limited to these:

- Trauma

- Dark thoughts—both about yourself and toward others

- Strong impulses—particularly the ones you *know* are not good for you

- Distractibility

- Rage

- Agony

- Intense determination

- Source of energy and power

The Beast is responsible for both the most evil and destructive and the most heroic & constructive acts of mankind, simultaneously. From the most unsuspecting and good men becoming cold-blooded murderers to hardened criminals channeling their efforts to save entire communities, The Beast is the common denominator.

Some of you have either said yourself or have heard people say, "Oh, I could never be a murderer. Hell, I couldn't hurt a fly." No, my dear reader, you absolutely could, and to think otherwise is a sign of naivete—sorry, not sorry. You're simply not murdering because you're controlling your impulses. Your environment is such that you don't have to resort to those impulses. Otherwise, if the motive was strong enough, with consequence or without—believe me—you're going to kill.

A compelling example from history that illustrates how ordinary people can be transformed into perpetrators of extreme violence under certain circumstances is the story of the Reserve Police Battalion 101. This battalion was a Nazi German paramilitary formation composed largely of middle-aged reserve policemen from Hamburg who were deployed to Poland during World War II. The men of Battalion 101 were not initially hardened killers; many were family men, ordinary citizens who were too old for regular military duty. Upon arrival in Poland, these men were ordered to participate in mass shootings and round-ups of Jewish civilians for deportation to death camps. Despite some initial reluctance, the vast majority of them followed orders. They executed thousands of Jewish civilians during their time in Poland and were instrumental in the implementation of the Final Solution. Their transformation from average citizens into agents of genocide was largely driven by a combination of peer pressure, obedience to authority, and gradual desensitization to violence (Browning, 1992).

So yes, you could turn into a monster because it's within you to do so—everyone's got that bit of Chaos in them. Some of you may naturally find it terrifying to realize what a monster you can potentially become—what actually exists within. But, of course, in a more civil society—especially when your environment or your circumstances don't bring that out of you or push you to animalistic behavior—The Beast within is less likely to reveal itself so prominently, though it still growls when necessary to protect you (and you should not suppress that). Highly agreeable people, especially those who haven't practiced much introspection, might completely deny that aspect of themselves—that it's even a *potential* reality, some will deny—which may very well contribute to their already decreased likelihood of successfully negotiating better outcomes or fighting for themselves. And since they are less likely to successfully negotiate with their Beast as a result, it seems natural to assume they are at greater risk of being consumed by it, of becoming bitter, resentful, even spiteful.

But don't let any of this scare you; The Beast isn't something to fear. On the contrary, it's something to understand and integrate. It's a source of power that, when controlled, can be used for great good. But if neglected or repressed, it *can* turn against you, becoming a force of destruction. Finding that balance between acknowledging The Beast and keeping it in check is essential for growth in the right direction. As we move into the next chapter, we'll dive deeper into the concept of The Beast. We'll explore its manifestations, how to befriend and tame it without losing the raw power it provides, and how to use it constructively. Understanding The Beast is key to mastering yourself, and mastering yourself is key to mastering your life.

Negotiating with The Beast

In the film Venom (spoiler alert), Eddie Brock's journey with Venom can be considered a strong metaphor for understanding, befriending, and ultimately negotiating with The Beast within us all—a concept deeply relevant to both fitness and personal development. The idea behind this connection is similar to that of the Hulk, Jekyll and Hyde, and the age-old Werewolf—the connection between the man and The Beast. Eddie's initial experience with Venom is one of chaos, fear, and loss of control, mirroring the feelings many of us have when we first confront our own dark impulses and chaotic thoughts. These impulses, much like Venom, can feel overwhelming and even terrifying when they emerge suddenly, revealing aspects of ourselves that we might prefer to ignore or suppress.

At first, Eddie resists and denies the reality of Venom, just as we often deny or suppress our darker instincts and impulses—domination, aggression, indulgence, etc. But as Eddie's story shows, completely rejecting these parts of ourselves can lead to greater inner disturbances and a loss of control. As the story progresses though, Eddie begins to realize that Venom, though dangerous and unpredictable, also possesses incredible strength and power—qualities that can be harnessed for good if properly understood and controlled. The crucial turning point in Eddie's relationship with Venom is the moment he stops fighting against The Beast and begins to engage with it, which leads him to understand its motives and with which he can negotiate terms.

In fitness, The Beast often reveals itself as the raw, primal energy that pushes us to lift heavier, run faster, or endure more pain than we thought possible. It's the voice inside that says, "You can do more," even when our bodies are screaming for us to stop. But just like in Eddie's journey, the major drawback that comes with this power is that if it's not controlled, it can lead to burnout, injury, and other kinds of trouble. Eddie's first encounter with Venom shows us this struggle quite vividly. Venom takes partial control of Eddie's body, protecting him with abilities Eddie had never experienced before, but with a serious drawback: extreme hunger and impulsivity—manifestations of The Beast's animalistic nature.

As Eddie continues to interact with Venom, he realizes that he needs to start setting boundaries. When Venom impulsively (though necessarily) scares Eddie's inconsiderate neighbor, Eddie starts to negotiate with Venom, expressing disapproval when Venom's instincts go too far. This moment marks a turning point, where Eddie realizes that he can exert some control over Venom and guide his actions more constructively. Similarly, in fitness, we must learn to negotiate with our own Beast. Recognizing the immense power and drive that our darker side can provide, we must also set boundaries to ensure that this power is used to enhance our journey rather than derail it.

For instance, when Eddie is faced with a situation in which he has no way out, he voluntarily allows Venom to take full control, recognizing that, in that moment, Venom's power is necessary. This is very much like pushing yourself in the gym when you know you need to break through a plateau—allowing your inner Beast to take over, but in a controlled and purposeful way. However, Eddie also learns to set limits on Venom's behavior, particularly when Venom insists on eating people. Venom's desire to eat people is like the darkest intrusive thoughts that present themselves in moments of passion, agitation, stress, etc., which—though we don't consciously take them seriously or ever act on—still do, in fact, come from within us. Because I'm a hyper-protective guy when it comes to the love of my life, my own example would be the desire to kill the bastard that checks out my girl while we're out and about. By negotiating with Venom, Eddie manages to channel Venom's hunger and aggression in a way that aligns with his values, setting a rule that Venom can only hurt or eat bad people.

This negotiation process is critical in fitness as well. If you have a tendency to push yourself too hard or find that your Beast takes over more than necessary, it's essential to negotiate with it. This might involve setting realistic goals, allowing for recovery days, or consciously deciding when to push your limits, when to hold back, and when to indulge a little. The concept I like to refer to as "conscious indulgence" is particularly relevant here. Just as Eddie learns to allow Venom controlled moments of expression—like defending Eddie or satisfying his cravings under specific conditions—we too can find ways to satisfy our darker impulses within the context of fitness. This might mean allowing yourself some calorie-dense treats you've been craving but doing so in a way that is mindful and controlled, rather than reckless.

By negotiating with The Beast, we can transform it from a source of chaos into a powerful ally not just in our fitness journey but in the various domains of our lives. Just as Venom tells Eddie that if he cooperates, he will survive, so it is with our Beast—if we don't cooperate, it will swallow us whole. Venom also tells Eddie that alone, each of them is a loser, but that together, they are unstoppable. In the context of our lives, this, too, holds true. Alone, our Beast is just a wild animal more inclined toward destruction, and we are defenseless doormats without it. Together, however, this partnership enables us to harness the strength, determination, and resilience that The Beast provides while keeping its more destructive tendencies at bay. Befriending and negotiating with The Beast is much more about the integration of which into our whole being, rather than trying to suppress it, through which we become more complete, more powerful, and more capable of achieving our goals. It becomes one of the most powerful sources of inner strength that, when properly channeled, can help us reach our highest potential both in fitness and life in general.

To better understand and negotiate with *your* Beast, consider the following questions:

- **What does The Beast truly desire?** Beyond the surface-level impulses, what deeper needs or fears drive The Beast's actions? Is it seeking power, control, security, or something more primal, like recognition or survival?

- **How does The Beast influence my decisions?** In what ways does The Beast subtly steer my choices, even when I believe I'm acting rationally? Are there patterns in my behavior that reveal its presence—like moments of sudden anger, defensiveness, or overwhelming drive?

- **What am I resisting by trying to control The Beast?** Am I suppressing emotions or desires that The Beast embodies? What would happen if I stopped resisting and let myself fully experience and understand these feelings instead? Could they hold the key to my deeper motivations or even my greater potential?

- **How does The Beast react to my fears and insecurities?** When I feel threatened or vulnerable, does The Beast come out to protect me, or does it amplify my fears? How can I acknowledge these fears without letting The Beast take control?

- **What would happen if I completely unleashed The Beast?** What would be the consequences if I just let The Beast completely take over? What might I gain, and what might I lose? How does this potential reality influence the way I choose to interact with The Beast?

- **Can I trust The Beast to act in my best interest?** Is The Beast truly an enemy, or can it be a misunderstood ally? How can I learn to trust this part of myself and build a relationship in a way that supports rather than undermines my goals?

- **What does The Beast reveal about my true nature?** In what ways does The Beast reflect my deepest, perhaps hidden, aspects of myself—those parts I might not be willing to confront or accept? How can embracing The Beast lead to a fuller, more authentic understanding of who I am?

- **How does The Beast respond to acts of compassion and understanding?** What happens when I approach The Beast not with fear or aggression but with empathy and a desire to understand? What about when I show compassion and understanding to others? Can I find common ground with this darker part of myself?

- **What role does The Beast play in my pursuit of optimization?** Does The Beast push me toward my full potential, or does it prevent me from achieving it? How can I harness its energy in a way that drives me forward without letting it consume me?

- **How can I honor The Beast without letting it dominate?** What rituals, practices, or boundaries can I establish to acknowledge The Beast's presence without allowing it to take over? How can I create a balance where The Beast feels heard and respected, yet remains under my control?

Channeling the Fuel

My best workout sessions happen when I'm **boiling inside** (not literally). I'm not talking about basic irritants like itchy mosquito bites or traffic, although you *could* use those too—they're just not nearly as powerful because traffic is meaningless rage. Fuck traffic.

The key is this. The source of the frustration must be meaningfully and emotionally bonded to you. It has to feel like it's embracing you, clinging on to you, and gnawing at you. You'll know you have it because it feels **raw** and **visceral** when the distress starts to creep up. At first, it may feel like a knife being driven through your stomach; for others, it feels more like claws clenching and squeezing the gastric juices out of your intestines. At full capacity, the fuel from this source has the **potential for massive construction or destruction**—and how you use that is all up to you.

Here's an example of a potential fuel source buildup:

You're clocking 40–60 hours a week, but life isn't just your job; it's a whirlwind of obligations, leaving hardly any moments for yourself. Home is meant to be a sanctuary but often becomes the source of most of your stress. Family members keep fighting over the same dumb shit. There are family issues that you want to solve but the solutions to which feel like sand slipping through your fingers. No one listens. No one wants to truly understand. Perhaps with enough money, at least some of those issues can be solved.

Payday rolls along. You see your check and are reminded how much of your earnings are deducted for taxes and such. You close your eyes, take a deep breath, and feel the air being exhaled through your flared nostrils. A punch in the gut, and all you can do is take it. You pay your bills—student loans, car, rent, credit cards, insurance, etc.—then you look at your balance, and almost all of it is gone. You're left with just enough for the bare essentials. At the same time, you were hoping to give some money to your folks to help them out. Well, that has to wait. Again. The guilt starts to eat at you. Your friends ask you to join them on a night out, and you can't afford the time or the finances to go, and you don't want to take their offer to cover you. The voices begin, "Such a fuckin' loser."

You want to move out and start a family... and you want your grandparents to see that happen while they're still around... well how the hell *could* you when you can barely afford yourself? Prices are going up faster than hamsters fuck, and you're not making enough to catch up. Feels like you're letting them all down. Desperation builds. You know you need to do something—SOMETHING—to break out of this hellish cycle. You've known this for a while, so why haven't you done anything? Why haven't you figured it out, HUH? Haunting voices start up again, "Maybe you're just stupid. Maybe you're just not smart enough. Maybe you're just dreaming." AHHH, FUCK! MAKE IT STOP!

By this point—especially if you've been simmering in this for long enough—you'd likely be a volcano, just waiting to erupt. You're HOT. You are so full of potential and energy that if you don't intentionally find an outlet for this pressure, you *will* explode.

This explosion is extremely destructive, and, in extreme cases, it can kill via highly impulsive, uninhibited, and dangerous decisions—drugs, careless spending, reckless driving, and suicide (just to name a few). And, most times, individuals who reach this point aren't just hurting themselves; they are likewise hurting those who love and care for them. How do you feel when you see a beloved friend or family member struggling? Now imagine if they engaged in any of the aforementioned self-destructive behaviors. Imagine how you'd feel.

Let's consider the following hypothetical. What would it feel like to see your mom depressed and upset all the time? Say she's having some financial difficulties, but then you start seeing her constantly making impulsive purchases, feeling bad for it, lying to herself that it made her happy, feeling worse inside because she knows she couldn't afford it, watching TV to escape, not getting her work done, feeling worse about that, and then repeating the cycle. It's painful to watch. It hurts when you try to help, and nothing changes, even more so when you can't figure out how to help to begin with or when nothing you do is enough to make some difference.

So if you know how it feels to watch someone go through that, then you can empathize with those who watch you squirm around in *your* own little hell. And if you can empathize, would you want to give them more than they already have to worry about? "Well it's not my fault they worry. Let them stop worrying." My dear reader, it is true that, although others' feelings may not necessarily be your responsibility, being able to truly empathize with them means you know their pain and empathy toward *your* situation are inevitable. So, the best chance you can give yourself, and thus your beloved, is by channeling the pain, rage, and fuel in some constructive manner. By doing so, you may develop the power, experience, and fortitude to do something about your situation.

So how do we find an outlet? What are some ways to relieve this pressure constructively? And how does fitness fit into all this?

Fitness is one of the best outlets there is. There is a ton of scientific and anecdotal evidence to support that—some of which

I will share with you in this book. I am one of those sources of anecdotal evidence. I will explain exactly how and why the gym works as such an effective outlet through which to channel the rage and release the pressure. Once you've successfully learned how to do so, then—and only then—will you have the chance to position yourself as not just an example, not just a beacon of hope, but perhaps even someone capable of saving your beloved from their little hellholes. At that point, you'll likely have what it takes to inspire and impact others in society.

But let's not get too cute and mushy. As we all know, life isn't exactly fair, but it also doesn't have to be horrible. Most of that is in your control—albeit it's easier for some and harder for others, naturally—and how well you control your life depends on both nature *and* nurture. There is no excuse, however, for deciding to completely give up, and how you play the cards you were dealt is your responsibility. This last part may have been a slight but seemingly worthy digression, so I will return to discussing sources of fuel to be channeled—starting with mine

Some of my sources of fuel have been:

- Being broke multiple times

- Family issues that I can't seem to get control over

- I can't seem to help the people I want to help in the way I want to help them

- The lifestyle I want to create for my wife-to-be and future kids

- Feeling like I'm not competent, capable, or intelligent enough to figure out and do what I need to do to hit my goals

When I'm at the gym, I'm thinking about these things, and I'll say things to myself, such as, "I'm not giving up. I'm not just gonna take this shit. I'm gonna push harder. I'm gonna push further. I'm gonna do whatever it takes to get out of this shit state that I'm in." *That's* the fuel. So channeling the fuel toward whatever thing you deem most important can lead to hyper-productivity toward that thing.

That fuel doesn't necessarily have to come from negative emotions, but those are often the most powerful ones. Positive emotions could be sources of fuel, though they can't match the power of their negative counterparts. An example of such a positive emotion that provided me such fuel would be the time I went to the gym after kissing my fiancé for the first time because kissing the person you truly love is unlike any other feeling in the world—and if you haven't experienced that yet, I wish you would someday. But the reason why negative emotions are so much more powerful is because the more you think about the things that cause them, the more it boils within you, and the more fuel you channel right onto whatever you're doing. This is where you let The Beast take over a little because it feeds on that fuel—concerns, rage, pain, etc.—and distracts you, all while being constructive.

I'm also not saying that you should never give in to distractions, though. We all need distractions from our daily problems, but in the fuel-channeling process, the problems that seem impossible to drown out or be distracted from mean that those problems are serious and need to be dealt with as soon as possible. You can think of that process like a filter; only the problems with enough pain and significance will still be felt along with (and after) the pain of the workout, while the smaller, insignificant problems will seem to get lost. At least *then* you will know which problems require your immediate attention.

But let's dive a little deeper and explore the line between constructively channeling your pain and subconsciously seeking self-punishment. Sometimes, when life throws its most sour lemons, there's a part of many of us that feels we deserve the pain. It may be due to guilt, anger, regret, or a sense of failure—it's different for each of us. Whatever the cause, the gym (or wherever *your* fitness space is) can become not just a place of development but an arena wherein we can duke it out with those inner demons of ours. It can become a place where we can distract ourselves from our emotional pain by using the pain we feel from pushing our bodies to their limits—a convenient way to transfer pain from one domain to another.

I'd like to use The Punisher (Frank Castle), as an example of someone who mastered The Beast within (spoiler alert). The man witnessed his family get slaughtered, yet didn't allow himself to give in to the weight of his grief and give up on life, even though anyone in his position would have every right to. What did he do instead? He channeled all of his fuel—pain, rage, confusion, and agony—into relentlessly avenging his family. Every fight and mission afterwards became an outlet for the intense, destructive energy within him—energy that, if not handled appropriately, can wreak havoc on its host. What makes Frank such a prime example is that, given the unimaginably immense energy naturally stemming from such pain, he still didn't let his inner Beast or its destructive energy destroy him—he tamed it and used it best he could. He could have easily become bitter and self-destructive, but he instead harnessed that power for a cause greater than himself. I'll discuss The Punisher in more detail later in the section, but there is more to consider beforehand.

Regardless of when or where we push ourselves, we need to figure out whether we are doing it for genuine development or subconsciously punishing ourselves for our perceived shortcomings because it isn't clear to many. We may feel that the pain is a consequence we deserve, perhaps some way to atone for failures or mistakes. Atonement as a motive is not necessarily wrong, but if it isn't recognized and managed, the behavior that it motivates can become intense enough to hurt us. I myself had this problem, and I only realized it *after* hitting a burnout point. Once I recognized it, however, I decided instead to use the pain as a catalyst for genuine development instead of self-punishment.

I reached my realization by considering the following questions, and I encourage you to do the same:

- What do I feel when pushing myself? How would I describe the pain that naturally follows?

- Am I channeling my pain constructively, or am I letting it consume me?

- Do I associate growth or suffering to the pain I experience? If suffering, do I feel as if I deserve it? If so, why?

- What would happen if I shifted my focus from punishment to empowerment?

Answering these questions can help you better understand where you stand on the fine line between self-improvement and self-destruction.

However, there *does* exist a somewhat practical aspect of self-punishment, so to speak, where you want to get to the point where it hurts more than it ever hurt before. But that's kind of a slippery slope because you don't want to injure yourself either. It's just that **the pain in that moment is something you really want to feel so that it swallows the pain of whatever you're thinking about**. Now, I need to clarify that I am not by any means trying to suggest this as a solution or long-term coping mechanism toward whatever pains or problems you may be facing in your life—I'm merely suggesting from my own experience that this may, for some of you, be as much a stimulating and cathartic experience as it has been for me. It was through moments like these that I've conjured up solutions to—or at least the strength to handle—some of the toughest issues in other domains of my life.

It's natural to wonder whether this mindset applies to everyone who steps into the gym or whether it applies to a particular group of people. Does the use of rage or frustration as fuel apply to everyone, to those who are deeply passionate about working out, or to bodybuilders alone? Well, I really can't speak for any of these folks, but what I *can* say is that I'm definitely not the only one who uses my fuel this way. Some people, especially men, go to the gym with their heads full of rage, and they take it out on the iron, but you can't always tell just by looking at them. Though they may seem pissed off, you really have no idea what's going on in their head. When they push as hard as they do, there is a lot of focus involved—from which the outward expression can be easily mistaken for anger.

Of course, there's a potential danger here. Sometimes, that anger can exacerbate the problems, fueling them instead of making things better. There's a reason why "roid rage" is a stereotype. Not everyone who works out to get as strong as possible has noble intentions. Some might like the feeling of power it gives them or even the ability to bully others. It's like handing someone a sword. What matters is *who* you're giving it to because some people will use it for the wrong reasons. Of course, this isn't to say that everyone with roid rage has malice in mind or that those with malicious intent are necessarily on roids, but it's a natural association.

In a nutshell, though, the point is to understand and control that fuel so that the behaviors it leads to will actually serve your goals and values—not hurt them. And though, for me, the gym has proved most effective, it doesn't have to be limited to that. You could grab a canvas and some paint, let your emotions pour out through the brush, and see what happens. The reason why I chose the gym, though, is because I know from experience that the endorphin rush you get from lifting is different from what you get by doing something creative, like painting or writing.

While these can all be cathartic, they trigger different hormonal responses. The physical act of lifting weights releases a unique blend of hormones and other chemicals—such as endorphins, adrenaline, and dopamine—that can provide a more immediate and intense sense of relief. With that said, go ahead and take some time to think about what might work best for you. Think about what feels good and gives you that sense of release without turning to self-destructive habits.

The Punisher: A Lesson in Resilience and Transformation (Spoiler Alert)

The first time I watched "The Punisher" (the 2004 film), I was just a small 13-year-old kid who was often teased and bullied. That movie sparked my Will to grow, though I was too young to think deeply about it at the time. Unlike other superhero movies that didn't quite have the same impact on me, "The Punisher" felt more realistic—his story, his character, his approach, etc. The unfairness of what happened to him—much like Batman, whose parents were killed—wasn't directly his fault, but he knew his job carried dangerous risks.

The real trouble started not when Frank Castle killed the bad guy's son—because he didn't; it was the police—but when Howard Saint's wife decided Frank's entire family should pay, leading to that brutal massacre at Frank's party. That moment, seeing his son and wife dead on the pier, transformed him. At that moment, he didn't just become the avenger; he became the monster. Then, it hit me: **sometimes, you *have* to become the monster, not out of malice but *necessity*.**

So unleashing The Beast is not inherently evil. There's a good beast and a bad beast. There's a primal drive within us, the capacity for dark actions like killing or torture. The difference is in controlling this beast, knowing when and how to unleash it, and really understanding the difference between mindless violence and necessary action. For instance, Frank Castle, the Punisher, **channels his grief and rage not into *senseless* destruction but into** sensible destruction—fighting those who spread evil—an idea similar to one which posits that the burning of deadwood is necessary to allow new trees to grow, or that killing aspects of yourself or your surrounding is necessary for your own growth and survival. The Punisher is a prime example of one who has mastered his Beast, of which he displays appropriate use and full control.

After handling the people who massacred his family—and, safe to say, in his darkest moment—he was gonna kill himself, but he didn't. He didn't fall into the victim mentality, which he very easily could have. I mean, he witnessed his entire family get slaughtered. If there was *any* reason that would make it sensible for someone to kill themselves, I think that's a pretty damn good reason. Still, despite the unimaginable weight of his trauma, he decides to live on and own his fate. It seems sensible to assume his thought process likely came to something along the lines of, "All right, this happened. I took care of this problem for myself. If I'm capable of doing this, then I'm not going to stop here. I'm going to continue doing this so that other people don't go through what I went through." And Jordan Peterson makes a remarkable point—one which I found profoundly insightful—when it comes to heroes and villains, positing that they've both experienced some tragedy, except the villain thinks, "The world did this to me, so I'm going to do this to the world," and a hero like Frank thinks, "The world did this to me, so I'm going to make sure others don't suffer the same fate."

Reflecting on real-life scenarios, I've personally seen how different people respond differently to the same challenges—such as siblings with a problematic father. One mimics their father, while the other takes a completely opposite path. And what's interesting is that the one who takes the opposite path does so in a strict or extreme manner. This form of opposition—a complete intolerance to anything that may resemble the ways of his father or sibling—may be due to the attempt to avoid anything that is a reminder of what led to family dysfunctionality, pain, trauma, or even the fall of a beloved sibling. But however extreme, the sibling that took this path is a lot more likely to guide others away from similar, painful experiences.

It comes down to choice and perspective, and the Punisher's journey showed me that no matter the trauma, we can still choose our path. Instead of succumbing to grief or anger, we can use our experiences to make the difference we'd like to see in the world. Again, part of what drew me to the military was my desire to be that protector. But although my plans to join the SEALs were foiled by health issues, the underlying motivation—to protect and positively influence—remains.

Whether it's using physical strength or the power of the pen, the goal is to impact the world constructively. The Punisher, despite the name, is *not* just about punishment. He is an example of what it means to own our circumstances, step up, take control, and make sure we're a force for good in the world.

Worthy Digression: The Punisher vs Batman

Although Batman overcame the murder of his parents, got really physically tough, capable, resilient, and all these other things I praise about the Punisher, I will never put him in the same category or consider him a shining example of something to live up to. He's unrealistically optimized and he's naive, and I'll get to that in a moment. Batman doesn't kill, and I'm a strong believer in that, "No, he should." Because the bastards he captures but refuses to kill are killing innocent people—or inevitably will. Why just put them in prison? Fuck that. More excessive punishment is warranted, not even equal; I'm sure crime rates will drop like turd from a bird if the morons knew what's coming. However, I still highly admire Batman's character—as well as that of other heroes who overcame similar trials.

Now, typically, people say that the Punisher is Batman if Batman loses control of himself, or something along those lines—that Batman is all about self-control, which is why he doesn't let himself get into killing, and that the Punisher is essentially a version of Batman who has lost that limitation. Batman says that there has to be a line between him and the criminals he refuses to kill—believing that killing is that very line.

Now, there definitely must be a degree of self-control regarding your rage and the given circumstances, and I understand where Batman is coming from, but I'd say it's still a naïve perspective. It's naïve for Batman to think that killing is the line between him and the criminal. There are so many criminals that don't kill, but they destroy people's lives without killing them—and in some cases, that's worse than if they had just killed them.

It's not just about murder. So, tell me then, the cops that are pushed to shoot and kill a guy that's a major threat, who has killed a bunch of people, who is still a direct threat and will continue his evil deeds until his very last breath—that makes those cops criminals because they "crossed that line"? No, it does not. Though there is so much more I'd love to share on this topic, it would be too much of a digression, and I plan on starting an entirely different project that discusses topics like this one anyway.

The Bitter Price of Freedom

You pay a price for everything that you do. Whether you tell the truth or lie, whether you make the right decision or the wrong one, whether you take the easy path or the hard one, you're paying a price. And though it may seem like the short-term gains or instant gratification, might be cheaper, it's not—you're gonna pay the remaining balance, with heavily accrued interest, down the line. There is no escape from or form of bankruptcy for it— very much like student loans. You're delaying pain in the short run, submitting to impulse for instant relief, without realizing how much torture you're going to endure later on. And, when it comes to lying and telling the truth, it's the same thing.

Why do people lie? It's like a short-term save. But the truth usually comes out, and if it doesn't, you're living with that shit on your conscience, and it's not very light. When I was a kid, I lied, a lot, but never to harm anyone. It was more to save face among people I loved and respected. If I wasn't doing too well in school with a couple of classes, and someone I loved and respected would ask me how that class was going, I'd lie and say, "It's great. Yeah, things are good." And then they would find out. These are people who are willing to help me. They would eventually find out that I had failed, and they would get upset—not so much because I failed the class but more so because I lied to them and didn't ask for help. So then they would ask, "Well, why did you lie?" I said, "Well, I was afraid that you would see me as stupid, or lesser than, or incapable, or whatever. And you might get upset, like, at the fact that I'm failing or still not doing well. The concepts that for you might be primitive, for me are hard to wrap my head around" (though this does not excuse the lie). And so they'd respond with something like, "Okay, was that short-term upset or moment of anger worth failing your class?! I could have helped you!"

But, for a lot of people, it *is* worth it. And for me, at that point, I probably would have said yes as well because I didn't care as much about the class as I did their potential reaction and judgment of me. But then you need to ask, "Well, how much better is it now?" Because now *you* know that *they* know you failed, *and* you lied to them. So you're a liar *and* a failure. The truth came out, and you paid a hefty price on both ends. So just pay up in the beginning. Make the right decision upfront, no matter the consequences—it's very much worth the investment because the punishment that follows is usually much more expensive otherwise.

In fitness, the price is the willingness to confront the untamed Beast, to face your demons, and to choose truth, even when it's painful. It's important to understand that every lie, every cheat and shortcut, is a chain that binds you. The only way to break free is to pay the price in full, upfront—otherwise, interest accrues, and it's a bitch.

Paying the price in fitness translates directly to other domains of life. Your willingness to push through discomfort, to delay gratification, and stay committed are the same qualities that will help you face challenges in your relationships, your career, and your personal growth. The willingness to overcome physical limits develops into a willingness to overcome mental barriers and other obstacles in life—the freedom from which allows you to be your true self, even in the face of fear. When you've faced your Beast, when you've made your hardest choices and paid the price, you unlock a level of authenticity, power, and confidence that you probably never thought possible.

But why is the price of this freedom so bitter? Well, as is usually the case, if it was sweet and easy, everyone would do it. But, to be more specific, confronting the hardest truths, decisions, and demons in your life will feel like going through a sewer full of shit on the hottest day of summer—every last cell in your body is going to fight to escape. If it were me, I'd say it's a price worth paying because the alternative is a lifetime of bondage by fear, regret, and mediocrity. Unless you're a masochist or have some sort of twisted fetish, I know that's not the life you want. I'd rather assume you want to realize your full potential, and *that's* worth *every* ounce of discomfort, *every* drop of sweat, and *every* hard truth or decision you'll ever have to face. If we think of freedom as the prize and discomfort as the currency, then it means we need to embrace discomfort because it's the only thing through which we can get what we want.

Embracing Discomfort

Start doing things—starting with small things—that make you uncomfortable and get used to that discomfort. Embracing small discomforts is a crucial step toward personal growth. For instance, consider the simple act of taking cold showers. Stepping into a cold shower, especially right out of a warm bed, can be jarring. However, this shock isn't pointless; it desensitizes you and trains your mind to handle discomfort, reinforcing the idea that growth requires stepping out of your comfort zone. Over time, consistently facing these small challenges can significantly improve your resilience.

Now let's see what this looks like in the context of fitness. You might naturally think the first sign of pain occurs upon the first workout, but it really first occurs upon the thought of starting your routine. It's the anticipation and mental preparation for something new. And the thing is, for me, along with many others I've worked with, that's the hardest part. Not to say that it's all cake after that, but it gets easier with each time you overcome that anticipatory discomfort. You get used to it. Every time I face this, I personify it. I used to cuss it out, but then I began to thank it after realizing that, "Would I cuss out someone that's making me stronger? No... I should be thanking them instead." Then I began loving it, embracing it; it felt like I had even more control over my Beast, and it gave me the kind of pump that made me feel as if I can take on the world. At that point, I started to not only welcome it but also began actively seeking all the uncomfortable things I had been avoiding that I needed to face.

Here's my experience step-by-step:

- The first week, I began making my bed first thing every morning.

- The second week, after making my bed, I went straight to a cold shower. The anticipation sucked, but then I thought, "Well, I know I'm going to do it anyway, so just fuckin do it already—step in, damn it!" At first, I'd take a deep breath just before stepping in, but after a couple days of this, I decided to tell myself that it's just a normal shower and stepped in without thinking about it. Sure, I always felt the shock anyway, but the intensity of the shock decreased with each instance. **This was the hardest of all steps to get used to.** Once or twice a week, I allowed myself a hot, comfy shower, but never consecutively—so as not to risk falling back into comfort.

- The same week, I started going to the gym for an hour even though I didn't feel like it—whether that was early before work, or late after work. I also started my calorie deficit by limiting the use of creamer in my coffee to one cup, once or twice a week. For someone that drinks about 5-6 cups of coffee a day, that shit adds up quickly. The creamer alone cut 300 calories from my daily intake— that's 2100 calories a week!

- The third week, I started adding more time to my workouts—more sets and more workouts, including cardio, which is something I never liked... I still don't. I also had an easier time saying no to things that don't serve me (except for cigarettes and the occasional drink)

- By the fourth week and beyond, I started asking others to spot me when attempting heavy weight that I hadn't attempted before, and asking strangers for help was not something I was comfortable doing before... until one day, it became natural.

By the time the month was over, I felt more comfortable with things I would normally avoid. I felt far more confident in my ability and willingness to face problems. I became more inclined to stand my ground, speak up, and do something about things I wasn't good with. Those initial pains and discomforts that you feel and endure are the signs that you're growing. Every burning rep, every drop of sweat, every moment you want to quit but don't is what transforms discomfort into strength. The more I experienced this in the gym, the more it bled into the rest of my life. Suddenly, tough conversations didn't seem so tough, and reaching for bigger goals than I'm used to didn't feel so impossible. Discomfort was the companion I needed on the road to actualizing my potential.

Novel experiences are usually gonna seem intimidating, especially for those of us who are generally hesitant, risk-averse, or conflict-avoidant—our natural temperament will always have its influence on our behavior. It's something you can work on, but it'll always be there to a degree. For example, a highly agreeable personality, though not typically observed in men, can pose a challenge for them because they'd be less inclined to stand up or negotiate for themselves or face certain—perhaps, in some cases, necessary—challenges. I had this problem, but the way I overcame the disadvantageous aspects of those traits was by putting myself in situations where I had to face the discomfort

I was avoiding. There were many times it was risky, but there is hardly ever any reward without risk.

Of course, not everyone reacts to risk in the same way. Traits like risk aversion and conflict avoidance often tie back to fundamental aspects of our personality, such as the aforementioned level of agreeableness prevalent in the Big Five personality traits. However, these traits *can* be worked on and managed through deliberate practice and self-awareness.

By this point, you may be asking questions like:

- So should I just do anything just because it's uncomfortable?

- Should I whip myself at night or light myself on fire?

- Should I just make my life difficult for the sake of making it more difficult?

No. None of the difficulties or discomforts should be such that they cause harm, like self-flagellation, unless that's some kind of cathartic kink you may have... but that's not what I'm getting at. When selecting challenges, **it's essential to differentiate between *mere* difficulty and *meaningful* difficulty**. Not all uncomfortable or challenging actions are worth pursuing. **The key is to select challenges that are not only hard but also offer tangible benefits or align with** personal values. For example, while cold showers are uncomfortable, they are harmless and bring health benefits such as boosted immunity and enhanced recovery.

This concept of selecting the right challenges applies broadly. For someone who dislikes hiking, a difficult hike might not offer the same value as it would to an avid hiker. Similarly, if improving social interactions is a goal, starting with simple steps like saying "hi" to someone in line at the supermarket can be a more relevant and manageable challenge as opposed to going to a party. The key is to progressively increase your comfort with these situations while keeping your overarching end goal in mind. **By identifying the areas in your life where you seek improvement and choosing discomforts that align with these goals, you can effectively tailor your growth experiences to ensure they are both challenging and beneficial.**

Consider the following hypothetical:

I want to get better at social interactions, especially with people I'm interested in. As mentioned above, I'll need to start with small steps. If talking to a girl in person feels too overwhelming, I'll begin with a smaller step. Maybe I decide to go on Facebook, find friends of friends who I think are cute, and simply send a message saying, "Hi, how are you? I noticed that you also know [mutual friend's name]. How do you know them?" If that still feels like too much, I might just start with a simple "Hi." If I'm too afraid to even message them online, then I might try talking to or connecting with male friends of those friends. If my social skills are severely lacking, or I'm just a hardcore introvert, starting with interactions with my closest friends will be less intimidating than talking to someone new—let alone a woman I'm interested in. But I have to remind myself that there was a time when I didn't know some of my closest people either, yet

I managed to have those first few interactions and build those relationships.

However, if someone already lives online and is desensitized to online interaction, this example won't work—it may even backfire. If being online is this person's comfort zone, chances are they'll be less willing to break out of their online habits because this example would just confirm their existing comfort zone. The example of online interaction as a first step is meant for those who have serious trouble with interacting at all—because for them, making that first uncomfortable move of saying "Hi" online can be a manageable step before moving on to saying "Hi" in person.

CHAPTER 7

What You've Got & What You Want

Taking Inventory

Taking inventory of your life involves a deep dive into understanding not just your limitations but also the resources available to you, both tangible and intangible. It's about acknowledging everything from the skills you possess, the people in your life—even those you might consider adversaries—to the physical possessions that support your daily activities. For instance, owning a car isn't just about having transportation; it's a tool that extends your reach and capabilities. Similarly, recognizing the strengths of your family members can transform them into a network of support and expertise.

For example, your father might have particular skills you can learn from, or you may have an aunt with whom you can discuss specific issues. Even something like a nearby library can be a bank of knowledge if you can't afford to buy books. Understanding and appreciating the value of these resources, which are often taken for granted, can significantly enhance your ability to leverage them effectively. If you need advice or support, knowing who to turn to in your circle can expedite your progress and prevent wasted efforts. Many people overlook the assets they already possess, continually searching for what they think they lack. This oversight is not just a wasted effort but a blind spot that keeps them from fully utilizing their potential. It's crucial to break this cycle of confirmation bias—seeing only what you expect to see—and instead, develop a habit of seeing with intention.

This principle applies just as crucially in the realm of fitness, but here, it dives deeper into the core of self-awareness. Taking inventory in this context means more than just knowing your physical strengths and weaknesses or keeping track of your numbers, supplements, etc. Though those are important, you should also consider resources such as your motivations, relationships, habits, choices, and experiences—all of which have their own as well as collective impact on your fitness. Once you do that, you will be able to decide in exactly what way each of them have their impact. After coming up with your list, ask yourself:

- Which of them already contribute to my growth? In what way?

- Are any of these not being utilized? Why not? In what way can they contribute?

- Which of them hinder my growth and should thus be eliminated? Can I change any one of these in a way that may serve my growth rather than hinder it?

The answers to these questions will give you a much better idea of what you have to work with. They will provide you the clarity that will aid in the formation of an achievable goal toward which you can move with clear intention. Dr. Jordan Peterson talks about the power of intention, saying that when you focus intently on a goal, everything unrelated becomes a blur. This focus sharpens your perception of what's necessary to achieve your aims but can also lead to tunnel vision. While this concentration is beneficial in driving toward your goals, it's equally important to occasionally pause and broaden your view. This ensures you don't miss other vital aspects of life, such as significant moments in the lives of loved ones. Getting overly absorbed in work, for instance, might cause you to undervalue or overlook an important personal event, conveying indifference instead of support.

You may have heard of or experienced tunnel vision in fitness. It can occur during a particular workout, where you're so hyper-focused on the rep, the muscle, and everything else involved in that specific action, everything else becomes a blur. It can also occur at the goal level, where you might be so obsessed with hitting a particular goal that other important aspects of your life start to decay. I've had experience with both forms of tunnel vision, and it feels amazing. However, before my ability to control it (which requires a solid degree of self-awareness), the drawbacks I experienced from tunnel vision included:

- Significant decrease in short-term memory formation and recall

- Loss of awareness of my surrounding

- An almost indifferent reaction to everything else—which kinda scared me because I'm normally very empathetic as long as I'm not stuck in my head, fixated on concerns. And as a result,

- Loss of some relationships

By consciously expanding your awareness beyond the immediate path to your goals, you can cultivate a more balanced approach that values both personal and professional fulfillment. Also, regularly taking inventory not only sharpens your focus but also helps gain control over tunnel vision and prevents it from clouding your judgment. Doing so provides the clarity necessary to maintain a clear intention without losing sight of other important aspects of your life, which then allows you to pursue your goals more precisely while making sure you don't overlook the support systems and personal connections that contribute to your overall success.

Defining Failure, Success, Good Enough, Ideals, & Where You Stand

We have our generally imagined ideals (e.g., of success, relationship, happiness, etc.) but oftentimes lack the following:

- A precise definition of your ideals.

- Why and how you came to these defined ideals.

- A precise definition of failure. Not having your defined ideal does not necessarily mean you've failed—many of us fail to realize there is an in-between. Just because you're not where you want to be doesn't mean you're still where you started or worse.

- Why and how you came to your definition of failure.

- The realization of how much you've achieved, improved (albeit incrementally), and how far you've come, so far, from your starting (or lowest) point. If you're there, good; starting from ground zero has major advantages.

And the point of all that is to know exactly where you stand; if you don't know where you are and how to know when you've reached your destination, you will always remain lost and confused. The best way to begin finding your answers to these crucial and introspective questions is to **AIM— Align, Investigate, and Mobilize.**

Align: To what degree are your thoughts, actions, spoken words, and daily habits aligned with your goals? All of these matter because they manifest themselves into reality. If I'm constantly thinking I'm not good enough, then I will never be. But if I start thinking, "I will be good enough; it's just a matter of time." Then, indeed, it will just be a matter of time when you will become as good as you believe you can be. I can hear some people scoffing, "Oh, yeah, right, I'll just think I can do it and then sit back and wait." That's not what that means. Thinking that way, aligning your thoughts to what you want, will inevitably shift your attention toward detecting things around you that will serve your goal, and due to cognitive consonance, you will want to act in ways that align with your thoughts.

Investigate: Dig deep enough to uncover the reasons behind your fears and ideals. Why do these particular ideals matter to you? Why does this particular failure scare you? Through this investigative process, you uncover layers of yourself that you may have otherwise not been aware of before. By looking deeper into the root causes of your fears and desires, you can discover the subconscious programming that controls how you define failure and success. You might notice that some of those definitions have been inherited from society, family, or even past traumas rather than truly being your own. In fitness, this could mean exploring why you want to build a certain physique or reach some incredible physical capacity. Is it because you genuinely value it because you're trying to live up to others' expectations, or because you're compensating for some aspect of yourself that you're not happy with or think you're lacking? But don't limit yourself to those questions. The discoveries made through this introspection will help you redefine your goals, as well as your behavior, in a way that resonates with who you truly are, making the process more meaningful and less burdensome.

Mobilize: Once you're clear on your ideals and the reasons behind them, it's time to move—to act with intention. I've found that intention works well with precision, and to be precise, you need to be specific. But it's still not enough to have specific goals because you should have a way to measure your progress. The goal also needs to be realistically attainable and should ideally align with what you uncovered while investigating your motives. If the goal is bigger than you're used to, remember that it's *your* goal, and you know what it's made of. So, you can break down the goal into its parts, which can be further divided into bite-sized steps. But having a bunch of loose parts can also be overwhelming. It's like a car that's completely disassembled with its parts spread out all over the place—you know what the whole should be, and you know the parts, but grouping similar parts together will make the assembly much easier. This means that the next step is to organize them in a way that makes most sense for you. One step toward that goal might be coming up with a regime that not only targets your physical goals but also factors in your mental and emotional well-being. And if, for example, you've discovered through your introspection that your motivation for fitness stems from a desire for mental clarity, you might want to prioritize a combination of cardio and meditation over resistance training alone. Again, the goal here is to mobilize all your resources toward actions that harmonize with you.

But it's not enough to have your ideals defined because your ideals are your successes, relationships, etc. in their perfect form. We can AIM toward perfection, but to see anything less as failure would be unwise, to say the least.

So, how do we prevent ourselves from this foolish trap? How can we be satisfied with less-than-perfect results? How can we be happy and fulfilled in a less-than-ideal life? These are not easy questions to answer, but we may begin with the following:

- As mentioned earlier, take inventory. This includes experience, assets, skills, material goods (not talking knick-knacks), relationships, networks, and other resources—everything that makes up your life.

- Valuation of current possessions. Write a brief description about the value each item provides to you—and, perhaps, even to those around you. Consider the associated costs. Consider what life would be like without them. How would the loss impact you? What was life like before them? Why?

    ☐ E.g., My car: I love my car. It's not my favorite one, but it's an amazing machine and it's the best one I've had so far. There are many others like it, but this one's mine. It provides quick and comfortable transportation, as opposed to traveling by foot, horse, or bus, or having to rely on someone else. I can transport goods and provide services outside of my locality. I can listen to audiobooks and music during my drives to learn new things or relax when I otherwise may not have the time to do so. I can comfortably take naps—the seat reclines all the way down, windows are tinted (providing more shade), and it has air-conditioning—which allows me to recharge my mind and body, thus making me more productive. Charging ports keep my devices alive, which are crucial to my livelihood. It's fast and handles well, which is fun and allows easy maneuvering through traffic. It is integrated with my smartphone, thus providing full and convenient access to my navigation, communication, and media apps hands free, hence keeping me and others safer on the road. This car costs me more than I can comfortably afford financially, but it provides me with enough to justify itself. I work very hard and reward myself accordingly, which keeps me motivated to continue working as hard as I do toward my goals. Every time I approach my car, every time I drive it, it reminds me how far I've come, how I did it, and how I can enjoy the fruits of my labor.

- Set defined milestones that aren't too far from each other, so you can still see it clearly in the distance, but that aren't so close to each other that they're just a hop, skip, and an arm's reach away. However, the first milestone is usually the farthest and most challenging one to get to; and with each one reached, it becomes easier to reach the next. It's like exponential growth: The more skills and experience you acquire and apply, the more you gain with less effort because the past becomes your new base, and your collective experience from all prior milestones makes it easier to reach the next one, each one becoming even easier to hit but with its own, unique challenges that add to your skillset and mental arsenal.

Each time we reach a milestone, we often forget—or don't realize—how far we've come, and upon reaching them, we often tend to form even higher goals and ideals, which may make it seem like we haven't come very far at all, like we're not even close. We create for ourselves a never-ending adventure. We get tired of the constant chasing of our ideals, we burnout, and we still don't give ourselves a fucking break. Would you treat your best-performing employee like this? Would you be surprised if one day they throw up their hands, call you a sadistic, ungrateful prick, and quit?! Most of us wouldn't be (and for those that would... well, wakey wakey).

This is why it's so important to track your progress, give yourself due credit, reward yourself, and give yourself a break. Chill. Have a popsicle or something, whatever tickles you—you get the point. It's up to you to decide what is enough and actually mean it. But, if you choose to play the game of "Enough Never Is (ENI-way, as I like to call it)," then you need to be ready to pay the price, and **you can't bitch about it because you're gonna keep playing ENI-way**. This is especially true for us folks with ADHD and addictive personalities.

But let's get back to giving ourselves a break. A lot of us get stuck here because of one or more of the following reasons:

- Fear of falling behind

- Fear of losing momentum

- Avoiding other aspects of our reality

We need to negotiate with ourselves the way we would if we worked for someone we love and respect. The fact that many of us don't think that way naturally is sad. We overwork ourselves like animals, and we often treat animals better than ourselves. People will pamper the shit out of their pets—and good on them for giving that soul a beautiful life—but they won't do anything close to that for themselves!

On the Naivete of Comparing What We Have to Our Ideals

My uncle Armen opened my eyes to the understanding that it is naive to compare what we have to our ideals. In this small but important section, I discuss what I learned through my conversation with him on this topic, combined with my own experience and perspective.

It's easy to fall into the trap of comparing what you have with the ideals you've set for yourself—whether it's your career, relationships, or personal achievements. This comparison may naturally feel like a necessary measure of progress, but it can also be a double-edged sword. The problem with comparing your current state to your ideals is that it assumes a linear relationship between where you are and where you want to be. This is a naive assumption because life is rarely that straightforward. In reality, you may sometimes have to compromise one ideal while in the pursuit of another, or while trying to protect what you have that isn't exactly tied to the ideal you were pursuing or currently are. It's also quite normal for the importance of certain values to shift as you grow and evolve, so don't be surprised by these changes—and, actually, instead of seeing this as instability, think of it as adaptability.

Because ideals act as a guiding beacon for your thoughts, actions, and decisions, they are imperative to your success as you strive toward them. Ideals drive your ambitions. They motivate you to push through challenges you otherwise wouldn't be motivated enough to even consider facing. However, take extra care not to lose yourself and become so obsessed with these ideals that you ignore your progress. When you move like a predator locked onto prey for so long, it's easy to fall into a constant state of dissatisfaction where nothing you achieve feels good enough, which is usually because it isn't on par with the ideals in your mind. I've made this mistake myself, and my goodness, it can easily take you to a dark place. If you start to feel like the finish line isn't getting closer no matter how much you move, you're at a dangerous point at which you should ask yourself the following questions:

- What if I'm the one pushing the finish line further out? If so, why?

- What if I'm not moving as fast as I think I am? Or could it be that I underestimated the distance between me and the finish line?

- What if I'm moving in the wrong direction?

- What obstacles have I faced? Did I overcome them? If not, why not? If so, how? Perhaps I should celebrate those victories.

- When's the last time I looked back at my starting point?

Both my mentors, Dr. Jack Bayramyan and my brother Ara, told me to always remember to look back and see how many steps you've climbed and how far forward you've moved from where you originally started. They're right. I, along with so many others, often forget where we started and instead become fixated on what is so far ahead. Even if you haven't gotten far, appreciate that at least you're not where you started, or worse, further behind—in which case, you should seriously consider the thoughts and actions that got you there. The pursuit of "more" can easily turn into a relentless chase for perfection, leaving you in a perpetual state of unrest, which leads to chronic stress, which in turn makes you vulnerable to a variety of undesirable side effects. So, yes, your ideals are crucial for direction and motivation, but don't let them rob you of the joy and satisfaction in your current progress.

It's also important to understand that as you advance toward one goal, you might find that other priorities shift. What once felt non-negotiable might lose its weight. That weight may shift to other values, or new values may emerge entirely. This may seem like I'm promoting inconsistency, but that's not what this is—this is growth, evolution, and adaptability. It's both human and natural for the experiences through your journey to reshape your ideals, just as it is for your ideals to reshape your experiences and perhaps even the journey itself. I ask that you appreciate the dynamic nature of the relationship between your ideals, values, results, and experiences. They should all evolve with you, reflecting the person you are on your way to becoming. Understanding this dynamic is key to diligently navigating your path without being blind to everything else, as well as embracing the way you evolve along the way.

A Little About My Experiences with These Concepts

I used to be much harder on myself because I hadn't defined what failure or success necessarily meant to me, or even what my ideals were. The way I thought about success was kind of a general, grandiose idea—one that society typically has, like, "Oh, you're a millionaire, and you've got everything you want." And if I couldn't live the luxury lifestyle I dreamed of, then I was a failure. But that's not what success means to everyone, and though I thought that's what it meant to me then, I know that's not what it means to me now.

Not defining these things made me vulnerable to the trap of comparison, and, like most people, I compared myself to "hyper-successful" guys in a single domain—usually finance or intelligence. I wouldn't consider what they might lack that I have or what they might trade to have what I possess. They might be a lot more intelligent or have the cunning that I wish I had, but maybe I'm not willing to utilize the same means through which they acquired their riches. Maybe I'm not that guy. Maybe I don't want to be that guy.

But it didn't stop there. I would then look for others whose characteristics were more like mine, yet who still succeeded—at least within the domain I was fixated on. It was crippling. I couldn't help but think, "What do they do, or what do they have that I don't?" And I'd pity myself and feel like a fuckin' loser while at the same time thinking, "Okay, I am willing to put in the work, but I don't know what the hell to do so that I won't just give up again in the face of inevitable challenges. Or what if I get bored again?!" But I wasn't asking the right questions. I should instead have asked myself the following questions (which I later did):

1. What are my unique strengths? If I don't have any, perhaps I need to create more experiences and explore to learn more about my strengths. If I do, how can I leverage them to serve me?

2. What specific processes led them to their success? Which aspects of that process can I realistically apply to my own life without hurting myself or becoming someone I'm not?

3. What do I genuinely want? Why is that important to me?

4. What potential obstacles might I face? Am I capable enough to face them? If not, how can I prepare, and which of my resources can help me?

5. How can I stay motivated throughout the process, even when it gets tough or boring? There is no one-size-fits-all solution to this, but one of the major things that work for me is reminding myself why I'm doing it, becoming frustrated, and using that fuel to keep going.

Eventually, I stopped feeling bad about it altogether. I stopped focusing on what I'm lacking or what I feel like I *can't* do and started focusing on what I *can* do instead. I began questioning whether I was really doing the best I could or pushing myself as much as I could. Am I wasting time? Am I being as effective as I possibly can? And I often found myself becoming defensive when I realized I had been mostly ineffective and inefficient—that I had underperformed—and that was painful, to say the least. At that point, I started listing my limitations, setbacks, etc. (like ADD and hypothyroidism, in my case), which do impact my performance—there's no denying it. I strongly encourage you to do the same. The whole point of the introspective process, acknowledging aspects of yourself and your life, and listing these things is so that you know what you're working with—so that you know the cards you're dealt.

Okay, well now I know my cards. So what can I do with these cards that I'm dealt? Play them the best you can, even if it's a shit hand. I can hear you saying, "If it's a shit hand, one would normally fold. Why would I risk a bet on a shit hand?" That's a fair and reasonable response for a normal card game, but that's not what this is. This is the game of life, and in life, things aren't as clear-cut and nearly as predictable as a card game, and the rules are different for everyone. You have no idea how life will respond to your cards or to the way you decide to play them. Consider the possibility that you can trade cards and perhaps even pick up more cards. Maybe you can see how other people who've played similar cards well did so. Whatever the outcome, however, it's your responsibility to own it. Also remember that no one likes playing with those who just fold all the time—they're typically not very fun folks.

How Fitness Helped Me Realize This

For a while, I had been going to the gym kind of aimlessly. I knew I wanted to build a better physique and get stronger, but I hadn't specified what "better physique" or "stronger" meant for me exactly. I'd see some guys with incredible physiques and think, "Man, I'd love to look like that," or see some other guys who didn't have such a physique but were incredibly strong and think, "Man, I'd love to be that strong." I kept comparing myself to these men and I was nowhere even close to their level of strength or physique, despite already having invested a significant amount of time and energy at the gym by that point. The goal seemed so far away. I felt as though I hadn't moved an inch from where I started, but I hadn't even stopped to look back to see exactly how far I'd actually come. People would even comment, saying things like, "Wow, you've been working out? You got leaner," but I'd completely dismiss it.

Then, one day, I was looking through some family photos and came across a picture of me from when I had just started working out. I thought, "Christ, that's how I used to look? God forbid I ever go back to that." And that's when it hit me. That's when I realized I had actually come much further than I thought. Sure, still far from what I wanted ideally, but not too far from good enough either—I had established where I stood. And then I thought, "Alright, fine. At what point, then, will I feel like I'm good enough? What exactly do I consider ideal? Do I absolutely *have* to reach that to be happy? Would it mean failure if I don't?" I then decided I couldn't go back to the gym until I answered these questions, and since I wanted to go back as soon as possible, I immediately began thinking deeply about these questions and spent the rest of the day doing so until I had all my answers.

Learning to look back and realize where I stand, as well as defining what I want and what I considered failure was one of the most important lessons that fitness taught me. When I had my answers, I was able to more effectively and efficiently pursue my goal, as well as more accurately measure my progress. I even implemented this thought process into the smaller aspects of the whole goal, such as how many sets of a particular workout would be considered not enough, good enough, or ideal. I began to notice that the more I improved through the use of this process, the easier it became to improve until I reached the point where I was genuinely satisfied with my results. Then, naturally, though not so consciously, these thought processes made their way into the other aspects of my life, which led to similar results. So, I will ask you now: Do you know where you are, what you have, what you want, and what you won't accept?

CHAPTER 8

People, Please

People Pleasing & Judgement

Let's say, for example, there's a family friend's house that my folks are gonna go to. The friends of my parents have two sons with whom I've spent a decent amount of time growing up. Back then, we were kind of close, but now we just don't connect, and our values are not aligned, and we don't provide each other any value. Then, at some point I began to realize that relationships are much like webs and ecosystems; each interaction, each connection, serves a purpose within that system that affects other aspects of that system. Each of those has their own identity, and each identity its own dynamic. When the ecosystem is balanced, it flourishes. But when its elements no longer serve each other, the system starts to fall apart. I'm not saying relationships should be thrown out at the first sign of imbalance. I'm just saying that they need to be evaluated for mutual value. This may feel as if relationships are transactional, and the truth is, they are.

When you're with someone, there is always a reason, which is that the person makes you feel a certain way or provides some other value that you want or need. It's human nature to seek reciprocity with those we interact with and with whom we choose to spend our precious time and energy. It's the give and take that keeps us connected, and when that's not balanced or is lost entirely, the relationship becomes more about obligation than genuine connection. Even when you think you're being selfless, purely altruistic, and expecting nothing in return, you're doing it because it will make you feel good. "No, I'm doing it for them to feel good." Right because knowing they feel good makes *you* feel good. This is not necessarily bad; we are all naturally selfish. It's how far you take it and what you do with it that matters. If we were to put it on a scale from 0 to 100, here's what 0 and 100 would look like:

- 0 – The Bitter Martyr: Sacrifices all of their own, but with heavy resentment and self-pity.

- 100 – The Ruthless Exploiter: Willingly and purely uses people for personal gain, even manipulating and potentially hurting them to do so, without remorse.

By now, you might be asking, "Okay, Manny, but where is the line between maintaining relationships and maintaining my sense of self?" Great question. I'm not saying completely disregard what people think of you because that does matter. Why do you wear clothes when you step out of the house and go to the store? Because otherwise, people are gonna think you're a little crazy—and maybe there are some of you who *do* want people to think you're a little crazy. Fine, but I imagine there must be a less extreme way of achieving such an outcome. We are social beings, yet our social nature may sometimes conflict with our individual wants and needs, and I imagine that trying to balance these aspects is one of the core struggles of human existence.

However, it's still necessary to have at least *some* regard to people's perception of you; it's important for survival, and because, after all, social acceptance can increase the likelihood and availability of more opportunities. Yet, on the contrary, it can also be a glue that binds you to others' expectations. And it would be a mistake to let the fear of judgment dictate every one of your decisions. We can't make every single decision based on "Oh, what will this person think? What will that person think?" Chances are they don't care, and they often share the same concern about themselves—almost like a dance of insecurities. It's actually kind of paradoxical. And if someone's gonna judge you negatively for doing what you want to do, or for having more valuable things to do than to come and entertain them, then they shouldn't be in your life. It's a good way of filtering people, in which case judgment becomes a valuable tool rather than something to fear.

If someone told me, "Hey, I'm not going to make it man. There's this project I'm working on," I would support them. I wouldn't think, "What a prick. He's not coming." Who am I, his master? Plus, why would I want to push someone to come if they'd rather do something else? If they come just for formality, or just so they don't turn you down, they're not going to be fully present, their mind will be on the thing they'd rather be doing, and they'll be less inclined to pick up your next call, or even more inclined to lie about what they're doing (which is kind of cowardice if they're afraid of dealing with the consequences of telling the truth). Though it may be obvious to some, many should understand or remember that any relationship built on pretense will crumble under the weight of truth. That's why it's worth establishing a foundation of honesty right from the start, even if it means some relationships will fail the test. We must also acknowledge that people have different values, and while you don't have to respect them, you ought to respect their right to choose and stand for their values.

Even with this understanding, many people fall into the trap of pleasing others without considering the cost of doing so, and even if they do consider the cost, it may either be because it's seemingly less costly to stay trapped or because it's being used as a form of procrastination, and then would become the perfect thing to blame when something's not done. How convenient. Is it possible we could be using this as a way to avoid facing uncomfortable truths about our needs and desires? Are we seeking justification for our inaction through the illusion of selflessness? These questions could be far-fetched—I can't be sure because I do have a tendency to look too deeply into things—but I imagine they're relative enough to be worth considering. Anyway, there's quite a bit of cowardice and deceit involved in pleasing people, though I'm not saying that that applies to everyone or that those are necessarily a part of it—just saying that in most cases, it's there to some degree. People get resentful. Say you're one of these types of people. You're there physically, but you're not *actually* there, not *actually* present. You're thinking about what you *could* have been doing instead. So is that fair to the person that you're there for? No, it's not. That's not fair to them, and it's not fair to you because you could have been doing something more productive and more valuable to you, and you're not giving your full attention, or at least genuine attention, to the person or people you're with. It starts this negative cycle where you start to question your own worth, your decisions, and, eventually, the very relationships you tried to preserve.

This cycle starts with sacrificing your own needs and desires to meet the expectations of others, which leads to a slow degradation of your self-respect and autonomy. Over time, this self-neglect turns into resentment—both toward others for their requests and toward yourself for allowing it to happen. As the resentment builds, you will likely start losing both your motivation and whatever degree of trust you have left in yourself. By this point, you might start engaging in self-destructive behaviors because you have little to no respect, trust, or agency left in yourself. The only end to this perpetual cycle is either through your own decision to end the cycle and change or to let it consume you entirely until you break and go postal. You decide.

How fitness helped me overcome this trap and how it may help you:

My progress toward overcoming this cycle began soon after I started being able to say no to myself. For some time, I wasn't seeing the results I wanted in the time I wanted them. I began paying more attention to what I allowed myself that I knew I shouldn't, purely because I didn't want to feel the discomfort of denying myself the thing I allowed. By doing so, I slowly began resenting myself. But once the fitness goal became a much higher priority, I knew that either I had to start saying no to the things I knew didn't add value to my goal, or I was going to break and forget about the goal entirely.

No. I wanted a nice physique, and I wanted it badly. The first few times I said no were to things as simple as my favorite creamer or condiment. Once I got used to that, the next challenge was to say no to skipping the gym when I felt tired or had a more exciting alternative activity, especially if I had planned to go that day. Then, I noticed myself saying "No" when I was reaching failure on a set and wanted to stop short because of the pain. After enough difficult "No's" to myself, I was finally able to say "No" to particular family members who offered me a drink or a particularly tasty but calorie-heavy meal. Those were some of the most difficult times to say No because not only did I not want to crush their spirits, but also because:

a. They weren't used to me saying no or standing for my values

b. They didn't understand the reasons behind my response

c. They were people with whom I normally enjoyed all those things

d. I feared their judgment of me and my priorities

e. I felt like I was risking damaging my relationship with them, or like I was neglecting them by doing so

Then I remembered that I had started feeling an annoyance toward these people because I knew I was going to be offered or expected to partake in things that hindered my progress, and I didn't like that. But that wasn't their fault. How could they respect me and my wishes if I myself wasn't respecting myself enough to stand up for my values and priorities, no matter how much resistance I faced? How could they know it's a problem if I've never let them know or confronted them about it? If they are so adamant on hindering my progress and are clearly not adding value to my life, then perhaps they don't need to be a part of it. So through each time I said no to myself, the more resilient I became and the better I felt about myself in the long run. As a result, I started to respect myself more and felt free from originally trying to please every one of my desires. Saying no to others then reduced the annoyance I had toward them and restored my full and genuine desire to be around them when I had the chance. Ultimately, I was free, and the relief was more satisfying and longer lasting than that of the procreative process.

Social Resistance & Sabotage

You will eventually, without a doubt, face some degree of resistance from those around you when making significant changes to your life, which is why staying confident in your values and goals is crucial. This is because whatever goal you decide to pursue—whether that's sculpting your body or advancing your career—the people around you might have a hard time understanding or supporting your efforts. Writing a book, for example, is a time-consuming and mentally exhausting project that doesn't provide immediate, tangible results. And since it takes months or years before you see any rewards, which is also the case with many other endeavors, it may easily seem to others like you're wasting your time or neglecting those who are used to having you around more often. The same can be said for fitness, and it's also something I personally experienced—especially since I was working on my physique and writing this book simultaneously. The moment you decide to make the necessary adjustments to serve your pursuit, such as changing your diet and regularly hitting the gym, those around you who are accustomed to your former lifestyle might be confused, unsupportive, or even actively against your new direction. I've noticed that the most common response, however, is the devaluation of efforts.

Those who dismiss your hard work will usually attribute your progress to luck or genetics rather than the intense effort you put in. At first, it was insulting and very frustrating to me, but the more I thought about it, it made some sense. How would they know what it takes if they only see your results and not the amount of time, energy, and resources you consistently invest to produce those results? This is a common experience for many who pursue fitness seriously. Though it's not their intention, friends and relatives of my own have tried downplaying my progress by saying I was always muscular or that I was born with a good build. But that's simply not true; I've seen pictures and videos of myself when I was younger—I wasn't born this way. They think this way because they think they've done what they're supposed to and perhaps have a hard time imagining anyone would work more intensively or effectively than they did to attain that goal. The transformation takes a level of hard work and dedication most people aren't used to (or willing to) endure, something many don't see or appreciate until they try to compete with you, as was the case when I started using an Apple Watch to track my activity alongside others.

By tracking and sharing our progress with each other, they finally realized just how much effort I was putting in. My goals were set higher, and I was consistently surpassing them, which left them amazed—and it wasn't like I didn't have a busy schedule because I sure as hell did. Still, I managed. And I'd love to give major credit to those who competed with me because they did an amazing job themselves, and they became more motivated to keep pushing. It became clear to them that results aren't just about genetics but about intense, disciplined work. This is something many people often fail to understand until they experience what it takes, even for a short time. They have to feel what it's like to feel the sting and beast through it. They might say, "Oh, it's just your genes," but even good genetics require effort to reach their full potential. You might not have the genetics to look like Chris Pratt as Star-Lord in *Guardians of the Galaxy*, but everyone has their optimal build, and it takes work to achieve that.

Why People Devalue Your Efforts

Malicious intent in people's resistance or devaluation of your effort exists but isn't as common. This is more so when people are consciously and actively trying to stop you, either simply out of spite, hate, or fear. However, it's more common for people's resistance to be subconscious and innocent rather than out of malice, and more likely that your actions and results highlight their weaknesses, fears, or insecurities. And sometimes even, the resistance may simply come from a lack of understanding why you changed, especially if those changes or the reasons behind them go against what they think they know or believe.

For example, there was a time when my grandma made me a style of omelet called "Oche" (pronounced *O-cheh*, but with a quick *ch*) using butter. When I asked her if she could use olive oil instead, she brushed it off, even joked about it, and continued using butter. It was as if my dietary choices were an inconvenience to her, something not worth respecting. She even went as far as suggesting my mother lie to me about the ingredients just to get me to eat it. Now, to be clear, this wasn't done out of malice, and I love grams; she just didn't understand or respect the importance of my dietary restrictions. The best part is she was more than willing to accommodate other family members' dietary preferences that aligned with her own beliefs, like avoiding beef for a relative who doesn't eat it for religious purposes. But when it came to my fitness goals, those were seen as less valid.

Why is it so difficult for the people we love to support the changes we're making?

Fear plays a serious role here; deep down, people are often scared and the majority of them choose to stay victims to their fears. The most common among these fears might include the following:

- Fear of change

- Fear of losing the connection that was once shared

- Fear that your commitment reflects poorly on their own choices

- Fear of failing

- Fear of not living up to their own potential and

- Fear of what *your* success says about *their* lack of progress

It can be intimidating for them to see you pushing past limits they've accepted for themselves. I've personally felt this way when seeing someone I know push a barrier that I couldn't in work life, and I did catch myself saying, "I mean, probably not worth it, but up to you" while also coming up with some reasons for which. But I said that because I didn't think *I* could because the effort wasn't worth it for *me*, and because seeing him do what I *wish* I could, that I *feared* I couldn't, made me feel weak. What I should have said instead was, "Man, I would if I could but hats off to you." There's a certain comfort in believing that someone else's success is due to something out of their control, like genetics or some extraneous factor, because it absolves them of the responsibility to strive for more. This isn't true for everyone, of course.

Sometimes, people even try to excuse themselves from putting in the work by lying to themselves, saying things like, "I could do that too. I just don't want to," when, in reality, they may just be scared of failure. There are also those who genuinely don't care about achieving certain goals, and that's fine. But for those who do care and see someone else succeeding, it can create a sense of discomfort that manifests as criticism—like a natural defense mechanism. At the end of the day, it's a reminder for people that they could be more than they are but that it would require the kind of effort, change, and vulnerability they're not used to.

Social Resistance in Fitness

I've found that this resistance can be particularly strong when it comes to fitness, probably because it's such a visible transformation. People begin to question why you're so focused on your physique, or why you're not indulging in the same habits as you did before. It's possible that the underlying thought may be, "Why are you changing? And why aren't I?" For example, when I was on a particular diet and was avoiding carbs, I often heard comments like, "Oh my God, here he goes again, this time he's avoiding carbs. What's wrong with carbs? You need carbs!" This is a form of peer pressure. It's very annoying, and the discomfort from which is enough to sway a lot of people from adhering to their goals. Solution? Stop giving a fuck. Because either they don't give a fuck about your goals, or they're ignorant to what you need to do. Sure, that's easier said, but the more weight your goals carry over their opinions, the easier it becomes to stay anchored to them. Your priorities are yours alone, and if they matter to you, then that's all that matters.

What people don't realize is that your commitment to your goals is not a judgment on their choices. It's simply a reflection of what you've decided is important in your life. But because we're social creatures, their discomfort with your choices can be felt deeply—especially if they are people very close to you, people you love. This may even get you to question whether you're doing the right thing, or whether you should just conform to avoid the tension. But conformity, especially when it goes against your values, is the death of your own agency and your personal growth.

Even now, as someone who's writing a book, working on his physique, working his day job, and trying to build a business, I still get some criticism or nagging from folks who expect me to do the things they do—whether it's partying, going out for drinks and dinners, etc. They don't get why I spend my nights writing or why I spend every waking moment working or thinking toward my goals. They are baffled by the thought of someone not watching shows or playing video games. And don't get me wrong, I enjoy those things but not when I know there are more important and more meaningful priorities to tend to. Those who expect you to conform to their expectations are usually the most confused by your dedication because it reminds them of, or shines light on, the areas in their own lives where they lack commitment. They might even see your dedication as a silent judgment of their own lack of purpose or direction. I say this not so you start focusing on or taking responsibility for others' thoughts and feelings but instead to make it easier to understand where the resistance comes from so that you can more easily focus on yourself and stick to your goals.

Risk of Alienation and the Importance of Filtering Relationships

Understanding the source of people's resistance to your changes is sometimes not enough. The resistance from some of those people may be intolerable for you, and your lifestyle changes may be intolerable for them—in either case, one of you drops the other. If you're aiming to become exceptional at something, you need to accept the risk of alienation. Excellence can often be a lonely road because it requires investments and sacrifices that most others aren't willing to make. This reminds me of an accurate and motivational quote I saw printed on canvas in the bathroom of a very successful brother of mine: "In Order To Become The 1% You Must Do What The Other 99% Won't."

The moment you decide to get fit and change your lifestyle, you might lose friends who are not on the same path, especially if their lifestyle is particularly poisonous to the one you've adopted that is conducive to your goals. So if your friends are into unhealthy and unproductive habits, if they're enablers of which, or if they hold you back or drag you down in any way, be prepared and willing to lose those friends. And honestly, that's a good thing. Your close circle has a major impact on your life. If they're not supporting your growth, they're holding you back. And I know it's not easy to cut people out, especially if you care about them, but sometimes it's not just necessary but critical to do so. There are a variety of traditional proverbs that touch on this concept:

- The Biblical text of Proverbs 13:20, which advises that walking with the wise leads to wisdom, whereas associating with fools leads to suffering.

- Greek philosopher Euripides, who was believed to have written, "Tell me who you consort with, and I will tell you who you are."

- From the play *Don Quixote* by Miguel de Cervantes, where Don Quixote himself states that one can know a man by the company he keeps.

It may come as a harsh truth, but sometimes, you may need to cut off the parts of your life that no longer serve you—even if those parts are people. There are those who won't really agree with your choices, but they won't constantly give you a hard time about them, either. They might tease or dish some insults to give you a hard time, but it's all in good taste, and you can serve it back to them. However, there are people who will actively try to slow you down. It's *those* silly geese that you need to get rid of. You don't have to be a prick about it; just stop responding to them. Recognize that not everyone who starts with you will finish with you, and that's okay. Remember that even a single rotten apple can spoil the whole basket.

Breaking Through Social Resistance Using Fitness

For a while, my own social resistance had an influence on me. When I first started my regime, that influence was strongest; I would catch myself giving in to the pressure from time to time. As I continued my regime though, my focus and discipline within which, as well as my ability to ignore external noise, started presenting themselves in all other areas of my life outside the gym. The gym became a controlled microcosm of the larger world—a playground where I can experiment with both my mind and body. The same principles that helped me push through the resistance of a tough workout helped me push through the social resistance, such as criticism and negativity, in other areas of my life. Also, anytime I'm going through a heavy lift or pushing to the edge of my past limits, the noise of the world fades into the background, and all that matters is the weight in my hands and the determination in my heart. Developing this mindset in fitness helped me filter the bullshit and focus on what truly matters to me.

Now, of course, not all the people around you are sources of resistance—at least, I hope not. That's why we'll move on to discussing the people in your life that offer support rather than resistance.

Social Support

Though I've discussed the significance of The Will, social support likewise plays a crucial role in your willingness to set, pursue, and reach a given goal. Willpower is great, but the people around you can either have the influence to support you or sabotage you. And if you're someone who values harmony in your relationships, you may naturally be attributing more weight to the opinions and behaviors of those in your social circle—sometimes even more than you might realize.

But what is it about social support that's so vital? Of course, it's nice having people cheer you on, but although that's important, it's still too topical. I'm more so referring to having the kind of people around you who truly understand and respect the path you're on, even if they're not walking the same one. You can even think of them as mirrors; when they reflect encouragement and positivity, that energy can be fed back into your efforts and reinforce your commitment. And when it comes to showing support, I've found the more subtle gestures to be more profound in signifying true respect and understanding. I'm talking about an instance where a family member who respects your new lifestyle changes might start prepping meals that align with your new diet plan—not because they've been asked but solely from their own recognition of the importance of your goals. It's things like this that speak the loudest—their acknowledgment of your efforts and silent agreement to stand by you.

Think about what it means to have those close to you adapt their behaviors to support your goals. Imagine how much they must love and care about you, and how much you mean to them. This also means you have influence over one another, and that your dynamic creates a feedback loop that can either strengthen or weaken your resolve, depending on the nature of your interactions of course. But so what? Why does that matter? Well, at the core, we're still social creatures no matter how introspective or introverted we might be. That is why our identities are, to some degree, shaped by those we surround ourselves with or groups we belong to. So being surrounded by people who genuinely support your growth is very much like having a safety net to catch you—to help you regain your balance and keep moving forward if you ever happen to stumble. And knowing you're not alone may even give you the courage to take risks and push beyond your perceived limits.

The first time I felt this support system was at the gym because it was an environment full of people who, more or less, get why I'm pushing myself the way I am and see the value in my sacrifices. For you, this might be at the track, the yoga studio, or the martial arts class—wherever it is, these spaces can end up being our sanctuaries because that's where we feel the most understood. If you have no one else, you can be sure to find someone in that space for whom it would be a pleasure to partner up. By teaming up with such an individual, you can encourage each other, hold each other accountable, and celebrate each other's achievements—no matter how small. Don't be shy; approach people. You never know; you may end up meeting someone who supports you in ways you've never experienced or teaches you things you may have otherwise never learned. I've met, helped, and learned from so many people I've met at various gyms I've been to over the last 10 or so years—some of whom I approached, and some of whom approached me. As a result, I have at least one supporter at almost every gym I go to.

When you have that kind of support in one area of your life, it doesn't just stay there—it begins to seep into other areas of your life. Depending on the strength of the connections you form in your space, you might even begin to notice that the same people who support your goals in one domain may very likely also be the ones who support you in other domains as well—whether that's your personal growth, your career, your projects, etc. **Social support, then, is the environment that nurtures your transformation**, regardless in what domain. You'll know you have the right support system when it feels like your goals are becoming not only more achievable but sustainable too.

So, as you pursue your goals, really take a moment to think about the people you've surrounded yourself with.

- Are they lifting you up? How? To what degree?

- Are they holding you back? How? To what degree?

- Are they aiding your efforts to become the best version of yourself, or are they reinforcing the doubts and fears that hold you in place?

Whatever your answers are to those questions, and if you don't already have social support, surround yourself with those who see your potential and are willing to help you realize it. By doing so, you will find that the path forward, while still challenging, is far more rewarding.

The Role of Community

Remember my coworker, John, from chapter 2? His initial inspiration to get back into shape occurred when he kept seeing my progress at work, day after day. What really led to his transformation, though, was the ongoing reinforcement, as well as the subtle nudges he received, both from me, from other coworkers, and from the changes he saw in himself. These included comments on his diet, comments on his physique, suggestions during our workouts, and celebrations of even his smallest victories. With enough time, these elements built up momentum, but even still, his progress wasn't linear. He had his ups and downs, periods of self-doubt, and moments where he thought, "Fuck it." But what kept him going was the realization that he wasn't alone in this. The office became a supportive community that believed in his potential and wanted to see him reach it. And when John got to the gym, he felt good about the fact that everyone there had something important in common—the Will to work on themselves. The how or why didn't matter.

Outside of your immediate support system, the communities you're a part of, or even frequently exposed to, can also have a significant impact on deciding whether to start or continue working toward a particular goal. They will also determine how difficult doing so would be. I've personally been among different groups of people who have either made doing so a pain in the ass or a walk in the park for me and others. If you've set a fitness goal, and you spend the majority of your day in the company of academics or overly pragmatic folks, they might not see the value of going to the gym or lifting weights and may throw fun little jabs at your lifestyle changes. You'd have the same experience if you set an academic goal but spend most of your day among tradesmen. I've had experience with both scenarios, and I'm not being absolute, just saying that it's common and that you shouldn't be surprised.

It can be easy to let the majority influence you toward conformity if your lifestyle is abnormal within that space. However, it's in these moments that it's most imperative to stay focused on what truly matters to you. Is it more important to fit in with the crowd, or to achieve the goals you've set for yourself? If you keep allowing the opinions of others to dictate your actions, you'll inevitably lose sight of what you're working toward—you might as well live for others and work toward *their* goals. Does that sound fair to you? I'm sure it doesn't. So stick to your guns, even in the face of social resistance. You'll build resilience and gain the respect from those who matter—and you will give hope to those who didn't dare rise above before you.

Friends and family are the communities most people are exposed to most frequently, and when you start making changes that set you apart, it can feel like you're distancing yourself from them. They might not say it aloud, but the thought of you becoming "better" than them can create a divide. If not addressed carefully, this can spiral into jealousy, resentment, and perhaps even a variety of other negative emotions that might eventually lead to their attempts at holding you back. So then you might need to have some tough conversations with some of these members or make difficult choices about who you spend your time with. This could even mean going at it alone for a while, but that's okay—I'd even say doing so for some time is healthy—because the rewards are totally worth it.

CHAPTER 9

Rest & Recovery

Rethinking Recovery, the Overlooked Necessity

Up to this point, it's mostly been about the push, the drive, and all the work. Now it's time to discuss their byproducts and the recovery from which because no human can continue to work effectively without setting time aside for rest and recovery. "Ahhh, jeez, another chapter on recovery—dude, we know!" Yeah yeah, I'm sure you do. I imagine most people recognize its importance, but not nearly as many act in accordance with that recognition, probably due to the likelihood that they don't immediately experience the side effects of not doing so. Also, of all the books I've read or influencers I've watched on fitness, recovery *was* discussed, but none of them were thorough enough on the matter for my liking. None of them dove deep enough into the underlying details and why they matter, which is what I aim to do here.

When I ask people what they know about rest and recovery, most of them mention sleep, time off, and proper nutrition—which are all valid—but they usually only go so far as, "I know they're important," and usually without understanding the deeper impact each of those has on them and how each one affects the other. This isn't good and likely also contributes, among many other factors, to their neglect of this concept. But they cannot be blamed because no one has educated them on the deeper aspects I'm talking about, and it only occurs to just a few of them to think about the impacts of which and what they might currently know about them either. Some of the things I discuss in this chapter include, but are not limited to, stress, sleep, self-respect, and forms of recovery—just to name a few. Before I dive in, however, I'll tell you a little bit about how *I* realized the importance of this concept the hard way. I will also share my attempts at the application of each aspect of recovery in my own life as we go through them across the chapter.

When it comes to things I want, I tend to be a bit impatient, and so I do everything I can to get what I want as soon as possible. So it was with my goals in fitness—I wanted to reach my ideal physique as fast as possible while working two jobs and going to school. Then, and even now, it upsets me that there are only 24 hours in a day, most of which are spent on necessary human functions—nutrient consumption, excretion, restoration—and in LA traffic. So, really, I'm left with something more like 10 to 12 hours, and that's just not enough time for me to do all the things. At the time, I thought I could win more time and outsmart my body by manipulating it with caffeine, nootropics, and other supplements. There were many nights where I slept an average of three to five hours, and some days where I stayed awake for 36 hours. This did not come without consequences. For starters, it led me to make poor decisions in all aspects of life.

My cognitive faculties obviously took a hit as a result, so to find a way to combat that, I became my own guinea pig and started experimenting with various combinations of different substances in hopes of staying on top of my game. There were times where I stumbled upon combinations that seemed to work, and other times when it would have hurt less to be stuck behind a Prius on the 405 freeway at the peak of rush hour on the hottest day of summer—like the time one of my concoctions had me nauseous, dizzy, and bedridden all day. Unfortunately, I can't remember *exactly* what was in that concoction, but I roughly remember combining a hormonal stress management supplement with a stimulant so that I can stay up while keeping my nerves calm. I learned quickly that I needed to be a lot more careful with my experiments and that the body isn't something we can really outwit; it's a system that demands our respect.

During my sleep-deprived experimentation period, I experienced some brief spikes of enhanced cognition from one of my magic potions, but I noticed that I had generally become weaker, slower, dumber, hyper-irritable, forgetful, sensitive to pain, and vulnerable to injury and illness. But wait, there's more! Most of the time and effort invested into my workouts were going to waste because I wasn't getting any sleep, which is absolutely crucial for optimal muscle repair and hormone production. Still, I continued pushing forward despite the consequences. I became a mess and went into a dark place again. I wasn't really being effective in any domain, which led to negative feedback from people at work, which added to my stress, which in turn kept me from falling asleep.

It was reckless and nonsensical, and detrimental to both my physical and mental health. What I was doing was nothing short of disrespecting myself and somewhat unconsciously killing myself—a slow and passive suicide. I say *"somewhat* unconsciously" because I didn't *actively* decide to kill myself, but I knew that what I was doing was harmful and dangerous and completely ignored or suppressed the potential reality of an adverse reaction being fatal. I knew I wouldn't harm anyone I respected, so by harming myself, it could have only meant I didn't respect myself. If this is where you find yourself, make it your top priority to figure out why, and then take steps towards its resolution—not doing so will negatively impact everything else over time.

Whether or not we like or understand it, sleep must be vital if nature forces the entire animal kingdom to do so and presents serious consequences to those who don't—torturing you first and then killing you.

"Sleep, bitch."
—Mother Nature.

Stressing Stress

Poor sleep causes an increase in the stress hormone cortisol, which can further negatively impact your sleep, which can then become a vicious cycle—more stress, less sleep, even more stress, even less sleep, and so on. Research supports this point and also states that impaired cognitive functions resulting from elevated cortisol levels lead to mood disturbances like irritability and depression, and they even affect physical health by increasing appetite and weakening the immune system (Cortisol: How it Affects Your Sleep, 2024)[1]—all of which negatively impact sleep, contribute to stress, and perpetuate the harmful cycle. So, let's talk more about stress, its contributing factors, as well as the impact each has on the other.

When you think of stress, what comes to mind? I imagine it may be things like getting the bills paid, worrying about your kids, hitting deadlines at work, or wishing you had a few more inches... to reach the top cabinet—these are mental and emotional stresses. But you may often fail to consider the stresses that come from physical activities like working out, working construction, or working the garden as such. The reason it's important to acknowledge and approach physical stress in the same way, and to the same degree, that we do so with mental and emotional stress is because we normally only attribute the side effects of stress to the latter, while somewhat neglecting those of the former. We just typically don't think that the side effects of stress are coming from the physical. However, I'm letting you know now that stress has the same response on us, no matter its source.

Whatever the source of stress—whether physical, mental, or emotional—your cortisol levels begin to rise. Now, for those who aren't aware, stress isn't entirely bad; brief spikes of cortisol actually do provide benefits—such as increased alertness (Lovallo, 2006)[2], reduced sensitivity to pain, and enhanced memory—which I've personally experienced (McEwen, 2007)[3]. However, if they remain elevated for long periods of time, cortisol levels can cause serious damage to your nerves, organs, and immune system, making you more vulnerable to diseases, disorders, infections, and illnesses. In fact, stress from one source can lead to stress in another. To give you a better idea of what this means, I'll provide an example from my own experience. I've noticed a pattern where anytime there's some problem that's become a cause for serious concern, if left unresolved for even just a few days, it leads to the development of physical pains of sorts. So, here, my mental or emotional stress leads to physical stress. This personal observation is supported by research, showing that chronic stress can manifest in several physical symptoms such as headaches, muscle tension, and fatigue, which then further exacerbate the stress, creating a detrimental cycle (Mayo Clinic, 2023)[4].

Likewise, I've found that this can also happen the other way around, where physical stresses can lead to mental ones, and this can manifest in a couple different ways. In one instance, the wrist pain I developed during my time as a massage therapist led to my need to take time off, which led to a lower paycheck, which inevitably led to my mental stress. In another case, I had a constant, aching back pain that didn't let me focus on my work or the professor's lecture, which led to much frustration, making me irritable and undesirable to be around. These personal experiences align with research that shows physical health issues can significantly affect mental well-being, leading to stress and reduced quality of life (Mayo Clinic, 2023)[5]. Chronic pain, specifically, is known to interfere with daily activities and mental focus, potentially leading to emotional distress (American Psychological Association)[6].

So how do you cope with these stresses? How *should* you cope? Do you, or should you, use the same approach for each kind? Finding an appropriate approach to deal with stress in a way that works best for you is essential to optimal recovery. The best way *I've* found to do so is to reflect on the following:

- How I've approached stress so far

- The results of that approach

- Resources among my inventory that can help me, perhaps someone similar to me who has had similar stresses and has dealt with it appropriately

- Aspects of my personality: tailoring my approach to fit my nature made it more effective, more genuine, and more sustainable

"Okay, so are you going to give us some actual techniques or not?" Not exactly the kind you may have hoped for. The purpose of this book is not to give you techniques on how to cope, nor to give any other kinds of advice that should be left to medical professionals. It is instead meant to present the benefits of adopting and applying a more introspective perspective, so that you can hopefully come to the answers you seek on your own. And since I'm *not* a medical professional—not yet at least—all I *can* tell you is that I would *not* recommend *any* method that involves some form of escape, health risk, or self-destruction, such as the use of drugs, which falls under all those criteria. I say that because I've experimented with all sorts of coping methods and found that the ones falling under that criteria, though they were momentarily soothing, only exacerbated my problems— maybe not always immediately but always eventually.

Another significant aspect to consider in the interconnectedness of stress and sleep is diet. "Manny, what the hell does food have to do with stress?" Just stay with me. We've already established what happens when you don't sleep well—your irritability and stress are increased, so things that wouldn't normally trigger you suddenly do. When this happens, it leads to an increase in the hunger hormone, ghrelin, which leads to what I like to call "stress eating," during which our dietary choices are usually of the poor sort. We usually go for comfort food, which is usually shit if we factor in its nutritional value. There's a nicer, I guess more PC term for that... Oh yeah, "junk food." Constantly eating that shit will negatively affect your hormones—cortisol, dopamine, testosterone, all of it—and some of which may even lead to inflammation of sorts. And if you didn't know, hormonal imbalance can contribute to various kinds of stresses, inevitably impacting sleep and putting you back in the same loop.

Personally, I love a late-night run to Carl's Jr., some extra hot Cheetos, and some form of dessert. Having it once in a while, I still feel like shit afterward, but when I have this stuff a bit more often than I should, I really do feel a drop in sleep quality, mental clarity, and emotional regulation. Besides that, such indulgences have led me to experience more heartburn and joint pain. So, yes, a shit diet can lead to both physical *and* mental stress. And because stress, sleep, and diet are all interconnected, you can't just focus on one area—you have to address all of them. I'll dive into more of the details of diet and nutrition later on.

Recovery Is Nurture, Nurture Is Feminine, and Feminine Does Not Mean Weakness

Both men and women have masculine and feminine energies, though men are predominantly masculine, and women more feminine—I'm not talking about the exceptions right now. I like to think of masculine energy as the active force, and feminine energy as the passive one. Regarding the active force, I'm referring to the drive to act, to push, to endure, and to lift the burdens on your shoulders. Regarding the passive force, I'm referring to the natural yearning for and practice of nurture, peace, rest, and recovery. It feels as though there's a huge overemphasis on the active, masculine side—working as hard as possible, becoming as strong as possible, picking up as much responsibility as possible, etc.—and not so much on the passive, feminine side. However, I'm much more certain that this is the case in the realm of fitness, particularly. It's unfortunate that many people see rest and recovery—the passive, nurturing, feminine side—as some form of weakness, though it is equally as important as its active and masculine counterpart.

Now, for those of you who have had the blessed experience of being raised by both a mother-figure and father-figure—those you can basically call "mom" and "dad"—let me ask you the following:

- Who do you call out to when you're in serious pain? Whether it's me, people I've witnessed, or even people on TV, the answer has usually been some exclaimed form of the word, "Mom." In Armenian, when something goes wrong, we often exclaim, "Vay *mama* jan!"

- How does it feel, or did it feel, to be taken care of by mom? Perhaps she has treated your wound when you scraped your knee during soccer or basketball practice. Maybe she aided in your recovery when you were sick.

Perhaps she was the one with whom you experienced your first and maybe most frequent release of oxytocin—the hormone associated with love, trust, and attachment.

- What would life be like without her? Or, for some, what has life been like without her? Perhaps it feels a bit colder, especially if there are no other women in your life that supply the necessary warmth and care that we naturally seek.

The reason why I mention both figures and not just mother alone, is because the significance of one relies on the other—on their own, without their counterbalancing force, each would be too much.

"Alright, Manny, we get it. You need to balance these out, but you still haven't told us how femininity does not mean weakness..." Right. Well, if you understand that you need to balance the energies out, then you understand that there's strength in the feminine as well. And though you may acknowledge its strength and importance, you may still not imagine exactly how so. Imagine what would happen if you went to work, day in and day out, without taking a break. Imagine never showing or receiving warmth from anyone ever again—not even a simple bro hug. Imagine lifting and pushing at the gym without breaks between sets. See just how long you will last. Some people will last longer than others, but everyone will inevitably become weak and break down. So, how can that nurturing, feminine quality that saves your ass really be a weakness? In the case I just mentioned, the purely active masculine force led to weakness, not strength.

The only case in which the passive feminine would become a weakness is if that's *all* you had.

So, now, since you have a better understanding of both the differences in roles and importance of the active masculine and the passive feminine energies, you must acknowledge, embrace, and balance these within yourself. This takes us to the discussion and importance of self-love and self-respect, and how rest and recovery are a major part of that, especially in the context of fitness.

And just to be even more clear, feminine does not equal female—they are two separate things. Guys, the bit of feminine energy that exists within you comes from your experiences with mother-figures growing up, as well as from the bit of estrogen you naturally have. Testosterone leads to masculinity, and estrogen leads to femininity. Both males and females produce both those hormones. And what makes you weak is the cowardice to fear, deny, and neglect a part of you that exists whether you like it or not. Femininity in itself is not weakness. It's what you do with it that makes it so. Loving, caring for, and respecting yourself is not weakness—it is strength.

Love Thyself, Respect Thyself

The concept of self-love and self-respect often gets tossed around, but it seems, so far, that it's rarely discussed in the context of fitness and recovery. What if true respect for yourself means knowing when to stop? What if the highest form of self-love is learning to rest, to recover, and to treat your body with the care it actually deserves? It's easy to get caught up in the grind and to tell yourself that rest can wait. Sometimes, it's not so much that you're caught up as much as it is that you're in the flow and don't want to stop. But ignoring the need for recovery hurts your progress and thus betrays the very idea of self-respect. Prioritizing the need to continuously push ourselves without taking time to heal has to be corrected. Whatever your definition of strength, I'd like you to also think of it as the balance between discipline and self-care, while seeing the latter as an essential part of optimizing your performance—not as a sign of weakness.

Consider yourself as both your own employee and employer. Would you work for anyone who doesn't respect you, your needs, or your well-being after all the work you put in? I'd like to think not. Then, my dear reader, I strongly encourage you to respect your own needs and give yourself the time and space to heal and grow, so that you can come back stronger. And, as an employer, you need your employee to trust you when you speak of rest. Otherwise, the employee will stop giving a shit, since they have no idea if and when they'll ever actually catch a break. Building trust in yourself in the context of recovery is crucial. You need to know that when you say you'll take time to rest after working hard, you'll actually do it. If you constantly push through without taking the breaks you said you would, you'll quickly lose trust in yourself. You'll start to wonder when you'll ever get to relax. I can't stress enough just how important it is to stay consistent with the promises you make to yourself. If something's not working, fine, but don't just brush it off—do something about it. Change it, renegotiate with yourself, but whatever you do, be sure to keep that trust intact.

You have to treat yourself like your best employee because if you had an employee consistently performing at peak levels, I'd like to hope you're a good leader who recognizes the importance of rewarding that individual with the necessary time off to prevent burnout. Now ask yourself: Why don't I treat myself the same way? Do I have something against myself, or am I just a masochist? If you are, isn't it more exciting to get back to the self-torture once you've at least given yourself a chance to catch your breath? If I were a masochist, I'd wait 'til I refresh myself and make myself believe that the torture is over, that I've fully healed, before I come back in and surprise myself once more. At the very least, I would take a break so that I can deliver optimal torture when I'm back; I would imagine that's more exciting. A small digression, but we see that, even through a dark, grim perspective, rest and recovery still benefit you in the end.

Now, though I do stress discipline, forcing it into every corner of your life is not healthy. Some people manage to stay strict on their diet even when they're heavily stressed, convincing themselves that discipline alone will carry them through. Others will force themselves to sleep on schedule despite their stress, often turning to quick fixes such as melatonin, cannabis, alcohol, or other substances. But you know, deep down, that those are band-aids at best. That's not to say that you should never use a quick fix or experiment—experimentation is necessary to find what works well for you, especially long-term—but don't just resort to quick little escapes. Because, really, there *is* no quick fix, especially not a long-term one. That's why they're called quick fixes, not lasting solutions. There's an entire billion-dollar industry built around quick fixes because everyone wants fast results, and delayed gratification is damn near non-existent.

They want that bulge, and they want it now—those pecs aren't gonna wait for the countless hours of work required otherwise. But if you want something lasting, something sustainable, you need to understand that it's going to take work, introspection, and experimentation. I've always been an experimenter, even with food. I'll sometimes mix things that make people look at me like I'm crazy, but some of my mixes work really well. You just never really know until you try.

Anyway, building self-trust, familiarizing yourself with your stresses, and finding lasting solutions to each form is not an easy thing to do. You may not like dealing with your own inner chaos, but if you don't face it, it'll catch up to you. If you don't feel like dealing with it when the stress is in its infancy, how do you think you'll feel—how do you expect to deal with it—when it becomes monstrous? Don't brush it under the rug. Whether it's through thought-tracking, kayaking, or lifting heavy weight, you need something to ground you. Whatever your method, it needs to help keep your mind and body in check.

The drive for success can blind you to your own limitations. When you're in overdrive, you might be riding high on progress, results, and perhaps even some monetary gains. And it does feel amazing. But the mistake many of us make is when we start to think, "I can keep this up forever." You'll inevitably hit a wall, and the very work you used to love will start to feel like a burden. Eventually, you'll resent the things that gave you that high because they'll no longer feel worth the effort. If you push yourself to that point, no kind of reward will feel satisfying. It becomes very similar to anhedonia—a condition in which you don't feel like doing or enjoying things that were once enjoyable. You don't want to reach that breaking point.

Sorry to break it to you, but your body will force you to rest if you don't do it voluntarily. It'll throw its hands up and say, "Alright, I'm done," whether you're ready for it or not. This is thanks to homeostasis, the body's natural balancing system, which works both biologically and psychologically. Homeostatic mechanisms, such as the HPA axis, help regulate the body's response to stress, but prolonged stress can disrupt this balance and lead to exhaustion (McEwen, 1998; Maslach et al., 2001)[7]. The mind and body need balance, and if you don't give them that, nature will take its course and restore it for you.

So why are we so afraid to give ourselves permission to rest? This fear is, again, largely due to our naive idea that rest is weakness. We've internalized the belief that discomfort is the only path to success. That's what many of us have been told growing up.

- "No time to rest, boy. Keep your nose to the grindstone."

- "Wanna be rich? Make every second productive."

- "I'll rest when I'm dead."

Do these sound familiar? But what's the point of grinding yourself into the ground if, in the end, you have nothing left to give? "But Manny, what about these 'gurus' telling me I need to do all the things and that there are these super methods to optimize sleep so I can run on four hours of sleep and feel like I slept eight?" Please. Don't be so gullible, McFly. They all know people are looking for solutions to cheat life and nature. You can't. You can only learn to negotiate and work with it. Cleanse yourself of all the shit you see on social media. How many opinions from self-proclaimed "gurus" can you keep up with, especially when so many of them have contradicting ideas? Stop.

A deeper issue is often a lack of self-respect. Again, would you overwork someone you respect? Probably not. So, if you think you don't deserve rest and are willing to hurt yourself, then it likely means you don't respect yourself. Perhaps you see yourself as a machine that should run 24/7. But you're *not* a machine, and even machines break down when overworked, usually due to overheating or the wear and tear of their parts. Maybe it's the fear that slowing down will lead to a loss in momentum. It might even be guilt that resting somehow means you don't care enough about why you're doing what you're doing. Maybe you feel like you haven't *earned* rest yet, so you keep pushing. But pushing through doesn't make you stronger if you're breaking yourself in the process because when you start disintegrating and thus slowing, you may be even *more* inclined to think you haven't earned it.

Another common fear people have is that while they rest, others are outworking them, getting ahead, and gaining the edge. This mindset is yet another trap. How far behind will you fall when you burn out? You already know what happens then. In this case, you're not competing against anyone but yourself, and the only person who loses when you burn out and crash is you. What's the point of pushing so hard if it comes at the cost of your health and, thus, your progress, happiness, and so on? You might be getting a lot done at the moment, maybe for a few weeks or months—but what about the longer run? Is it really worth sacrificing your long-term potential for short-term gains? "I get it, Manny, but I've been at this for a while—I'll be fine." You know how naive you sound, Kay?

Respecting yourself means recognizing that rest is a necessity to develop true discipline. True discipline means knowing when to push and when to step back. Try to think about all of this as a strategy that makes sure that your hard work actually pays off and that *you're still able to give your best when it matters most*; you can't function at your highest level if you're constantly depleted. Learning to respect yourself, to love yourself, and to give yourself the necessary nurture is a major investment in your future self.

Personalized Recovery

Personally, what I do to rest and recover is usually very different from what I imagine when I hear the words uttered by someone else—especially by social media influencers. I think of zen, meditation, spa, and other seemingly typical shit like that. Sure, I absolutely love massages, but zen stuff and meditation drive me crazy. I get bored from not doing anything, it bothers the hell out of me, and I just end up becoming hyperirritable. So, I'm not going to list a bunch of ways to recover because different things work differently for different people. That's why **personalizing your recovery is essential**.

Everyone's capacity to operate at peak is different, as is everyone's recovery time. Some people can go at peak for two or three months straight and only need a week off, while others can keep going or might need a much longer break. Some prefer intermittent breaks—working a day, taking a day off, working a day, taking a day off. And then there are some for whom short bursts work best—working eight hours a day and then spending the rest of the day in pure relaxation. You need to experiment to find what works best for you, and it's critical that you take the time to do so. That's how I found what works for me.

I tried *scheduling* breaks, but that didn't work for me. I thought I could work at peak for four or five days a week and then have the weekends to myself, but that didn't work either. Certain days were supposed to be for relaxation, but they were still part of the peak schedule. I couldn't freely make plans because certain things had to be done on those days, and I just felt locked in. I've even had periods where I took no breaks for months and performed wonderfully, but then I needed an extended period of time to let myself go. The most recent approach that's been effective for me involves going with the flow—more or less—while maintaining a general structure. I set weekly tasks and deadlines—some of which are hard and others soft—but I still allow myself flexibility within that structure.

For example, if I have tasks that need to be done by a certain day, I prioritize them, but I also leave room for spontaneity. If something comes up that I want to do—like visiting my grandfather or spending time with my girl—I make *that* a priority, knowing I can complete the task later. "Isn't that procrastination?" Not if I've built the self-trust and discipline to know that I will get it done by what I define as "later" and actually getting it done when I say so. This flexibility gives me a sense of control and satisfaction, which is an important part of my recovery.

It's important to prioritize figuring out what causes you stress, as well as what allows you to recover from each type of stress most effectively. A form of recovery that works well for one form of stress may not work as well with another. For example, if I'm worried about finances, I can't comfortably watch a movie, but going for a night drive might do it. If I'm mentally exhausted from work but not necessarily worried, a movie with my girl will do the trick. You *can* use band-aid solutions, but be careful not to become reliant on them. After all, they wouldn't be a thing if they didn't serve a purpose, and even though they're not an actual solution, they *can* be useful as quick recovery techniques or temporary cover-ups once in a while. However, you need to actually *treat* the wound, not just keep slapping Band-Aids on it. Sure, you can stop the bleeding for now, but you'll need to address the underlying issue eventually. And once you *do* find a way to successfully treat and heal it, you'll know what to do if, God forbid, you run into the same issue again. You'll know where to go and how to get it treated because you've already done so once before and thus will have the experience to handle it once more.

Everyone finds their own form of relaxation or recovery. Personally, spending time with my girl recharges me quickly, and it's my favorite form of rest and recovery for pretty much all forms of stress. I also enjoy driving around at night while listening to music—it helps me unwind, clear my mind, and feel at peace. At other times, I shut down completely. I'll have a cigarette, watch a light comedy, chew some sunflower seeds, and go into my nothing box. Even *then*, however, it can be hard to truly turn off my thoughts. If I *still* find my mind racing, I might go to the gym and push to the point where the only thing my mind can think of is, "Fuck, I just want to sleep already,"—and those usually turn out to be awesome sessions.

There are times when going to the gym feels like work, especially if I don't feel like going, but I know I need to maintain my physique. And then there are times when I've already worked out for the day, but I feel the need to go back to get something off my chest. After a session like that, I might listen to music on the drive back, have a nice meal, and then fall asleep to music. "Alright, Manny, we get it: You love music! Jeeesusss..." Yes. Yes, I do. It's a huge part of my life, and I couldn't live without it. In fact, if I could play more instruments, I would. I'd love to learn how to play Armenian-style clarinet, for example. Point is, everyone has their own unique way of relaxing or recovering—of doing something that brings peace to their mind. What strums your soul's string? If you don't really know, I promise it's worth spending the time to find that peace of the puzzle.

The Peace You've Been Looking For

What role does spirituality play in people's lives? For some, it's a source of comfort, hope, and strength amid the chaos. For some others, it fills in the gaps they couldn't fill themselves—it provides closure of sorts. Ultimately, it's where they find peace, a sense of grounding when everything else feels uncertain. Peace is something we all seek, consciously or unconsciously because it's essential for our well-being. It almost seems like everything we do is to get a little closer to peace. We might work hard to make money to provide our kids the opportunity to live a better life. We might work hard to stay fit so that we can live a long and healthy life without worrying about being a burden to our loved ones. You see how both of these provide everyone involved a peace of mind?

"But Manny, what about all that talk about The Beast and rage? How does this search for peace fit with the idea of channeling rage and powering through challenges? How could you possibly have peace while embracing such intense emotions?" Those are all valid questions. And it definitely seems contradictory on the surface, but the truth is, they're not mutually exclusive. It's really quite the opposite because, as surprising as it may be, the two can actually complement each other. When The Beast comes out, and your raw, intense energy that comes with it is channeled—whether it's rage, determination, or sheer willpower—you're not letting it consume you because, by now, you've hopefully learned to work with it. Instead, you're using it as a way to clear your mental clutter, and when the clutter is gone, you will feel the same sense of relief that you do when your messy room has finally been cleaned up. Sometimes, it may even feel similar to the calm and quiet peace you might feel when a storm is finally over. Every time I've pushed myself to the edge, whether in the gym or in life, I've found a strange kind of peace come over me afterward. It's almost like that release allows me to reassure myself that, "Yeah, I can handle this," whatever "this" may be.

Please understand, this does not mean you must live in a constant state of rage or tension—that would just be a form of slow and torturous suicide. Chronic stress is a patient, determined, and often silent assassin. High levels of cortisol mess with your body on a fundamental level—your nerves are heavily taxed, your muscles tighten up, your organs don't function properly, and your mind becomes a hot shit mess. When I'm on edge for long periods of time, I develop digestive issues, it becomes harder to breathe, I become very forgetful and hyper-irritable, and I can't concentrate on anything if my life depended on it. I become incredibly undesirable to be around. When you're constantly on edge, every part of you pays the price, and so do others around you. So, while it's okay to tap into those intense emotions when you need a quick spike of fuel, I suggest you learn to appreciate and prolong the peaceful state that follows immediately after.

Outside of the post-storm peace, people have all sorts of other ways to try and achieve internal peace, but obviously, not all of them are healthy or sustainable. Drugs are amazing escapes but only offer temporary relief, a momentary sense of calm, but it's bullshit because the shit you're trying to escape will only haunt you harder upon the come down—not considering their other negative impacts. To be clear, I'm not saying you'll throw your life away if you smoke a joint once in a while. However, anything that makes you feel good can easily become a gateway to worse habits later on, especially if you're not in a good place or have an addictive personality. It's like slapping a band-aid on a wound without cleaning it first. It might feel similar to "Out of sight, out of mind," but that wound is becoming disgusting, and when the band-aid falls off, you're just going to be scrambling for another quick fix. Either use what you have to treat the wound yourself or go to a hospital if you don't know how.

So is there a way to achieve lasting peace of mind? Well, maybe, but the way that works for me is not easy, and it's certainly not something you achieve overnight. One of the best ways I've found is to anchor yourself to something truly meaningful to you, and that's usually something beyond your immediate concerns. When you're working toward something that resonates that deeply with who you are and what you value, it gives you a real sense of purpose. That purpose may not only give you a sense of lasting peace, but it may very likely also be what keeps you going when everything else feels like it's falling apart. The only time the peace found through purpose may disintegrate is when some other far more valuable factor takes a hit, and there is little to nothing you can do about it. I've experienced this, and it feels like you're neck deep in shit and cannot breathe, kind of like a panic attack. God forbid you experience this, but if you do, Good Luck. It's not impossible to get through—you just need to endure the torture and ride the wave until it passes with time.

However, there may be many people for whom peace can feel so foreign that they may not even know how to experience it and may even thus feel uncomfortable. In this case, not having peace is all they know, all they are used to. It may sound absurd, and such people will not consciously realize or acknowledge it. Does this mean it's impossible for them to experience peace? No, but attempting to do so will actually take some serious work on their part. And upon achieving some peace, they might enjoy it for a moment, but then they might begin to feel weird and uneasy and will inevitably find a way to step back into the chaos they're so familiar with, often unconsciously. I imagine some of these folks may even feel that they don't *deserve* to be at peace—

that's a much deeper issue to be investigated and won't fit into this book.

Peace isn't something that just happens because you want it to. It cannot be achieved by avoiding conflict or pretending everything is fine when it's not. You need to confront what's in front of you, deal with it, and *then*, *maybe*, you will find your way back to peace. The more you go through this, the easier it becomes until it eventually becomes second nature. **You cannot have peace without conflict**—and believe me, your mind, among other things, will fight you every step of the way. It may try to convince you that what you're doing is pointless, that perhaps you don't deserve it, and that you're just going to fall back to square one eventually which will make the entire thing a waste of time and energy. You may even scoff or laugh at the idea of peace, denying its potential reality. Laugh and scoff all you like, but your disbelief—probably stemming from the possibility that you haven't seen or experienced it yet—doesn't change the fact that peace *is* real and *can*, indeed, be achieved. If you can push through that resistance, you'll find that it gets easier over time. Eventually, you'll reach a point where it's easier to stay in that peaceful, clear-minded state than it is to slip back into the chaos.

I've found that when I'm in my most chaotic state of mind, the only way I can feel some peace and recalibrate my mind is through the kind of workout or any activity that requires all my focus and energy. When I'm at the gym, pushing myself through such a workout, there's a moment when everything else fades away. It's the same feeling I experience when I'm on the road, alone, driving at ridiculously high speeds, especially at night.

Most people experience an adrenaline rush, or something similar, from such a stimulation, but it has the opposite effect on me—it calms me down. I'm not thinking about the insignificant stresses of the day or other forms of shit that live in my mind rent-free, like junkie squatters. I'm fully present, focused on the task at hand because not being so can mean serious injury... or even death in the case of my driving. That's just one of my forms of peace, and the clarity that comes from these activities is unlike any other. In these moments, my mind gets used to a different kind of stress and learns to stay focused through it until it finds its peace.

Among all other forms, however, achieving a peaceful mind through fitness seems to be the most productive and most beneficial to your overall well-being; this has proven true for me as well as others I know and work with. I stress the importance of a peaceful mind because of how imperative it is for optimal recovery, both in and out of the gym. When your mind is at peace, your body follows suit, and you're able to recover faster, think more clearly, and perform better in every aspect of your life. Not being at peace can leave you weak and vulnerable, no matter how many plates or burdens you can lift; a state of chaos, confusion, and chronic stress can make you blind and reactive. It took years for me to realize that true strength isn't just about how much weight I can lift, both literally and figuratively speaking; it's about how well I'm able to maintain my inner peace, no matter what life throws at me.

Okay, so say you find peace working out, dancing, playing hide and seek, or whatever it might be for you—does it stay confined to just that activity? No, not normally. With time, as with the other developments I've discussed that can be achieved through fitness, it will spill over into other areas of your life. You may even find that you've become more patient, more thoughtful, and more intentional in everything you do. And when life throws its bag of mixed, raw, and unshelled nuts your way, you're better equipped to handle them without becoming something of a nut yourself.

Peace and fitness are interconnected a lot more than people might realize. The peace and clarity found through physical exertion is similar to the peace found in prayer, meditation, or deep reflection. Your mind gets used to staying calm under pressure, and one of the most important forms of strength you gain from fitness is learning how to keep your inner peace when life does what it can to break you.

Endnotes

1   Breus, M. (2024). Cortisol: How it affects your sleep. Sleep Doctor. Retrieved from https://www.sleepdoctor.com/2024/05/02/cortisol-and-sleep

2   Lovallo, W. R. (2006). Stress and health: Biological and psychological interactions. Sage Publications.

3   McEwen, B. S. (2007). Physiology and neurobiology of stress and adaptation: central role of the brain. Physiological reviews, 87(3), 873-904. https://doi.org/10.1152/physrev.00041.2006

4   Mayo Clinic. (2023). Stress symptoms: Effects on your body and behavior. Retrieved from Mayo Clinic Website

5   Mayo Clinic. (2023). Stress symptoms: Effects on your body and behavior. Retrieved from Mayo Clinic Website

6   American Psychological Association. (n.d.). The impact of stress. Retrieved from APA Website

7   Maslach, C., Schaufeli, W. B., & Leiter, M. P. (2001). Job burnout. Annual Review of Psychology, 52(1), 397-422. https://doi.org/10.1146/annurev.psych.52.1.397

McEwen, B. S. (1998). Protective and damaging effects of stress mediators. New England Journal of Medicine, 338(3), 171-179. https://doi.org/10.1056/NEJM199801153380307

CHAPTER 10

Starting Your Fitness Journey

Why Get into Fitness (If You're Already Inclined)

I know people who have, for a long time, thought of fitness as something shallow. Everything they were exposed to about fitness—the gym, lifting weights, yoga, supplements, etc.—was tied to the trendy social media influencer culture. That made them very hesitant; they didn't want to seem vain or shallow like the people who promoted that image. They cared about their body, but more from a standpoint of being the best version of themselves rather than just looking good in the mirror.

It's a common struggle for people who are already inclined toward fitness but can't quite get past the surface-level bullshit. They know fitness is valuable but don't want to fall into the trap of vanity that so much of the culture promotes. Now, there is nothing really wrong with vanity being a fitness goal, but honestly—and by now, I'm sure you've gotten the point—fitness is much deeper than aesthetics. It's a tool that improves and empowers every aspect of your life. The more optimized your body becomes, the more clarity you'll find in your goals and decision-making, and the more resilience you'll develop physically, mentally, and emotionally.

Again, it's better to approach fitness with the idea that it's more so a way of living and not so much a destination to be reached. When you're already inclined to start but haven't fully committed, the most valuable thing you can do is shift your mindset from one of overwhelming changes and instant results to incremental steps and a long-term investment. Consider how much of your daily energy is drained by small, seemingly insignificant habits such as doom scrolling. We often don't realize the compounding effect of our habits—some of which contribute to our progress, while some others hold us back.

Another one of the most important things to keep in mind is that **you don't have to follow a rigid, pre-made program to see results.** Fitness is about aligning your goals with your values, your lifestyle, and making the process work *for* you rather than *against* you. A lot of people assume that if they can't commit to an hour-long workout five days a week, then they might as well not even bother. But that's the wrong approach; you can start by introducing incremental changes that naturally fit into your day.

For example, if you're spending time gaming, bingeing a show, or scrolling on your phone, there are moments of downtime—loading screens, respawns, or even just breaks between sessions. Why not use that time to lift a dumbbell or do a few stretches? You can integrate movement into your existing life in ways that make sense for you that won't disrupt your entire routine. If you don't want to treat it like a separate task, you don't have to—just squeeze it into the time you're already spending on something else.

If you have a genuine desire to improve and really haven't found a way out of your box, the key is to shift your perspective. By doing so, once again, you wouldn't just build physical strength but mental fortitude as well. You'd be proving to yourself that you can find ways, even if slowly or in small increments, to improve, thus breaking through the bullshit excuses you may have had. Keep doing this, and one day, you'll look back and realize how much further you've come than you ever thought possible.

Diet and Nutrition: Discipline Without Deprivation

Everyone has their own take on nutrition, and it's one of those things on which every so-called expert seems to have a different opinion. So how can you give universal nutritional advice beyond the most basic, most obvious things? Well, I'm not here to tell you exactly what to eat, like whether you should eat more meat or cut carbs. Most of that is up to you, though I will, in a later supplemental work, include some pointers on macronutrients you should consider. For those of you who aren't aware, I can tell you this: if you want muscle growth, you need more protein for optimal recovery after tearing your muscles. If you want weight loss, you need a calorie deficit. It's up to you to figure out what fits your diet, your body, and your goals. What's key is understanding how what you eat affects you and your progress.

But where most people mess up is they either overcomplicate their diet with extreme approaches or they ignore important, seemingly insignificant aspects of it—such as the fine print on nutrition labels, which can be deceiving as hell. You might look at your favorite condiment and see "40 calories per serving" and think, "Oh, not bad." But what's the serving size? Because for many condiments, it's usually a teaspoon. And let's be real, most people are squirting a lot more of that stuff on their food than that. It's those little things that add up and sabotage your progress without you even noticing.

Now, let's talk about indulgences. I like doughnuts. Occasionally, I'll take a dozen to the office, and then I hear the same thing every time:

- "Wow. Okay, that's not fair. How do you eat that and look like that?"

- "I eat one M&M and gain 10 pounds. This guy eats doughnuts and has abs."

- "Fuck you, dude."

People see me eating doughnuts and think it's either magic, or pure genetics, or that I'm on drugs of some sort. But really, it's just discipline and sheer determination. I know how to indulge without it ruining my progress because I've earned that right through hard work and control. There's no quick and easy solution to reaching your fitness goals. One coworker once asked me to help him lose weight quickly. I told him the faster he wants results, the harder it's going to be, and it'll require changes and effort that he might not be used to. After I explained what it takes to eat what he wants while still maintaining a good physique, he literally said, "Ah, fuck that shit." Well, there you have it. Your goals depend on your priorities and your willingness to put in the work and make sacrifices.

Self-Trust and Indulgence

I will never tell you that you shouldn't eat a particular thing unless I know everything about your goal. However, if you're not even close to your fitness goal and you tell me you want to look a certain way, I'll be upfront with you. I'll tell you that you need to be much more careful about what you put in your mouth because what's going in right now isn't serving you. You can maybe afford a treat if you've reached your goal and are just maintaining. I can afford a treat because I know what I need to do to compensate for it. If it fits into my daily caloric needs, no problem. If it doesn't, I'll make up for it tomorrow or the next day. But the key here is that I have the discipline; I know I can do it, and I trust myself. You need to build trust in yourself because you'll spiral out of control otherwise.

Just like your muscles, trust is something you build over time—it doesn't appear overnight. Trust comes from repeatedly proving to yourself that you're capable of staying in control, even when it's tempting to let go. It builds when you say you're going to do something and you follow through to completion. Trust is built on discipline, which is built on decisions and the actions that follow. So, for example, when deciding whether to restrain or indulge when you know you shouldn't, you're either reinforcing that trust or chipping away at it. When you can look back and see that you've held the line consistently, you start to believe in yourself more deeply. You stop questioning whether you can handle it, and you start confidently trusting that you will. That's a quiet, internal strength—and it's fair to say it's far more valuable than any external result.

Regarding restraints, I don't restrict myself severely. I've been there and done that. I've tried extreme diets, fad diets, extreme routines, etc.—none of which were sustainable. It doesn't work. I've found that it's better off eating whatever you want in a controlled, disciplined, and moderate way. Craving a donut? Have a small piece and save the rest for later; you don't have to have the whole damn thing. Craving Flamin' Hot Cheetos? Take a few pieces and put that shit away.

It wasn't so easy for me to restrain myself as much as I needed to in the beginning. The way I got used to it was by using the following methods:

- Negotiating with my Beast

- Personifying the thing I was craving and then talking to it—something I also do with pain

- Reminding myself of the consequences of indulging

- Reminding myself that my weak decision here can show up in another domain

- Reminding myself that I'm not going to enjoy it more with the more I eat

- At first, not buying any of it. When I gained some more trust in myself, I bought some but kept it all out of sight and would only grant myself access when I deserved a treat. With enough trust in myself, I was able to keep them around, even at my desk because I built that degree of control.

Cravings usually feel bigger than they really are. It's not because you're hungry that you keep eating it—it's either the addiction to the dopamine hits that come from the flavor or just a nervous habit. Either way, your mind convinces you that you need more to feel satisfied, but in reality, the satisfaction comes before the food even touches your lips. Most people think more equals better, but each time they do that, they realize that having more just means more guilt, more discomfort, and more regret. For me, and most people I've asked, it's really the flavor you're after. Once you have a taste, it's not a positive correlation—your satisfaction doesn't increase with each bite.

It's actually a lot like sex—your satisfaction is highest just before the climax. You salivate the most and get the biggest dopamine hit just before that first bite when the Cheeto hits your taste buds. It's not going to be any better the more you eat. So why keep eating? You got the taste. Instead of blowing through the whole bag, you can have that same dopamine hit again in three hours with just a few more pieces, and with the added benefit of reveling in some post-nut clarity for a while. The best part is that you can repeat this process and give yourself multiple orgasms throughout the day. What more do you want?

Guilt and Guilty Pleasures

A lot of people refer to their indulgences as "guilty pleasures." But why are you feeling guilty? You should only feel guilty if you know you shouldn't have done it. If you're doing the right things then you shouldn't feel guilty. Those pleasures don't have to be guilty if you've earned them. If you change your actions, if you've put in the work and made the necessary sacrifices, you can enjoy those pleasures guilt-free—and you don't even have to go for the low-fat, low-calorie versions either. If you still feel guilty about it, thinking you canceled out your work, then really consider your goal and consider the efforts you put towards that goal. Sometimes, I've found it helpful to **think of it like going to Vegas**—setting aside "trash cash" that I don't expect to get back. Likewise with fitness, I **set aside calories I'm willing to burn only to be enjoyed**—not wasted—by foods I enjoy that I don't regularly have. You can't feel guilty about it; that'll just drive you crazy and make you sick. If you're disciplined and you've put in the necessary work, you deserve to treat yourself guilt free.

If thinking about any form of dietary restraints feels gut-wrenching, or if you just don't really care and don't want to deal with any of this, yet you keep telling others you feel guilty or that you're gonna start next week, it means you're not being honest with yourself about your goals. If you don't want it, be honest with yourself about your values. Once you acknowledge that you don't really care about getting into shape, then you could stop complaining that you're not in shape. But if getting into shape is a priority for you, then do something about it. Reorganize your life, your time, your tasks, to where you can work toward that priority. Just don't lie to yourself and others saying, "Oh, I want to get into shape, but oh, there are all these things that are in the way" because it's simply not that high of a priority for you. Then you *don't* want it bad enough, and that's okay. Why are you afraid of people judging you? Is it because fitness isn't at the top of your priority hierarchy? So what? It doesn't have to be. Maybe you're really judging yourself and projecting that judgment onto others. But in any case, **if you're still feeling guilty, then deep inside, you know you have to change**.

But think of guilt not as your enemy but more so as a messenger. I personally like to think of it as a warning light on the dashboard of my life, telling me that something's out of alignment. However you take it though, do not make the mistake of many others who let their guilt spiral into shame. They internalize it, beat themselves up, and feel like they've failed. But by seeing it as a message or warning light, it becomes a powerful tool that your mind and body are using to tell you, "Hey, genius, we're off course. Get our ass back on track." Don't wallow in it; listen to it and use its lesson to move forward.

The Dangers of Extreme Dieting

Now, let's get into something more dangerous: extreme dieting. This is something through which people I've known have gone into very dark places. I've seen people starve themselves to lose weight faster without realizing the damage they're doing to their minds and bodies.

Ron

I once worked with a very dear friend, Ron, who wanted to lose weight and get lean very quickly. This guy loves challenges—the harder it is, the harder *he* is. I told him what it would take to hit his goal, but that I wouldn't really recommend it—not because I knew the dangers at the time, but because I just knew it wasn't sustainable. I felt that if he failed, it might throw him off fitness entirely, and I didn't want to kill his motivation. He created such a huge calorie deficit that he dropped his intake to 1,200 calories a day while burning close to 3,000—a deficit of 1,800. That is dangerously low intake and much too great a deficit.

At first, he did lose a lot of weight, but that weight also included muscle. Then, he just became skinny. He didn't lose all muscle mass, but there was a noticeable loss. He started telling me that he feels "off," to which I suggested he increases his calorie intake so that the deficit isn't too great. But my warning was too late, his negative spiral had just begun. His testosterone levels plummeted, he lost muscle mass, and he fell into a depression. Why? Because the body can only handle so much deprivation before it snaps back and forces you to bring back balance. And when this happens, it snaps hard. He started binge-eating 8,000 to 10,000 calories a day because his body was extremely desperate for fuel. Binging made him feel even worse, and the cycle was terrible. I blamed myself for this. I hated to see Ron in this shape, and I felt responsible. I should have tried harder to stop him, and I should have been more educated on the impact of such a deficit on the body. It took a while, but Ron is good now. Do not make the same mistake.

Extreme dieting can negatively impact mental health in ways you probably can't imagine. When you deprive yourself to the point of starvation, or become extremely rigid with your restraints, it's not just your body that suffers—your mind starts to rebel too. You become obsessed with food, constantly thinking about what you can or can't have. This obsession can become dangerously intrusive, to the point where you won't be able to focus on anything else. So don't just think "calories in, calories out are all that matters" (that's too vague), but don't become so obsessive over your numbers either. The only people that need to be serious in their counting are bodybuilders who prepare about two weeks before a show, but then they return to their normal diet afterwards.

Extreme diets should not be associated with discipline because such diets are a lot closer in nature to desperation—a state of weakness. It's much more important to build an appropriate relationship with food. If that relationship becomes toxic, you'll start to feel out of control, not just with eating, but with everything else. That's why it's crucial that your relationship with food be one that's built on trust, discipline, and moderation.

Balance in Nom-Nom

Similar to the balance I discuss in other areas, if you're constantly in a state of restriction, constantly telling yourself "no," your mind will start fighting back or give out like an overworked muscle. But if you allow yourself small indulgences without swinging from one extreme to the other, you keep that mental muscle strong and flexible. You stay in control. Balance and moderation are signs of control. Good strength and control are when you can indulge in something you enjoy and not let it shit on your progress. Knowing that one doughnut, one slice of pizza, or one cheat meal isn't going to ruin everything you've worked for is an awesome kind of confidence. And that confidence comes from self-trust, which is the result of proving to yourself time and time again that you can handle it.

The way you approach your nutrition, your indulgences, and even your guilt will likely reflect the way you approach everything else. It's important to find a way to regulate yourself so that you stay on track without depriving yourself of life's pleasures. You might think, "Well, shit, how do I come up with this perfect system?" but it can never be perfect and it certainly doesn't have to be. You just need to learn how to stay in control as much as possible—not through force, but through balance.

Tools & Tech: The Impact of Technology on Fitness

We are all very lucky to live in a world with the technology we have today. We have more tools, tech, and overall resources on fitness than we have ever had before. Tech has given us easy access to educational content and made it easier than ever to track and measure progress. Whether you're just starting to consider fitness or you've already started, regardless how serious you are, these tools can be game-changers. If you just started considering fitness, you have access to videos and apps that can provide more info and perhaps fill the info gap that kept you hesitant. You can even use that content to learn more about what equipment you can order for home workouts, and you can have them delivered in just a couple days! If you're so worried about all the things you need to track, there are apps and devices specially built for that purpose, such as the MyFitnessPal app and the smartwatch—both of which I use regularly.

Before their existence, keeping track of how much you ate, how much you burned, or even your vitals required much more work—manual work. First, you'd have to learn what to measure and for what. Then you'd have to learn how; maybe there was some anatomy, physiology, and math you had to learn. You'd have to pay attention to so many things it would be annoying and likely difficult to focus on your workout. With all that, is it hard to imagine why people were more hesitant and anxious toward fitness? You'd have to write things down, calculate data by hand, and hope you weren't way off. But now, since the apps and smart devices sync up, you instantly have all your essential data at your fingertips. It's almost like having a personal trainer in your pocket, and it's a massive advantage if used wisely.

Once you start using tech to track your diet and workouts, it becomes habitual. Over time, your eyes get used to portions, burn rate, and your physiological state. You get a feel for what 200 calories looks like, or how much protein is in 8oz of chicken breast, without having to slap it on the scale every time. You'll get a feel for your average caloric burn rate during your training sessions. Once you experience this, you'll never want to go back. It feels like freedom, which comes from control, which is effortless relative to what it would be like without these tools. And that confidence, again, comes from self-trust. I'll get to how these tools can make it easier to build trust in yourself in just a bit.

After a while, I just started to eyeball most things, and I still do. People often ask me, "Are you cutting or bulking?" And sometimes, I don't even know the answer. One week, I might feel like leaning down, so I eat a little less. The following week, I might feel like getting bigger or stronger, so maybe I'll eat a bit more. Generally, however, I like to stay lean and light. You don't have to be so strict once you've really mastered your tracking and gained enough trust in yourself, but it's important to be so in the beginning. Believe it or not, even Arnold didn't track his intake obsessively. He either ate more or less of what he would normally eat, and he'd increase or decrease his workout volume, depending on his goal at the moment. The key here is awareness, not obsession, and technology seriously helps you build that awareness.

Remember John? I told him to start wearing his Apple Watch because it has a fitness app that tracks overall calories burned, as well as those burned from activities synced by the watch's exercise app. The watch takes into consideration your age, weight, movement, and heart rate. The count isn't perfect, but it's far more accurate than your own guesstimation. I told him to wear it constantly for at least a week—four days with training, and three days sedentary—so I could see his average daily burn rate in both conditions. Since he is just starting out, and he isn't in such a rush, I decided to recommend a mild cut—just 300-400 calories a day. All he had to do is skip a dessert, cut the sugar in his coffee, or leave out that bagel in the morning. Those small changes add up.

People don't realize how easy it is to cut 300 calories, especially when they're using things like creamer or condiments.

Technology will make you realize the stackup of those calories real quick. Once you see it and have a mini heart attack, you'll be more inclined to dial it back. Seeing your progress in real-time gives you a reflection of your effort, and that can be satisfying. When you see the numbers climb—whether it's calories burned, steps taken, or reps completed—you start to believe that you're capable of more, and it becomes a game in which you are more motivated to do more.

Outside of the tracking though, let's discuss how accessible fitness has become because of technology. There is no shortage of apps with workout programs, personal training templates, YouTube tutorials—you name it. And thus, there are no more excuses about not knowing how to work out or needing a gym membership because you can literally work out in your living room and still get results. This has changed the lives of many people. I've seen folks who were too anxious or introverted to step into a gym but suddenly succeed in their fitness journey simply by having the ability to work out in private. Technology gave these people a way to build their confidence without the pressure of performing in front of others.

So say you track every step, calorie, or rep, but what matters most at the end of the day is how you use that data to understand yourself. You need structure, sure. But if you're rigid all the time, you'll likely become obsessive, and that can have a detrimental impact on your mental health.

Control vs. Obsession

Technology can either be a tool for a healthy, productive form of control, or can turn into a source of unhealthy obsession (because being obsessed isn't necessarily a bad thing). It's important to be careful and aware of your state of mind because you could easily start feeling like a prisoner to the numbers where the data becomes a tyrant. You'll be able to tell when it's a problem when you get worried about numbers while you're working on a task at work, or not being able to track the bowl of soup your aunt offered you at her place. This obsessive approach can make its way into your other thought processes, and at that point you can go into a dangerous spiral. Why are you becoming so obsessive to begin with? Have you become obsessive about other things? **Does this feel like it makes up for a lack of control somewhere else?** Is it a distraction? Do you feel the need to have such a rigid structure? If so, why?

Technology and Self-Trust

Now, as I had mentioned earlier, I'll come back to how technology can be a way to build self-trust. If you've set a daily goal to hit 10,000 steps and burn 2,500 calories, imagine the difference between seeing it visually in real-time versus guessing or even quite possibly forgetting when relying on just your mind. With tech, the visuals are similar to progress bars and leveling up in video games. And as you see your numbers get closer to the goal you've set, you feel better and more inclined to do everything you can to hit it completely—which plays on the need for closure. When you do hit your numbers, the psychological reward feels incredible. At this point, you're not just seeing progress; you're reinforcing that trust in yourself because you kept your word to yourself. You're proving, over and over again, that you're capable of doing what you said you would do. The trust you build in yourself throughout this process likewise makes its way into your life's other domains. Getting used to holding yourself accountable in the gym or with your diet means you can do so at work, in relationships, etc. Fitness is very closely tied to building a relationship with yourself, learning what you're capable of, and proving it to yourself day by day.

Keep in mind, however, that you can have all the tools and tech in the world, giving you a major advantage, but **they won't do the work for you**. It's ultimately still up to you to put in the effort, stay disciplined, and make the necessary adjustments. And when you use these tools right, they can help you build a stronger connection to your own potential. Don't think of technology as a shortcut, but rather an augmentation or enhancer—like any other supplement. It's a way to make things more efficient, more accessible, and more measurable. Let the data guide you, but don't let it define or destroy you.

Gym Etiquette

If you've been to the gym, you've likely run into screamers, hoggers, hoarders, bangers, and all kinds of other messy, weird, inconsiderate species. This section is going to be fairly straightforward. It contains rules that many considerate folks and I abide by and wish everyone else did as well because not doing so leads to the gym becoming a shit-infested zoo full of animals no brighter than an ostrich. The aforementioned species either don't know better, or they think they own the gym, and/or they don't care at all about the impact they have on their surroundings. Some of them even complain about others just like them—it's fine when they do it, but not when others do. It's comical. Guys, most, if not all, of gym etiquette is common courtesy. You might think this is obvious, but to my great surprise, I haven't come across any book yet that covers the importance of gym etiquette and what it entails.

The Sperm Whale

The sperm whale is the loudest animal on the planet, and—surprise!—they don't belong in the gym or any public space for that matter. When you're using the rage I've discussed when you're really pushing hard, **it's natural to grunt or even to want to growl a bit, but you don't want to be the one people can hear across the gym**, in some cases even *with* their headphones on. It's obnoxious. If you can't do the workout without being so damn loud, then it's too heavy for you—take it down a notch.

Many of the ladies and gents I've trained with—who push very hard, mind you—are able to keep their moaning and groaning to themselves. When I'm pushing hard, people who have joined me at the gym haven't even been able to catch the difference between when I'm using the rage I've discussed and when I'm not. If you pay close enough attention to my face and micro-expressions for a long enough time, you *might* just catch a difference. Other than that, however, I never yell. Sometimes I'll do short, small grunts if I'm exerting a lot of force, but that's the most that'll ever come out—in a public space at least. Otherwise, I don't yell, I don't scream, I don't make mating calls, and neither should anyone else. **If you can't hold it in, use a ball gag.**

The Turkey Vulture

The turkey vulture is one of the messiest animals on the planet. They shit on their own feet. You may have seen these creatures at the gym. I'm referring to those who sweat on everything and don't wipe it down or those who leave plates and dumbbells lying around instead of putting them back on the rack. Leaving your sweat all over the benches is not hygienic and it's hazardous; it can cause slippage, it can harbor bacteria, and if you have any breakage in your skin, it can enter and lead to infections. When iron or other equipment is left lying around, they become obstructions and tripping hazards, and it becomes very annoying for anyone who may be looking for them.

How would you feel if you felt someone else's sweat on your skin or even clothes? How does it feel when you can't find any of the weights or equipment you're looking for? The weights you use aren't yours, and they don't belong scattered all over the gym floor. You wouldn't leave your dishes unwashed at a friend's dinner table, and you shouldn't leave the weights lying around after your set. It demonstrates respect for order and structure. If you can't take the time to return a 45-pound plate, this says a couple things. First, **it says, "I'm a lazy, inconsiderate prick,"** because you just did a whole-ass workout with those weights, and putting them back is the least you can do. Second, it says you half ass things and cut corners. So, Jimmy, where else in your life are you cutting corners? Putting things back in a clean and controlled manner helps you get used to finishing what you started and not half-assing life.

Think of all this as **returning things better than you found them**. You wouldn't leave a mess at someone else's house, would you? I'd like to think not. Then treat the gym the same way—it's a shared space. **Wipe down and re-rack!**

The Feral Swine

Feral swine are among the world's worst invasive species—they do not recognize boundaries, they take over space, and they damage the environment they invade. Unfortunately, you may likely come across this species at the gym as well—and of which there are three forms: the hoarder, and the hogger, and the combination of both, the hoardogger.

- **The Hoarder**: takes over multiple stations and/or multiple sets of dumbbells or other equipment and barks at those who try to use something he's not actively using.

- **The Hogger**: takes over a bench, machine, or dumbbells for half an hour without using it, and doesn't give it up for anyone else to use, while all he does is watches highlights of Peppa Pig.

- **The Hoardogger**: not only does he take over multiple sets of equipment, but he also holds on to them for too long, sometimes spending most of the time chatting or on his phone.

The gym is not yours, and you're not the only one paying to be there. The gym is a communal space, and **it's selfish to monopolize equipment, especially if you're not actively using it**. There have been many times when I wasn't done with a machine, but had to take a call. During those times, if I notice anyone looking or trying to use that equipment, I make it clear that they can use it. If I know I'm going to be switching between equipment, especially for a while, others are free to use the ones I'm not actively using. Any time I use dumbbells, even though I know I'm going to use them again a couple sets later, I still re-rack so others can use them until it's my turn again. Don't be greedy—**take only what you need at the moment, and leave what you're not using for others**. If you want it all to yourself, build a private gym. Also, consider the following question in the context of your life outside of fitness: are you taking too much time, space, or attention that should be shared?

The Imprudent Bull

You wouldn't be wrong if you walked up to your favorite machine at the gym, saw a sign that said it's broken due to misuse, and thought, "This is bullshit." That's because it is. Bulls are known to be aggressive, often associated with reckless force and destruction, charging forward without much regard for their surroundings. So, a broken machine would literally be the shit outcome of an empty-headed bull. Sure, lifting heavy is impressive, but only when you're able to truly control that weight. If you can't control the release of the weight, that means it's too heavy and you're ego lifting. If you're ego-lifting, you not only risk damaging the equipment, but you will also inevitably injure yourself.

But lack of control is not the only reason why people bang weights and break equipment. Some of these animals do it for attention and intimidation. Well, let me tell ya, it doesn't make you look stronger—it makes you look primitive and insecure. Some of the strongest guys I know, including myself, are almost undetectable at the gym—quiet, with every move focused and controlled. **True strength is silent**. True strength lies in focus and control. If you're slamming weights or making a scene, not only are you disrespecting the equipment and the people around you, but you're also showing a lack of control over yourself. **Control the weight, control your body, control your mind**. These principles apply to every aspect of your life. As Ice Cube once said, "Check yourself before you wreck yourself."

I hope to have painted a colorful enough picture of the zoo animals that you may so unfortunately come across at the gym. But please, do not let them deter you. If you just mind your business, they'll mind theirs—but whatever you do, don't pay any attention to the ones seeking it. These creatures are an example of how to disrespect the gym and its members. Gym etiquette goes beyond following rules just for the sake of doing so. It's a reflection of how you operate in other areas of life. Do you respect the environment, the people around you, and, ultimately, yourself? It also shows how disciplined, considerate, and mindful you are to yourself and your surroundings. Every aspect of this etiquette—cleaning up, sharing, controlling yourself, respecting equipment—translates directly into how you approach work, relationships, personal goals, and other domains. If you can learn to respect gym etiquette, you'll carry that discipline into everything else you do and it will be noticed and appreciated.

Techniques & Technicalities

Though I strongly believe everyone needs a tailored approach and could greatly benefit from consulting with a competent personal trainer, there are some general guidelines you can use to get started on your own—most of which can easily be found on YouTube or just anywhere online. I dedicated this section to include some practical, technical information that can be generally applied to fitness, particularly for those who want to start lifting—that's where my expertise is, after all. The following points are things I learned through research and personal experience. I've applied the following points to my own routine and have seen positive results. What I *can't* do is guarantee any results for you. I'll stress again that if something works for me and some others, it doesn't necessarily mean it will work the same for you. Everything here is based on peer-reviewed research studies, unless explicitly stated that it's my personal preference, experience, or opinion.

On Diet & Nutrition

Calories:[1]

You consume and expend calories. Calories are energy. Generally, 3,500 calories equal one pound of body weight, but of course the exact amount depends on each person's metabolism and adaptation (Hall et al., 2013). The more muscle mass you have, the more calories you burn at rest, since muscle tissue is more metabolically active than fat (ACE, 2020). Additionally, having more muscle mass increases thermogenesis—the body's heat production—due to muscle's higher energy requirements (Caro et al., 2019). This is because muscle needs fuel to grow or maintain itself, which increases caloric expenditure (Wolfe, 2006).

If you burn 2,000 calories a day:

- **To lose 10 lbs**: 1 lb = 3,500 kcal → 3,500 x 10 = 35,000 kcal. Divide that number by the number of days in which you want to lose that weight.

    If 100 days → 35,000 / 100 = 350 → This means you need to be at a *daily* caloric deficit of 350 calories. This means you have to eat 350 calories *less* than you burn per day. Or, burn 350 *more* calories than you consume per day. So, you'd have to consume 1650 calories a day. But if you want to consume 2,000, then you would have to burn 2350.

- **To maintain weight**: Calories consumed need to equal calories burned. If you're burning 2,000 kcal a day, then you need to consume 2,000 kcal a day.

- **To gain 10 lbs**: Same as losing, except instead of a deficit, you need a surplus. So if we use the same numbers, if you want to gain that weight in 100 days, it means you have to eat 350 calories *more* than you burn. Or, you have to burn 350 calories *less* than you consume. So, you'd either have to eat 2350 calories a day, or burn 1650 while eating at 2,000 kcal a day.

Macronutrients:

- **Protein[2] (4 calories per gram)**: The most important macro for increased metabolism, muscle repair and development, and a bunch of other important physiological functions (Phillips & Van Loon, 2011). This is the most satiating of all nutrients, keeping you full longer than both fat and carbs (Paddon-Jones et al., 2008). For optimal muscle protein synthesis (MPS)—the process your body uses to repair and build muscle after exercise by using protein to rebuild and strengthen muscle fibers—it's recommended to consume 20 to 30 grams of protein per meal, depending on your weight, activity level, and goals. Spreading your protein intake across meals throughout the day can help maintain MPS, particularly if you're involved in regular resistance training (Moore et al., 2009). While eating every 3 to 4 hours may help regulate energy levels and provide consistent protein intake, overall daily calorie and protein intake are the most critical factors for fat loss and metabolism (Schoenfeld et al., 2015; Moore et al., 2015).

- If you workout frequently and intensively, I strongly recommend consuming 1g of protein per pound of body weight (Jäger et al., 2017).

- If you're cutting and still just as active, I would increase that to 1.2g per pound, so that your muscles have enough to maintain or even continue to grow—albeit slowly (Helms et al., 2014).

- If you're not working out, but don't want to lose muscle mass, I recommend a maintenance intake of about 0.8g per pound (Phillips, 2014).

• **Carbohydrates**[3] **(4 calories per gram)**: a key macronutrient, essential for providing energy to fuel physical activities. Carbs are classified into two main types: simple and complex. **Simple carbohydrates**, like sugars, are quickly digested and provide immediate energy, which can be useful for short bursts of activity. **Complex carbohydrates**, such as those found in whole grains and vegetables, are digested more slowly, offering sustained energy that supports longer and more intense exercise sessions (Slavin, 2013). During physical activity, especially high-intensity workouts, **carbohydrates are the body's preferred source of fuel**. Research shows that *low carbohydrate* *availability can impair performance and delay recovery* (Burke, Hawley, Wong, & Jeukendrup, 2011). Additionally, carbohydrates help replenish glycogen stores post-exercise, which is critical for muscle recovery and performance in subsequent workouts (Ivy, 2004).

- Assuming you're active, **if cutting or maintaining**: 40-50% of your daily calories are recommended to be from carbohydrates. This amount supports energy levels while still allowing for fat loss (McArdle et al., 2015).

- **If bulking**: 50-60% of your daily calories are recommended to be from carbohydrates. This amount supports more growth and performance (Jäger et al., 2017; Thomas, Erdman, & Burke, 2016).

- **Fat**[4] **(9 calories per gram)**: also a crucial macronutrient that plays an important role in fitness by providing energy, supporting hormone production, and aiding in recovery. Fats are divided into two main categories: saturated and unsaturated. **Saturated fats**, found in animal products and certain oils, should be consumed in moderation due to their link to increased cholesterol levels and potential cardiovascular risks (Siri-Tarino et al., 2010). In contrast, **unsaturated fats**, especially **polyunsaturated** and **monounsaturated** fats, found in sources like fish, nuts, and avocados, have been shown to reduce inflammation and support heart health (Hu et al., 2001). Additionally, fats are **essential for hormone production, particularly**

testosterone and estrogen, which are key for muscle growth, repair, and overall physical performance (Volek et al., 1997). They also help in the absorption of fat-soluble vitamins (A, D, E, K), which are necessary for optimal body function and recovery.

Again, assuming high activity:

- **When cutting**: 20-30% of daily calories. Focus on unsaturated fats (avocados, nuts, seeds) for hormonal health (Burke & Deakin, 2015; Hu et al., 2001).

- **When maintaining**: 25-35% of daily calories. Balanced intake of healthy fats, moderate saturated fats (lean meats, eggs), and limited processed fats (Lichtenstein et al., 2012).

- **When bulking**: 30-40% of daily calories. Higher intake of unsaturated fats, and some saturated fats to support a calorie surplus for muscle growth (Phillips & Van Loon, 2011).

Personal Experience:

I focus primarily on protein. I weigh about 165 pounds at the moment, but since I don't eat much and I burn more than I do, I try to get in about 175g of protein a day. I usually have two 50g protein shakes and normally just one decent-sized meal a day. I tend to have more fats (most of which are unsaturated) than

I do carbs. No real reason—I love both, but fats have a greater impact on hormones than carbs do, and so they're especially important for me. I am constantly under lots of stress, I don't get much sleep, and I still train pretty hard, so the fats do a decent job at regulating my cortisol and testosterone levels. This doesn't mean you should ignore those things and rely on eating more fats. I don't get enough carbs in because by the time I've consumed the necessary amount of protein and then all the fat, there isn't really much of a caloric budget left for carbs.

I snack frequently, but my snacking is very careful and is done in micro-doses. For example, I might have a few CHEEZ-ITs®, roasted nuts or sunflower seeds, or a tiny piece of extra dark chocolate every 15-20 minutes while I'm at my desk. By the time I'm away from my desk, I probably consume between 250 and 500 calories in snacks alone. My meals are usually no larger than 1,000 calories. So with my single meal, my protein shakes, and my snacks, I normally hit about 2,000 calories and I don't go over very often. My average burn is 2,400 calories a day but can get up to 3,000 or more on very active days.

I may have some days where I just eat some shit food, like the double jalapeno cheeseburger and jalapeno poppers from Carl's Jr®. Maybe I'll even have some desserts here and there, I don't care. I either plan for it, or I know I can make up for it if I go over my budget.

On Lifting

There are different kinds of training, and you can't work towards all of them at the same time. I recommend training for no more than two, but everyone who is absolutely new to lifting or physical activity, in general, should work toward stabilization first; if you're not stable, you're more likely to hurt yourself. The primary training types, according to the National Academy of Sports Medicine (NASM), include stability, strength, hypertrophy, power, and endurance.

The following are general, widely accepted guidelines, particularly from sources like the National Strength and Conditioning Association (NSCA) and American College of Sports Medicine (ACSM). These organizations establish foundational principles for different training styles based on research on strength, hypertrophy, power, stability, and endurance training.

- **Strength Training** guidelines are based on working near maximal effort to improve neuromuscular adaptations.

    - **Sets**: 4-6 sets

    - **Reps**: 1-6 reps

    - **Weight**: 85-100% of 1 Rep Max (RM); very heavy weight, near maximum effort

- **Hypertrophy** recommendations focus on moderate rep ranges with moderate to heavy weight to promote muscle growth through time under tension.

  - **Sets**: 3-5 sets

  - **Reps**: 6-12 reps

  - **Weight**: 65-85% of 1RM; moderate to heavy weight

- **Power Training** emphasizes explosive movement with lighter weight and lower reps for speed and power development.

  - **Sets**: 3-6 sets

  - **Reps**: 1-5 reps

  - **Weight**: 30-70% of 1RM; lighter weight, focus on speed and explosiveness

- **Stability and Endurance** focus on higher reps with lighter weights to improve muscular endurance, joint stability, and control, especially for beginners or rehabilitation purposes.

  - **Stability**:

    - **Sets**: 1-3 sets

    - **Reps**: 12-20 reps

- **Weight**: 50-60% of 1RM; light weight, focus on control and balance

□ **Endurance**:

- **Sets**: 2-4 sets

- **Reps**: 15-25+ reps

- **Weight**: 40-60% of 1RM; light weight, focus on prolonged muscle contraction

Personal Experience:

My primary goal is hypertrophy for an aesthetic physique, and my secondary goal is strength. I have tried all kinds of commonly known splits and routines, but I didn't really care for any of them. I don't like doing the same thing over and over, even though that's what lifting weights is—seems very contradictory, I know. But what I mean is I decide on the fly what to do each day, so each session is a surprise. I've also found that not having a strict and predictable routine has helped me break certain plateaus. It's not completely random, of course—I need to keep track of which muscles I've worked on which days and for how many sets. Doing so is necessary to prevent overworking or underworking a particular muscle. I recommend using a dedicated notebook or at least a note file on your smartphone because there is no way you can accurately remember everything you do just from your own memory.

Typically, I like to choose one muscle from each section of the body—upper, mid, and lower. I might go in one day and decide, chest, erector spinae, hamstrings. Next day I might do back, abs, quads. There is no logic at all. I personally don't like the usual pull day, push day, etc., because if I'm working my chest, I'm already working my triceps, too—it's a helper muscle. And so, if I go on to triceps after my chest workout, I won't be able to lift as much as I normally would because they're already working but not in an isolated, effective manner. I like working opposites instead. For example, If I work chest and I also want to work my arms, I will choose to work on my biceps. Hell, sometimes I mix up the routine completely, and I'll do both a chest workout *and* a back workout the same day.

I typically do four to seven sets per muscle, and about eight to fifteen reps per set. It depends on the muscle, the weight, the set, and the goal. Usually, I like to start at a lower weight and do about 12 reps to warm up—the 12th rep being somewhat challenging. I'll rest about a minute between each set. Then I'll increase the weight and go until absolute failure. Rest, increase weight, repeat. Rest, decrease weight, repeat. And then the same thing once or twice more. Sometimes I will vary the speed of the reps, at times even holding the contraction, but I typically prefer slower, fully controlled reps with proper form. Before working the next muscle, I will rest no more than 3 minutes.

Everything I have done, whether some may think I'm right or wrong, has yielded the results I've wanted—all of which have been achieved naturally. I'm happy with my physique and I am pretty strong for my size. "So how much can you bench, Manny?" My max has been 300 lbs x 7 reps. I'm 5' 6", and I weighed 170 and was 31 years old at the time (around March 2024). I currently weigh 165 lbs, I haven't gotten taller, I'm 32, and I can push 250 lbs x 7 reps. I've definitely lost strength due to my lack of sleep, lack of enough carbs, maybe, and some other factors, but my Beast is full of fuel and drives me forward.

On Recovery

I've included five of the most effective techniques for muscle and nerve recovery, based primarily on research from the ACSM and NSCA, two of the most respected organizations in exercise science.

1. **Sleep**: Sleep is critical for muscle repair and recovery, influencing hormones such as growth hormone and testosterone (American College of Sports Medicine, 2021).

2. **Active Recovery**: Low-intensity activities such as walking or cycling promote blood flow and reduce muscle soreness (National Strength and Conditioning Association, 2020).

3. **Hydration and Nutrition**: Post-exercise nutrition, particularly a mix of adequate protein and carbohydrates, supports muscle glycogen restoration and tissue repair (American College of Sports Medicine, 2018).

4. **Massage and Myofascial Release**: Foam rolling and massage therapy improve blood flow, reduce muscle

tightness, and help alleviate delayed onset muscle soreness (Cheatham et al., 2015). This one is my favorite of them all.

5. **Cold and Heat Therapy**: Alternating between cold and heat therapies can reduce inflammation and support muscle and nerve recovery (American College of Sports Medicine, 2021).

Personal Experience:

We've covered sleep enough, and yes, it will make or break you. Regarding active recovery, I'm not a big fan of walking or cycling, but I've found that lightly working my sore muscles the following day actually helps speed up my recovery and reduces the soreness faster. When it comes to hydration, as long as I drink a lot more sparkling water than coffee, I feel great. I definitely feel better when I'm hydrated because I start twitching and fatiguing otherwise.

Massages are hands down one of my favorite recovery methods—they do wonders to the body. I particularly prefer the more painful sports or medical massages—as I find them more effective—followed by a softer, more relaxing massage to end the session. Whatever style you go with, it's always a happy ending. I haven't really tried the cold and heat therapy, mainly because I don't feel like doing it. Also, people have told me that either the cold or the heat exacerbated certain issues. If it doesn't feel amazing, I'd rather not risk it.

Endnotes

1 Hall, K. D., Sacks, G., Chandramohan, D., Chow, C. C., Wang, Y. C., Gortmaker, S. L., & Swinburn, B. A. (2013). Quantification of the effect of energy imbalance on bodyweight. The Lancet, 378(9793), 826-837. https://doi.org/10.1016/S0140-6736(11)60812-X

American Council on Exercise (ACE). (2020). Metabolism and weight loss: How you burn calories. Retrieved from https://www.acefitness.org/education-and-resources/lifestyle/blog/6785/metabolism-and-weight-loss-how-you-burn-calories/

Caro, C., Lopez-Jimenez, R., & Rea, R. (2019). Thermogenesis and muscle metabolism. The Journal of Clinical Endocrinology and Metabolism, 104(12), 5829-5835. https://doi.org/10.1210/jc.2019-00172

Wolfe, R. R. (2006). The underappreciated role of muscle in health and disease. The American Journal of Clinical Nutrition, 84(3), 475-482. https://doi.org/10.1093/ajcn/84.3.475

2 Phillips, S. M., & Van Loon, L. J. C. (2011). Dietary protein for athletes: From requirements to optimum adaptation. Journal of Sports Sciences, 29(sup1), S29-S38. https://doi.org/10.1080/02640414.2011.619204

Pesta, D. H., & Samuel, V. T. (2014). A high-protein diet for reducing body fat: Mechanisms and possible caveats. Nutrition & Metabolism, 11(1), 53. https://doi.org/10.1186/1743-7075-11-53

Paddon-Jones, D., Westman, E., Mattes, R. D., Wolfe, R. R., Astrup, A., & Westerterp-Plantenga, M. (2008). Protein, weight management, and satiety. The American Journal of Clinical Nutrition, 87(5), 1558S-1561S. https://doi.org/10.1093/

ajcn/87.5.1558S

Jäger, R., Kerksick, C. M., Campbell, B. I., Cribb, P. J., Wells, S. D., Skwiat, T. M., ... & Arent, S. M. (2017). International Society of Sports Nutrition position stand: Protein and exercise. Journal of the International Society of Sports Nutrition, 14(1), 20. https://doi.org/10.1186/s12970-017-0177-8

Helms, E. R., Aragon, A. A., & Fitschen, P. J. (2014). Evidence-based recommendations for natural bodybuilding contest preparation: Nutrition and supplementation. Journal of the International Society of Sports Nutrition, 11(1), 20. https://doi.org/10.1186/1550-2783-11-20

Phillips, S. M. (2014). A brief review of critical processes in exercise-induced muscular hypertrophy. Sports Medicine, 44(1), 71-77. https://doi.org/10.1007/s40279-014-0152-3

Schoenfeld, B. J., Aragon, A. A., & Krieger, J. W. (2015). Effects of meal frequency on weight loss and body composition: A meta-analysis. Nutrition Reviews, 73(2), 69-82. https://doi.org/10.1093/nutrit/nuv004

Moore, D. R., Robinson, M. J., Fry, J. L., Tang, J. E., Glover, E. I., Wilkinson, S. B., ... & Phillips, S. M. (2009). Ingested protein dose response of muscle and albumin protein synthesis after resistance exercise in young men. The American Journal of Clinical Nutrition, 89(1), 161-168. https://doi.org/10.3945/ajcn.2008.26401

Moore, D. R., Churchward-Venne, T. A., Witard, O., Breen, L., Burd, N. A., T

Burke, L. M., Hawley, J. A., Wong, S. H., & Jeukendrup, A. E. (2011). Carbohydrates for training and competition. Journal of Sports Sciences, 29(sup1), S17-S27. https://doi.org/10.1080/02640414.2011.585473

Ivy, J. L. (2004). Regulation of muscle glycogen repletion, muscle protein synthesis and repair following exercise. Journal of Sports Science & Medicine, 3(3), 131-138.

Slavin, J. L. (2013). Carbohydrates, dietary fiber, and resistant starch in white vegetables: links to health outcomes. Advances in Nutrition, 4(3), 351S-355S. https://doi.org/10.3945/an.112.003491

Thomas, D. T., Erdman, K. A., & Burke, L. M. (2016). Position of the Academy of Nutrition and Dietetics, Dietitians of Canada, and the American College of Sports Medicine: Nutrition and athletic performance. Journal of the Academy of Nutrition and Dietetics, 116(3), 501-528. https://doi.org/10.1016/j.jand.2015.12.006

Jäger, R., Kerksick, C. M., Campbell, B. I., Cribb, P. J., Wells, S. D., Skwiat, T. M., ... & Arent, S. M. (2017). International Society of Sports Nutrition position stand: Protein and exercise. Journal of the International Society of Sports Nutrition, 14(1), 20. https://doi.org/10.1186/s12970-017-0177-8

McArdle, W. D., Katch, F. I., & Katch, V. L. (2015). Exercise Physiology: Nutrition, Energy, and Human Performance. Wolters Kluwer Health

4   Siri-Tarino, P. W., Sun, Q., Hu, F. B., & Krauss, R. M. (2010). Meta-analysis of prospective cohort studies evaluating the association of saturated fat with cardiovascular disease. The American Journal of Clinical Nutrition, 91(3), 535-546. https://doi.org/10.3945/ajcn.2009.27725

Hu, F. B., Stampfer, M. J., Manson, J. E., Rimm, E. B., Colditz, G. A., Rosner, B. A., ... & Willett, W. C. (2001). Dietary fat intake and the risk of coronary heart disease in women. The New England Journal of Medicine, 337(21), 1491-1499. https://doi.org/10.1056/NEJM199711203372102

Volek, J. S., Gómez, A. L., & Kraemer, W. J. (1997). Fats in sports nutrition. Exercise and Sport Sciences Reviews, 25(1), 131-162. https://doi.org/10.1249/00003677-199700250-00011

Burke, L. M., & Deakin, V. (2015). Clinical Sports Nutrition (5th ed.). McGraw-Hill.

Lichtenstein, A. H., Appel, L. J., Brands, M., Carnethon, M., Daniels, S., Franch, H. A., ... & Sacks, F. M. (2012). Diet and lifestyle recommendations revision 2006: A scientific statement from the American Heart Association Nutrition Committee. Circulation, 114(1), 82-96. https://doi.org/10.1161/CIRCULATIONAHA.106.176158

Phillips, S. M., & Van Loon, L. J. C. (2011). Dietary protein for athletes: From requirements to optimum adaptation. Journal of Sports Sciences, 29(sup1), S29-S38. https://doi.org/10.1080/02640414.2011.619204

CHAPTER 11

Tailoring Fitness

Personalizing Your Path

Fitness includes all kinds of movement, whether it's martial arts, long-distance running, mountain climbing, or, hell, some good ol' fashioned procreation—each offering their own unique benefits depending on who you are and what you need. Whatever activity you choose should serve your goals and fit into the life you're trying to build. It's not likely that any activity will be an absolute perfect fit for you, but you can choose one that fits as closely as possible with your personality, values, needs, schedule, etc. For example, martial arts or boxing could potentially be a more suitable activity for someone timid or unsure of themselves who not only wants to get stronger but also feel more confident in their ability to stand up for themselves. If this sounds like you, you will learn how to stand your ground, handle confrontation, and build confidence in doing so. Someone with anxiety may not care much about strength or endurance but would do anything for peace of mind. For such folks, activities such as yoga or kayaking will likely offer more benefits. Fitness doesn't always have to be about pushing limits. Sometimes, finding some mental clarity is all you need.

There isn't only one way to achieve fitness. Many people fall into the trap of mimicking celebrity workouts, convinced that if they follow Chris Hemsworth's routine, they'll get the same results—but that's just not how this works. What makes those routines effective aren't the workouts or diets themselves; the context, motivations, and specific goals of the person doing them all matter. Maybe they thrive on certain dark experiences and push themselves to the edge because that's how they cope. If you don't share that same drive, you'll quit long before you see the results you want. Trying to copy someone else's approach without understanding why it works for them will only set you up for failure. Too many times, I've seen people try to copy Arnold's workouts or follow some other celebrity trainer's "blueprint," expecting to look just like them. Some of these "blueprints" are easily marketable because they know everyone wants to look like the celebrity they trained. Some others are offered by people who aren't aware that a specific routine won't work for everyone. Whatever the case, don't just blindly follow someone else's path—find your own.

Here's another example. Take a busy CEO who doesn't have time for a bodybuilder's routine but wants to stay fairly lean and maintain a decent physique without letting fitness take over their life. The following suggestions can be considered if you are a busy CEO—or have a similar lifestyle—and are truly looking for ways to fit your goals into your busy schedule:

- Try to schedule your calls or brainstorming sessions in a way where you can walk while you talk. Research has shown that walking can significantly enhance cognitive processes, including creative thinking and effective problem-solving. In fact, a study by Oppezzo and Schwartz (2014) found that walking boosts creative ideation in real-time and shortly after, suggesting that moving during discussions can lead to more productive and creative outcomes.

- If you have absolutely no way to schedule a block of time for your workouts, then have some resistance bands or dumbbells at the office so that you can fit your sets in when you can. It doesn't have to be intense at all, and it doesn't have to be daily either. However, setting aside 15-30 minutes specifically for your exercise would be optimal.

- Take the stairs as much as possible.

- If you don't want music, listen to podcasts or audiobooks. However, if you're constantly productive, I highly recommend at least using those 15-30 minutes to enjoy a little music and let your mind, body, and soul feel what they need to.

- Cut or at least limit your use of creamers, condiments, and other additives that seem insignificant—they're easy to cut and add up quite quickly.

- Cut or at least limit your use of juices (most have a ton of added sugar), alcohol, and full-sugar sodas. If you love carbonated beverages like me, have some sparkling water. If you want actual soda, I personally always go for the diet version. And if you're worried about aspartame, worry no more. Extensive research and regulatory reviews have consistently found aspartame to be safe for the general population, with no evidence linking it to cancer or other adverse health effects (Butchko & Stargel, 2001; Butchko et al., 2002; Lagiou et al., 2006)[1].

Now contrast that with someone who *can* dedicate time to fitness and who *thrives* in social settings. They may often find it difficult to work out at home because they prefer having people around. For them, the gym is so much more than just a place to lift—it's a place to meet people, influence others, connect with friends, and enjoy access to all kinds of equipment and amenities. It's an experience that detaches them from the humdrum of daily life. Social interaction is likely what keeps them coming back, even on days they don't feel like working out. The gym becomes an energy source they can feed off of. And their workout is just as important, but it's the people and the vibe that make it sustainable.

Then there are the more introverted folks who see the gym as an escape. They aren't there to socialize; they're there to focus, clear their mind, and channel that internal drive into something productive. This is more like me, except I don't mind making connections or quickly catching up (in more or less 30 seconds). The motivation for these types of folks usually doesn't come from the energy around them—it comes from within. However, there is a mix of these two types as well. This can be someone who enjoys being around people but not caring to chat; or someone who feeds off both external and internal energies. I can channel internal energy in private, but it's just not the same as being at the gym with other human beings around. Besides that, once I'm there, I want to make the most out of my visit since I've already invested the time and gas to get there after all.

If you're someone who finds the gym intimidating or simply doesn't like exercising in front of others, fitness can start at home. Investing in some adjustable dumbbells, resistance bands, or other equipment can give you enough to get started and may perhaps help you grow comfortable before gradually visiting the gym during quieter hours. Your personality traits and emotional triggers shouldn't be considered obstacles. You should instead see them as tools to craft a routine that fits your life.

If the workout you're doing doesn't resonate with you, you'll dread it, resent it, and eventually give up. That's why it's so important not to choose routines based on someone else's results without asking if it fits who you are and what you want. It needs to align with your values, goals, and personality. Once everything is clear and aligned, your fitness routine becomes something you look forward to.

Ultimately, fitness is deeply personal. It's incredibly important to understand what fuels you, what hinders you, and what environment allows you to grow. Knowing yourself is your greatest asset in designing a fitness routine that's not only effective but also sustainable. You don't need to fit into the gym's culture or anyone else's routine—you just need to create your own.

Fitness Across Life Stages

Physical fitness evolves through the different stages of life, and the role it plays becomes even more important as we age. I've seen guys who defy what most people would consider "normal" aging. I've come across men who, at first glance, I assumed were in their 40s or 50s, but as it turns out, they were in their mid-70s! When I ask them how they've managed to stay in such great shape, they all usually have the same answer: they never stopped moving, never stopped working out, and yet didn't become obsessive about being perfectly healthy either. All but one of them told me they never restricted themselves to anything, and the one that did never drank or smoked. They all still enjoyed life, had the occasional drink, maybe indulged in a few things that wouldn't be considered textbook "healthy," but they always did what they had to do—they moved. And, say what you want, but all the best-looking ones regularly lifted. It's easy for people to simply attribute some of their success to genetics—and sure, genetics do play a part—but if you don't take care of yourself consistently, the clock is going to catch up to you real quick, no matter how good your genes are.

How long do you think your car can run without regular maintenance? And how long do you think it can run if you take *great* care of it, especially if you got the car brand new, even if you get a bit rough with it here and there? If you think of fitness as maintenance, then perhaps you'll agree that the older the car is, the more care and maintenance it requires to continue looking great and performing well. And if we just make a habit of taking great care of it from the very beginning, it won't age as fast as it normally would. Your body isn't very different, so starting young can set you up for a long, healthy life.

There's this myth I had constantly been told by family members and other concerned parents that lifting weights or engaging in strength training when you're young stunts your growth. That's been debunked. In fact, strength training actually stimulates the release of growth hormone and testosterone, which play important roles in muscle development and bone density. Now, while these hormones contribute to overall physical development, their effect on height is limited and mainly influenced by genetics and overall health—especially in males during adolescence (Faigenbaum & Myer, 2012; Barbieri & Zaccagni, 2013)[2]. Research has also shown that the enhancement of bone density and muscle strength during resistance training contributes to overall physical development without affecting growth plates (Faigenbaum & Myer, 2012; Barbieri & Zaccagni, 2013). When your muscles contract under resistance, they *are* pulling on your bones, but the idea that your muscles are somehow stopping your bones from growing is just plain wrong. If anything, the strengthening of muscles and bones contributes to the overall physical development of both males and females, the benefits of which are even more pronounced during the teenage years, particularly in males.

From about 30 to 50, your testosterone peaks and can maintain itself fairly well if you're careful with your mind and body. During these years, you can still build plenty of muscle, burn fat, and achieve the physique you want. Take advantage while you can because things start to shift after 50. Testosterone levels start to decline, and while you can do your best to slow that process down through regular training, good nutrition, and proper sleep, you can't stop it. The difference between aging quickly or aging slowly—or looking 50 at 70 and vice versa—comes down to how well you take care of yourself during this critical period.

As you move into your later years, physical fitness becomes even more essential. I often hear people ask if they should slow down or change the way they exercise as they age. If you're fairly healthy and have no serious conditions, the only thing I'd recommend shifting is your intensity. Even if you're healthy, your age alone has a major impact on how much your heart can handle. One day, while I was on the treadmill at the gym, I witnessed a guy who was running on another treadmill to the right of and behind me have a heart attack. I hadn't noticed him taking any breaks. The guy was severely overweight, and his heart just couldn't handle the strain of the workout he was trying to do. He hadn't conditioned his body for that level of intensity, and it cost him his life. I found out he was just 40 years old. You should know that there's a maximum heart rate that people shouldn't exceed, especially as they get older. To determine your max heart rate, subtract your age from 220. This estimation method is endorsed by the American College of Sports Medicine (ACSM) (Tanaka, Monahan, & Seals, 2001)[3]. So if you're 40, your max heart rate is 180 beats per minute, but you shouldn't be pushing yourself to 100% of that anyway. Intense workouts should stay in the 70-85% range of your max heart rate to stay safe, depending on your health and fitness level—as recommended by the American Heart Association (AHA, 2020)[4].

If you've spent your life staying active, your body has adapted and is conditioned to that level of activity—in which case, you're generally safe. But if you're new to fitness or have taken a long break, you need to be careful about jumping straight into high-intensity workouts regardless how old you are. The body doesn't just bounce back the same way after extended periods of inactivity. Detraining, or the loss of fitness due to inactivity, can occur in a matter of weeks and significantly impacts muscle strength and cardiovascular health (Bosquet et al., 2013)[5]. You could've been an athlete for 10 years, but if you take a 10-year break and try to go back to your old training routine, you're setting yourself up for serious injury.

"What if I'm pushing 70? Is there any point in starting a fitness routine?" Yes. The *American Heart Association* (AHA) and the *Centers for Disease Control and Prevention* (CDC) both emphasize the importance of physical activity in older adults, as it reduces the risk of chronic diseases, improves mobility, and enhances cognitive function (Nelson et al., 2007)[6]. And if you're absolutely new to it, the routine could simply consist of a 10-minute walk, perhaps twice a day around the pool or garden. In later years, low-intensity cardio might take on a bigger role. You could even start or continue to lift weights but reducing intensity and incorporating more functional movements that support longevity and mobility would do you well. In fact, the *American College of Sports Medicine* (ACSM) *recommends* strength training for seniors, emphasizing the use of functional movements that improve balance and prevent falls. Lower-intensity resistance training is safe and beneficial for increasing bone density, muscle strength, and joint stability (ACSM, 2009)[7]. The older you get, the more important it becomes to listen to your body and adapt your routine to what your current state of health can handle. If you're in your 60s or 70s, pushing yourself too hard isn't just counterproductive—it's dangerous. The key is to maintain a consistent routine that works with where your body is right now.

Though we've established that fitness is as much mental as it is physical, this matters a lot more later in your silver years. This is closely tied to the psychologist Erik Erikson's concept of generativity versus stagnation—the seventh stage of psychosocial development. Stagnation generally refers to not being productive, not having purpose, not contributing to family or society, or not doing anything meaningful. Generativity, on the other hand, refers basically to the opposite of stagnation's characteristics. If you have nothing to live for, if you don't have any personal goals, family, or passions driving you, you're less likely to stay motivated to keep pushing forward. But if you're driven by the idea of being there for your grandkids, continuing to pursue your passions, or simply wanting to live a longer, healthier life, that drive can keep you moving. In fact, generativity has been linked to higher life satisfaction, better mental health, and a greater sense of purpose in older adults (McAdams & de St. Aubin, 1992)[8]. Pursuing your goals in those years keeps both your mind and body active, and an active body leads to a sharper mind. It becomes a positive feedback loop that slows your aging and keeps you young in mind, body, and spirit. This mutual reinforcement between mind and body creates a feedback loop that promotes healthier aging (Erickson et al., 2011)[9].

Lite Advice for Three Types of People

To someone just starting on this path—whether you're new to physical fitness or an introspective approach to life, there are a couple things you must realize. First, that it will take time to develop the right habits, and second, that you shouldn't rush it. I'm not saying you should dilly dally—the sooner you act, the sooner you'll reach development—but don't be so hasty. In this regard, haste makes waste. Most people mess up because they think they need to sprint toward a finish line that doesn't actually exist. Both fitness and introspection are lifelong, step-by-step processes. Just don't overtrain or overthink.

Start small and be intentional. If you've never touched a weight before, don't be afraid to pick one up. Everyone was new to this at some point. Focus on learning the essentials:

- How to move your body with intention and proper form

- How to think about your actions and then about your thinking

- How to recognize your limits, and

- How to push past them without breaking yourself

Whether you're lifting weights or journaling for half an hour to reflect on your day, it's the same principle: progress happens when you engage in habits that serve your goals, even when you don't feel like it. The more you do that, the easier it becomes to push a bit further each time. And because the physical and the mental are always at play with one another, the work you put into building your body mirrors the work you'll need to put into building your mind, and vice versa. You'll surely start to notice a shift in your approach to challenges. Fitness has been a gateway to understanding myself, and it may potentially be the same for you. Once you recognize how your body responds to stress, discipline, and effort, it becomes easier to act and plan accordingly.

For the typical gym goer—I understand that you've been lifting for years, and you may know how to count your macros, and maybe you even follow a decent routine. But are you really paying close enough attention to your actions and the deeper reasons behind them? Or are you just going through the motions?

If you're stuck in autopilot and lacking introspection, then you're really missing out on optimal development. I'm not knocking the work you're putting in physically. I'm just strongly suggesting that a healthy level of introspection can make a huge difference in both your current efforts and life in general. If you're mindless in your approach to something that matters to you, then you will likely be so in your approach to everything else.

Don't just lift to lift or think just to think. Lift to learn. Learn to think. Think to grow.

For the deep thinker who's never touched a weight—you might already be someone who loves spending hours in your head, diving deep into your thoughts, deconstructing ideas, and searching for the meaning behind things. You might even already have a strong mind. But you can't neglect the meat sack that your brain is a part of because if that's out of whack, then it won't be long before your noodles take a hit, too. As a deep thinker myself, I've personally found my mind to be more clear and focused after some light activity, and even more so after a full workout. If you've never really been active or touched a set of weights, you'd do yourself well to dedicate some time toward acquainting yourself with your physical side and how it fits into that mental prowess you've developed.

Philosophy, introspection, and deep thinking can take you far, but they're incomplete without the physical element. To balance things out with the complexities of your introspection, introducing something more straightforward and primal would work well. And there's something about intentionally engaging the body in strenuous activity that strips away the abstraction and brings you face to face with raw experience—at least, that's been *my* experience anyway. The same way a good philosophical debate can stretch your mind, a tough workout will stretch your body and, by extension, your mind as well. Lifting, or any other strenuous physical activity, challenges your mental strength. It forces you to confront your first mental barrier, to push through the pain, and to silence the voice that says, "I can't."

It's very natural for your philosophical mind to resist and question the meaning of it all. You may even argue why the mind is more important than the body. But instead of seeing one being more important than the other, understand that they need each other for both to stay in good shape. "Ahh what a load of crock. My body looks like a starving sailor, and my mind is still in great shape." It may be for now, but what if it can perform better? Or even if it's at peak performance, which I highly doubt, it won't be long before your body starts demanding attention from your mind—whether through pain or some other physical expression. You really can't fully explore one without engaging the other. You don't need to try and optimize both because that's impossible. You can give more importance to the mind but without neglecting the body. Physical fitness is a way to ground yourself and can perhaps be a way to experience the philosophy you spend so much time thinking about. There's a clarity that comes after a hard workout that you may have never experienced before—a peace that I feel you just can't achieve through hours of deep thought.

To all three types—whether you're completely new to fitness, a seasoned gym-goer, or a philosopher who's just starting to realize the importance of fitness, the fact remains. Fitness is a tool for self-discovery, and the discipline you develop in training your body becomes a gateway to understanding your mind. The more you push yourself physically, the more you'll understand who you are, what you're capable of, and where your limits truly lie. To do this, you need fuel, purpose, and raw emotions—and it should come as no surprise, by now, that the kind of fuel you have makes a difference. Motivations, depending on their source, have a different impact on us. Also, each of us has walls of varying thickness, made of different materials. That's why you need the kind of fuel that creates a strong enough drive to push through your walls. Otherwise, the effort required to do so won't make any sense to you.

The Role of Body Type, Genetics, & Physical Limitations

People often ask, "To what degree do genetics, body types, or physical limitations play into setting goals?" And quite frankly, it really is one of the most important questions to consider when you're starting your fitness journey. You need to know what you're working with. Maybe you don't have what it takes to craft a diamond, but maybe you can refine your wood, which you can then use to build something nice and solid. Many folks are constantly exposed to images of peak physiques, and for most of us, it creates a standard we think we need to hit. In reality, most of us will never look anything like Arnold in his prime, and that's okay. In fact, it's essential to realize that the pursuit of fitness is not at all about trying to mold yourself into some impossible version of a "perfect" body. But that's not to say we shouldn't *aim* for *our* peak physique.

Sorry if I burst your bubble here, but no amount of personal training, super duper diet plans, cutting-edge supplements, or hours in the gym is going to make you look like someone whose genetic blueprint is entirely different from yours. If you're naturally built like a Bruce Lee, chasing the body of someone like The Rock is going to make you feel like nothing works and there's something wrong with you. Well... that wouldn't be *entirely* wrong because what *would* be wrong in this case is the ignorance of your reality and your unrealistic expectations. However, understand that while genetics and body type do play a significant role in how you'll ultimately look, it doesn't mean you can't be successful in fitness. But they do set boundaries—real, fixed boundaries—that, if ignored, can easily lead to self-doubt, body dysmorphia, obsession, and even serious physical injury.

People don't consider that the physiques they see in social media, that they use as standards, were sculpted from a completely different foundation than their own. Both Arnold

Schwarzenegger and Bruce Lee had phenomenal physiques, yet they're entirely different from each other. Arnold was this massive figure—huge, muscular, and broad—while Bruce Lee was compact and lean, almost sculpted to perfection in a practical sense. All of this is what makes it so imperative to understand yourself.

Genetics determine a lot of what you're working with. It's why some people find it easy to pack on muscle or burn fat, while others struggle no matter how hard they push themselves. It even determines the literal shape of your muscles. That's why some guys have four-pack abs while others have eight or why one person's abs are aligned and symmetrical while others' are not. Genetics contribute to your body type as well, of which there are three forms: endo-, ecto-, and mesomorph.

- **Endomorphs** are naturally inclined to carry more body fat and tend to have a wider waist and hips than their counterparts. They might have to work twice as hard to achieve the same leanness an ecto- or mesomorph would achieve with half the effort. Think Chris Pratt.

- **Ectomorphs** can be considered the polar opposite of endomorphs in that they tend to carry both less fat and even less muscle mass. They are typically narrow at the shoulders and hips and can be described as long-limbed. These folks would have to try much harder than others to put on a significant amount of muscle. Think Bruce Lee.

- **Mesomorphs** are genetically the luckiest bunch when it comes to putting on muscle. They tend to have broad shoulders, a narrow waist, and a lower body fat percentage than the former two types. It's also much easier for them to put on muscle and burn fat. Think Arnold Schwarzenegger.

Each has its aesthetic potential, so be happy with what you've got. Just because your body type doesn't match the one you may have compared yourself to doesn't mean you can't achieve an impressive physique with your own. Being an ectomorph does not mean you can't bulk up, and being an endomorph does not mean you can't lean out. But trying to sculpt your body into something that resembles the potential of another body type is only going to frustrate you. Embrace your body type and set your goals accordingly. Understand that setting realistic goals does not mean lowering your standards—it simply means understanding what's achievable within the unique framework *you've* been given. Regardless of your body type, it's your habits, discipline, and choices that ultimately carve out your body's potential. Genetics will surely influence how your body looks, but how you treat your body over time will have the greatest impact on your results.

Aside from body types, we must also acknowledge that not everyone is starting from the same baseline. Some people are working with physical disabilities or chronic conditions that make some of the usual fitness routines seem daunting or even impossible. That just means that your version of fitness will be tailored to your abilities. Someone with physical limitations might not be able to do *every* exercise, but there are always adaptations. Training for strength or size, for example, can be done seated or even with resistance bands if dumbbells aren't an option. Cardiovascular health can still be improved through ergometers or other equipment designed for mobility challenges. It may also be very helpful for them to go with someone who can assist in their efforts, such as picking up, putting back, initiating, or releasing. Focus on what you *can* control, what your body *can* do, and what *can* be possible.

Everyone has a different path, shaped by their genetics, body type, limitations, and many other variables. Approach fitness with the idea that you can use it to become the best version of yourself instead of trying to squeeze yourself into an unrealistic mold. In the end, fitness is as much about understanding who you are as it is about becoming who you want to be, and you can't come to the latter without the former.

Endnotes

1   Butchko, H. H., Stargel, W. W., Comer, C. P., Mayhew, D. A., Benninger, C., Blackburn, G. L., ... & Tephly, T. R. (2002). Aspartame: review of safety. Regulatory Toxicology and Pharmacology, 35(2 Pt 2), S1-S93. https://www.sciencedirect.com/science/article/abs/pii/S0273230002915424

Butchko, H. H., & Stargel, W. W. (2001). Aspartame: Scientific evaluation in the postmarketing period. Regulatory Toxicology and Pharmacology, 34(3), 221-233. https://www.sciencedirect.com/science/article/abs/pii/S0273230001915368

Lagiou, P., Samoli, E., Lagiou, A., Peterson, J., Tzonou, A., Dwyer, J., & Trichopoulos, D. (2006). Flavored beverage consumption and cancer: A prospective study in Greece. European Journal of Cancer Prevention, 15(3), 195-199. https://journals.lww.com/eurjcancerprev/Abstract/2006/06000/Flavored_beverage_consumption_and_cancer__A.3.aspx

2   Faigenbaum, A. D., & Myer, G. D. (2012). Resistance training among young athletes: Safety, efficacy, and injury prevention effects. British Journal of Sports Medicine, 46(1), 14-20. https://doi.org/10.1136/bjsports-2011-090228

Barbieri, D., & Zaccagni, L. (2013). Strength training for children and adolescents: Benefits, risks, and practical implications. Journal of Strength and Conditioning Research, 27(4), 1071-1082. https://doi.org/10.1519/JSC.0b013e318286be55

3   Tanaka, H., Monahan, K. D., & Seals, D. R. (2001). Age-predicted maximal heart rate revisited. Journal of the American College of Cardiology, 37(1), 153-156. https://doi.org/10.1016/S0735-1097(00)01054-8

4   American Heart Association (AHA). (2020). Target Heart Rates. Retrieved from https://www.heart.org/en/healthy-living/fitness/fitness-basics/target-heart-rates

5   Bosquet, L., Berryman, N., & Dupuy, O. (2013). Effect of training cessation on muscular performance: A meta-analysis. Scandinavian Journal of Medicine & Science in Sports, 23(2), 140–149. https://doi.org/10.1111/sms.12047

6   Nelson, M. E., Rejeski, W. J., Blair, S. N., Duncan, P. W., Judge, J. O., King, A. C., ... & Castaneda-Sceppa, C. (2007). Physical activity and public health in older adults: Recommendation from the American College of Sports Medicine and the American Heart Association. Circulation, 116(9), 1094-1105. https://doi.org/10.1161/CIRCULATIONAHA.107.185650

7   American College of Sports Medicine (ACSM). (2009). Exercise and physical activity for older adults. Medicine & Science in Sports & Exercise, 41(7), 1510-1530. https://doi.org/10.1249/MSS.0b013e3181a0c95c

8   McAdams, D. P., & de St. Aubin, E. (1992). A theory of generativity and its assessment through self-report, behavioral acts, and narrative themes in autobiography. Journal of Personality and Social Psychology, 62(6), 1003-1015. https://doi.org/10.1037/0022-3514.62.6.1003

9   Erickson, K. I., Voss, M. W., Prakash, R. S., Basak, C., Szabo, A., Chaddock, L., ... & Kramer, A. F. (2011). Exercise training increases size of hippocampus and improves memory. Proceedings of the National Academy of Sciences, 108(7), 3017-3022. https://doi.org/10.1073/pnas.1015950108

CHAPTER 12

Ultimate Impact—The Ripple/Domino Effect

The Ultimate Impact on the Individual

At the core of everything discussed in this book is the fundamental belief that change begins within the individual—within you, my dear reader. Fitness is just the vehicle I've chosen to illustrate this concept because:

- It's what I know well.

- It's what led to my transformation and that of so many others.

- Its reach extends far beyond the walls of the gym.

To truly understand the ultimate impact of what we've explored together, you need to realize that every decision you make in your physical development ripples out into everything about you.

When we think of strength, many of us usually imagine it as something that comes from overcoming external obstacles, from physically pushing through weights or enduring physical strain. And even if we consider internal strength, we may only consider it in terms of enduring stress or being resilient. Strength is so much more than that. There's a war within you between what you know is right and wrong—between doing what serves your values and what doesn't. It lies in your ability to see, think, and act in the middle of all the chaos and introduce moments of peace. The gym—or wherever your fitness space—is merely a reflection of this deeply internal war. It's a controlled environment, or training ground, for your mind, your values, and your sense of self. The muscle you build is not just physical. You're likewise developing the muscle of the mind and soul.

What happens when you reach your limit during a workout, when your muscles and nerves are burning? Your mind and body beg you to stop. Yet, you may hear a faint voice within you that says, "No. Keep going." That voice is your potential, your soul, demanding to be heard, tested, and realized. Any time I've failed to listen to that voice, I've felt weaker. And every time I did listen, I became stronger.

Imagine the profound impact on your life if you could master your mind and wield your thoughts as tools. Not just to free yourself from insecurities or push through mental blocks but to fully *command* your mental faculties, using them deliberately to improve and move forward. I'm talking about self-mastery here. Once attained, you will feel that control is always within reach, no matter the situation; it'll be much easier to maintain clarity and control over your thoughts and actions, regardless of the chaos around you. And the first step toward such an achievement is understanding yourself on as deep a level as possible.

Take me, for example. I understand myself quite well—maybe not perfectly, but significantly. Through this self-understanding, I've positively transformed my life. I'm not saying everything is fuckin' daisies—the war never ends, and I have my deep lows and peak highs—but the developments have made me a better warrior, and thus, fighting has become easier. So, how did I begin to understand myself?

People always told me to pay attention to how I respond in various contexts, but I was always too caught up in the moment to do that. I couldn't figure out what to do and how to respond while also paying attention to how I do respond and why. The situation report, or sit-rep, which is when I would reflect on and analyze what happened, would happen long after the situation took place—and, in most cases, it was too late. "God dammit... why did I respond *that* way? I shoulda said '*this*' instead... Why didn't I think of that *then*?! God, why am I so slow?!" Another common and cliche piece of advice is, "Be strong. Don't give up." Really?! How profound! If someone *really* wanted something, do you think they'd really *want* to give up? You think if they *had* the tools and knew how to use them, they'd choose *not* to be strong? I don't think so. They may be afraid, inexperienced—something is holding them back, and it takes lots of effort to face whatever that might be. You may say I'm being too positive or too hopeful about people, but I *do* believe that reasonable people who want better for themselves and others *would* do what serves their values if they had the tools.

Then, one day at the gym, it hit me—I was focusing on how my mind and body are responding while I'm in the moment, right in the middle of a workout. I was fully aware of the sarcomeres within my muscles, each strand of my nerves, and all my thoughts and actions throughout my workout. I thought, "Fuck, if I could do this here, I should be able to do it anywhere." In my next conversation with someone, I completely forgot what I had told myself at the gym. And this happened a couple more times. But with each time I forgot, I kept reminding myself later at the gym, until one day I didn't forget, and I was actually able to pay attention to myself for a fraction of the conversation. My biggest problem during conversations was my distractibility, so I trained myself to keep redirecting my attention—and this felt like repetitions of weightlifting. Maintaining my attention, especially to conversations that weren't exactly stimulating, was very much like endurance training—how long can I hold the weight before my muscles and nerves give out? The more I thought of it that way, the more I trained, the better I got.

Besides approaching various other activities with the fitness lens, my best self-reflective tool for understanding myself was journaling. There were times where I'd just write out thoughts as they come without any structure and then circle a few things that caught my attention and dove deeper on those. Other times, I'd question thoughts about a particular thought, belief, motive, action, decision, conversation, outcome, etc. Sometimes I'd write for five minutes, and other times I'd end up writing for hours. And any time I hit a point where it felt like it was going to hurt to continue, I'd push myself to continue to dive deeper, and that's when I'd make my greatest self-discoveries.

There is no end to understanding yourself; it's an ongoing process that requires constant refinement. It requires the humility to admit there's always more to uncover. It would only benefit you to consistently strive for a better understanding and then use that knowledge to keep improving. As you uncover more about yourself, you learn more about what you truly believe, value, want, etc., which makes it easier to set clear, deeply internal standards for yourself; it's vital to the development of your character.

"But Manny, what if there isn't much about me to understand? What if there isn't much depth to me. Say I find out some things about myself. What if after all that, nothing changes?" It's natural to think that way, but what *if* you find something that may be useful? Time is passing anyway, and by not searching, things will definitely not change. *Not* searching, *not* acting, *not* trying is a waste of time. So many people live in fear of failure. And I was one of those people. "What if I can't? What if it's not worth it? All that time and effort would have gone to waste. I need a guarantee." Here are the only guarantees I've learned exist in this world:

- At some point, you're going to die.

- It takes strength to be happy and courage to seek happiness because that happiness (or whatever its cause is) can be taken from you.

- Time is passing, and you can't get it back.

- Not everything will go according to your preference.

- Nothing about your experience of the world will change unless you do. "But Manny, what if I lose my job? That's not in my control." Sometimes it's not, but that's not what I'm talking about. If you keep looking for people or things to blame for your situation, if you keep acting like a victim to life, nothing will change, and you will always remain a victim. Some people prefer being a victim because they think it's far easier than the price of responsibility and accountability. Is it really, though? You have stress either way, so it becomes a question of which one you'd rather have. One would be from crying about shit all day and nothing changing, and the second would be from facing reality, doing what you can with the cards you're dealt, and then learning from and owning your plays. You can blame the unhappiness of your body on genetics, the availability of junk food, and the animals you want to avoid at the gym. Or, you can do everything you can to care for and develop your body, *choose* not to eat shit, and *choose* not to be affected by those around you. You don't think everyone else at the gym doesn't get annoyed by those animals? Trust me, they do, but their will to be there is stronger than anything that may have otherwise deterred them.

- Results from consistently following the steps toward a better physique. I swear, if you just follow the science, eat right, lift right, recover right, development is inevitable. "Can't you say the same about business? If you just do all the right things, of course you'll succeed." Nope. Not that simple. Business has way more variables, those of which have a much greater impact on the outcome of your chances of succeeding. The "right" things themselves can vary. Your physical body, however, works pretty much the same as everyone else—your heart pumps, your muscles contract, your stomach digests nutrients. At different rates, yes, but with enough time and effort, development is inevitable. In business, you deal with people. People are different and hardly predictable. Say you have a startup going, and then start making moves based on an investor's promise to fund you $500,000 for your next phase. Suddenly, the investor changes his mind because he has another emergency for which he needs that money, or he simply changed his mind. You may have done everything right, but there was no way of knowing such an emergency would arise. If you don't get funding in time, you can't pay your employees, and then there's no company. You're fucked. In fitness, maybe you get injured badly, but unless you literally die, there are things you can do to recover, to continue developing, or to at least not get worse.

- And, lastly, if you wait for guarantees before you act on something, I guarantee you'll be disappointed. If you think the world is shit, if you wish people would be better people, the best thing you can do is to embody the ideals that you'd like to see more of in others. Be the example through your actions. You can't expect everyone to follow suit, but if you become someone respectable, admirable, someone people look up to, I can guarantee you will have a lot more influence than you would otherwise.

The ultimate impact on you as an individual is not the aesthetic reward of a muscular body with six-pack abs, although that may come too. It's knowing, deep inside, that you are capable of facing your demons, of tolerating and functioning despite a great amount of pain, of staying in control amidst your internal war, and of forging a stronger version of yourself. Once you're significantly more aware of and able to control yourself and fight for what you want—in other words, once you've transformed—people will notice. Then, everything changes. You move through the world and experience life differently because you've shown yourself and others what you're made of, what you're capable of, and what you're willing to do. By applying the concepts discussed in this book, I am confident that you will come closer to or actually reach these results. I am confident you will experience positive developments, perhaps even a total transformation, and that you will have a positive influence on those around you.

The Ultimate Impact on Society

When one person positively transforms, their influence causes a ripple effect which, in turn, affects the entire fabric of society. Now imagine what would happen if *more* people experienced these transformations. If even a *small* percentage of people begin to take their fitness—and by extension, their self-development—seriously, we will have a stronger, more capable, and more cooperative society as a result. At the very least, it'll lead to a less shitty society.

A society filled with individuals who have mastered their bodies and their minds is a society that can overcome its own internal chaos. Imagine a society in which its members actually cooperate, WOW! Think about the significant impact on the world if everyone learned to master their thoughts and use their cognitive faculties with the same precision as they use their physical ones. Imagine a world where people didn't just react to or escape from stress but consciously chose how to engage with it, asked for and received support, grew stronger from those experiences, and then helped others overcome similar ones. The very nature of human experience would be elevated. Each step forward, each improvement, raises the collective bar for human potential.

What happens when people learn to embrace discomfort, to see challenges not as threats but as opportunities? They become more inclined to face them. What happens when people stop feeling sorry for themselves, stop thinking of themselves as victims, and realize they have more control than they thought before? They stop making excuses. They stop blaming others for their failures. They take ownership of their lives, and by doing so, they contribute positively to the world around them. The father who pushes himself in the gym is better able to push himself through the difficulties of fatherhood. He's much more likely to be a better father for his children and a better husband for his wife. Maybe you're a father who leaves the diaper changing to your wife. Maybe she gives you shit for it. But then as you push through your discomfort in fitness, maybe you come home one day and decide, "You know what, honey? Let me handle that shit today." Or, perhaps you're having trouble understanding your mother-in-law (or "Zokanj," as they are commonly referred to by Armenians), which has been causing tension in the relationship with your wife, but it's been too heavy a matter to address. As you build up strength and endurance in your fitness space—lifting heavier, pushing through plateaus and pain barriers—you will likewise build up the nerve and strength to be better able to face such a heavy matter. If you're not used to putting yourself in others' shoes and trying to see things through their perspective—also known as empathizing—it might seem difficult at first. But because you value your relationship because you love your wife who loves her mom, and because, by extension, you love your Zokanj—because, after all, she gave birth to and raised the beauty you're lucky to call your wife—then you will do your best to lift this weight and push yourself to understand everyone's point of view and come to the most optimal resolution possible. The reward would be a better relationship with your wife, and potentially more respect from your Zokanj... or a very salty cup of coffee, God knows. The point is, at least your wife will appreciate your efforts in genuinely doing your best to resolve the matter carefully and respectfully.

Likewise, the entrepreneur who breaks through their physical barriers is better equipped to break through the uncertainties and obstacles of building a business. If this is you, you might need to hunt for funds, go through a ton of rejections, or deal with some harsh surprises. Not everyone can stomach those realities, let alone jump at them head-on. You can consider hunting for funds as attempting heavier weights to build more strength, rejections as endurance training, and dealing quickly with surprises as building both power and agility. The most difficult aspects of entrepreneurship, for me, personally, has been moving forward despite the following:

- Knowing that many people doubt me, look down on me, and hope I fail.

- My deep discomfort with administrative and bureaucratic processes.

- My fear of failure.

The more I push in the gym, the more I notice I'm able to push outside of it. The more I push outside the gym, the more fears and discomforts I face, the more problems I resolve, the stronger and more capable I become in every other domain. The developments from these battles produce in me qualities that make me a better leader. Likewise, both the father and the entrepreneur who apply these concepts become better leaders.

These individual transformations add up and can have a compounding effect on society. They can create a society where fitness, optimization, and introspection become the cultural standard. And, again, fitness isn't just confined to the physical; it includes spiritual, psychological, and intellectual fortitude. A strong society is one where people are resilient, adaptable, and capable of enduring hardship without collapsing under its weight. A society built on these values becomes one where people strive not just for personal gain but for collective growth. Such a societal impact can lead to a world where people don't shy away from the hard work of becoming better, where they don't flee from responsibility or the difficult path. That's what we could create if more of us took the principles of fitness and applied them to life.

But it starts with you. When you demand more of yourself, when you hit milestones you had set for yourself (especially if you'd been ridiculed for them), you challenge those around you to rise to the occasion. "Shit. He did it" might ideally lead to "Well, shit if he can do it, I guess I have no excuse." Lasting societal change can be achieved through individual evolutions rather than major revolutions because it would be genuine, stemming from the very core and Will of its members.

Ultimately, the strength of one becomes the strength of many, and the progress of the individual becomes the progress of the whole. That is the power of fitness, not just as a personal practice but as a societal revolution.

ABOUT THE AUTHOR

Manuel Gezalyan is a fitness expert and philosopher at heart with 15 years of dedicated personal development in the fitness world. Holding a BA in Psychology from CSU Channel Islands, he merges his academic background with his own experiences to explore the profound connections between physical fitness and mental well-being. Manuel's journey through personal challenges and his unwavering commitment to self-improvement have fueled his passion for guiding others on their own paths to growth. His unique perspective inspires readers to view fitness not just as a physical pursuit but as a holistic approach to life.